Fundamentals of
Creative Thinking

FUNDAMENTALS OF
CREATIVE THINKING

by

JOHN S. DACEY
Boston College

Lexington Books

D.C. Heath and Company · *Lexington, Massachusetts* · *Toronto*

Library of Congress Cataloging-in-Publication Data

Dacey, John S.
Fundamentals of creative thinking / John S. Dacey.
p. cm.
Includes index.
ISBN 0–669–16140–3 (alk. paper).
ISBN 0–669–16141–1 (pbk. : alk. paper)
1. Creative thinking. I. Title.
BF408.D32 1989   88–16879
153.3'5 – dc 19

Published simultaneously in Canada
Printed in the United States of America
Casebound International Standard Book Number: 0–669–16140–3
Paperbound International Standard Book Number: 0–669–16141–1
Library of Congress Catalog Card Number: 88–16879

The paper used in this publication meets
the minimum requirements of American National Standard
for Information Sciences – Permanence of Paper
for Printed Library Materials, ANSI Z39.48–1984.

ISBN 0–669–16140–3

89 90 91 92 8 7 6 5 4 3 2 1

To
Dr. Richard Ripple,
who helped me get started in research,
and to
Mr. Joseph Gerrity,
who helped me get this research finished,
this book is gratefully dedicated.

Contents

PART II
How Creativity Develops

Figures

Tables

What Creativity Is

1

A Model of Creativity

Chapter Highlights:

Creativity in Childhood

The First Characteristic
    The Person: Tolerant of Ambiguity/Original
    The Product: Unusual

The Second Characteristic
    The Person: Analytical and Intuitive/Sensitive
    The Product: Appropriate

The Third Characteristic
    The Person: Open-minded/Flexible
    The Product: Transformed

The Fourth Characteristic
    The Person: Reflective and Spontaneous/Poetic
    The Product: Condensed

Key Terms and Concepts:

Analysis	Constraints
Appropriateness	Flexible
Condensation	Intuition
Context	Norms

Open-mindedness   Stimulation
Originality   Summary power
Reflection   Surprise
Satisfaction   Tolerance of incongruity
Savoring   Transformation
Sensitivity   Unusualness
Spontaneity

Important People:

Phillip Jackson   Samuel Messick

What is a creative person like? For many people, the following vignette describes the typical childhood of such a person.

Creativity in Childhood

Tommy was an unkempt child, whose physical health was poor because of frequent bouts with viral infection. His teachers reported that the quality of his schoolwork was generally poor, and he had considerable difficulty with spelling and rote learning. He cared little for reading or writing and manifested a consistently negative attitude toward school in general. He frequently interrupted classes by "asking foolish questions," being rude to the teachers, and playing practical jokes on others.

He set fire to a portion of his home, and when asked why, he answered, "Because I wanted to see what the flames would do." The boy was given a beating by his father, in full view of the neighborhood. He attempted to hatch chicken eggs by sitting on them, and when this didn't work, he encouraged his playmates to swallow some raw. Neighbors frequently noted explosions coming from the basement of the boy's home, where his mother permitted him to play with chemical substances.

The boy's father had little regard for his son's intelligence, and stated that strong disciplinary intervention and obedience training were the best methods for dealing with Tommy. Nevertheless, his mother, a former schoolteacher, insisted that he be allowed to stay at home and receive the rest of his education from her. Ultimately, she had her way.

In fact, this boy did rather well. His full name is Thomas Edison.

As a child, Edison was plagued with stress and failure, and almost no one expected him to do well as an adult. He was socially inept, and he hated school but loved physical and technical knowledge. Edison had trouble reading and may have been dyslexic. Some theorists believe this is associated with dominance of the right hemisphere of the brain, which is also associated with high creative ability. In addition, his parents were not known to be highly creative.

Everyone would agree that this man was highly creative. Can we draw from these facts about his childhood some formula for producing a creative child? Absolutely not; for many creative persons, none of these factors were influential.

Which brings us to this question: "What do we mean by a creative person?" For people to be called creative, must their achievements be of the sort that brings national or international recognition? Must they be famous? I do not think so.

This book is not about extraordinarily creative geniuses like Edison. In fact, the ideas presented here are not restricted to highly creative persons in general. Instead, this book describes creativity as a cognitive, attitudinal, personal trait that every person has to some degree (unless in a coma or of very low intelligence).

The goal of the book is to describe what people who are high in creativity are like and how they may have gotten to be that way, so that readers can understand how to increase their own creativity and how to cultivate this trait in others. These others might include their children, their students, or their employees. The major premise is that all people may be helped to move from their present level of creative ability to one that is much higher. The higher the level a person has reached to begin with, the more he or she can hope to grow, but a study of the principles presented in this book should help anyone to make significant gains.

To begin with, it will be useful to study the most succinct model of creativity available today, which was developed by Phillip Jackson and Samuel Messick (1965). Table 1–1 provides a summary of the model, which includes cognitive and personal traits of creative people, characteristics of the products these people often produce, and the reflexive reactions observers usually have to those products.

The First Characteristic

Each characteristic in this model is represented by a complete row (see table 1–1). Thus there are five aspects of each of the four characteristics. The first characteristic has these aspects: tolerance of incongruity; originality; unusualness; norms; and surprise.

The Person: Tolerant of Ambiguity/Original

The intellectual trait suggested in the first row in table 1–1, **tolerance of incongruity,** is indeed a rare characteristic. Another term the authors might have used is *tolerance of ambiguity* (which is the term that will be used in chapter 2). This may well be the most crucial aspect of the creative mind. Its opposite is fear of the unknown or the unfamiliar.

The fear that most of us feel toward people and ideas significantly different from our own appears to have had evolutionary value. Avoiding strange situations must have helped animals and early humans stay alive. Unfortunately this tendency has become over-generalized. For example, most people of a different race, ethnic background, or political orientation are not really dangerous to us, yet we tend to view them suspiciously. Anthropologists tell us that it is common for preindustrial tribes to treat "those who live on the other side of the river" (other tribes who live in the vicinity) as enemies. But the person who is able to control this fear is far more likely to produce creative thoughts, and therefore products.

Tolerant persons are able to empathize with ideas that diverge from their own, and thus they are capable of combining their existing ideas with those that are new to them. The ability to produce unique intellectual combinations affects not only the mind, but also the person-

Table 1-1

JACKSON AND MESSICK'S FOUR CHARACTERISTICS OF CREATIVITY

Traits of the Person		*Traits of the Product*		
Intellectual Traits	*Personality Traits*	*Product Properties*	*Standards*	*Reflexive Reactions*
1. Tolerance of incongruity	Original	Unusualness	Norms	Surprise
2. Analysis and intuition	Sensitive	Appropriateness	Context	Satisfaction
3. Open-mindedness	Flexible	Transformation	Constraints	Stimulation
4. Reflection and spontaneity	Poetic	Condensation	Summary power	Savoring

Source: Jackson and Messick 1965. Copyright 1965 by Duke University Press. Reproduced with permission.

ality. Jackson and Messick believe that these tolerant individuals have an **original** life-style. Their social and emotional lives are imaginative, as are their ideas.

The Product: Unusual

When these individuals decide to produce something, it will often be unusual. We know it is unusual only because we can compare it to **norms** to find that it is rare. As Jackson and Messick put it, "No matter what other positive qualities it might possess, then, we generally insist as a first step that a product be novel before we are willing to call it creative" (p. 317).

If the product is really unusual, the reflexive response of most who experience it is one of instant **surprise.** No judgment occurs in this reaction; it is simply a matter of being startled, of having one's breath taken away by the originality of the product. This is the case whether the product is a painting, a building, a formula, or an omelet. Take, for example, Salvador Dali's painting *Crucifixion.* The viewer looks down on the cross as if perched on the top of a tall stepladder. Instead of nails, silver cubes affix the body of Christ to the cross. Many viewers gasp when they turn a corner and first see it.

The Second Characteristic

The Person: Analytical and Intuitive/Sensitive

Analytic and intuitive thinking is the cognitive trait for Jackson and Messick's second characteristic. Creativity is often linked to intuition, which is the ability to solve problems through the use of the subconscious. The fantastic leaps of imagination that lead to brilliant new concepts are usually considered intuitive. But high productivity almost never develops from the subconscious alone. The use of inductive and deductive logic typically plays a role in creating high-quality products. So does the careful checking of results against expectations. Analytic thinking may be seen to operate in the creative act in many ways.

Some years ago, one might hear that men are analytical and women intuitive. A friend once suggested to me that he thought this to be true because the expectations of society for the type of work the two sexes should perform is so different. His thinking went like this:

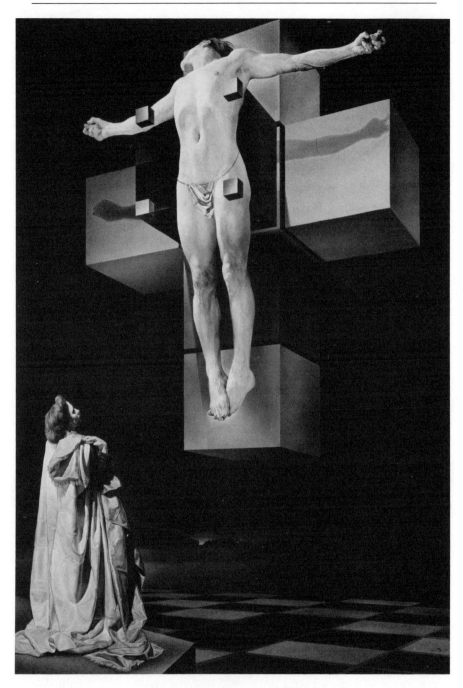

Figure 1–1. DALI'S *CRUCIFIXION*

We raise boys to understand that others who work with them will expect them to explain why they say what they do. Therefore boys are trained to think analytically—that is, logically, step by step—and to be consciously aware of the process. This way, they will be able to retrace for others the steps that brought them to their conclusions. Women, who work alone at home raising children, seldom have this requirement placed on them. Unhampered by the need to explain constantly the reasons for their decisions, they can afford to think intuitively.

Of course this is less likely to be the case today, since female gender roles are changing (see chapter 2).

At any rate, the point of Jackson and Messick's theory is that most creative acts are born of both analysis and intuition, and usually in the reverse order. Many creative persons have reported that they first get a strong feeling about an imaginative idea, and then must spend many hours pursuing it to fulfillment in the laboratory, on the canvas, or at the keyboard. Many people are relatively good at either analysis or intuition, but it is a rare person who does well at both and can use each to best advantage.

This cognitive trait is often found in people whose personalities may be described as highly **sensitive**. Such individuals seem to have special antennae the rest of us lack. They appear to have a sixth sense that allows them to delve into the heart of a situation and to be aware of the existence of problems before anyone else. In a groundbreaking study, Getzels and Csikszentmihalyi (1975) learned that although most gifted artists are excellent problem solvers, the best of them are also exceptionally good at problem finding.

The Product: Appropriate

Appropriateness is the second criterion of the creative product, and it results from this combination of intellect and personality. It refers to the correctness and goodness of the product, and is necessary in order to exclude those products that are original but serve no purpose. For example, the convoluted sentences of schizophrenics are unique but apparently have no meaning; they have been referred to as "verbal salad."

Correctness relates to the degree to which some specific objective has been satisfied. Goodness relates to the sense of value or worth the product evokes. Correctness is often the criterion used for scientific achievements, and goodness has more to do with the judgment of artistic productions. The former is probably easier to assess than the latter.

Jackson and Messick claim that "to be appropriate a product must fit its context; it must 'make sense' in the light of the demands of the situation and the desires of the producer" (p. 315). Thus it is only within a particular **context** that a product can be judged. When it has a distinct appropriateness, it generates a feeling of intense **satisfaction** in the observer. Many people find Handel's *Messiah*, for example, to be especially satisfying because of its ability to uplift them spiritually.

The Third Characteristic

The Person: Open-minded/Flexible

Open-mindedness, the ability to receive new information without prejudice, is obviously a critical aspect of creativity. Most people tend to view the new and different with a certain degree of fear. The unknown may or may not be dangerous to us, but we often treat it as potentially dangerous until we know more about it. This tendency is a more generalized version of the fear of strangers mentioned earlier. Creative persons differ in that they tend to treat the unknown or the unusual phenomenon as a challenge rather than as a threat, and thus they are more likely to come to an insightful understanding of it.

Why are some people genuinely open-minded? We don't know for sure, but it appears that an important cause is the lack of a learned generalized fearfulness. This theory concerns the relationship between the level of fear that is caused by the level of strangeness in a situation. The theory holds that open-minded people are those who are able to experience a higher than average level of strangeness before they reach a fearful reaction.

Why should this be so? The style of parenting is probably a major part of the answer. Most parents teach their children to avoid potentially dangerous situations by making them afraid of the consequences. In some cases this training is so severe that the child grows up filled with neuroses. Parents of the creative seem to be able to find more positive ways to protect their children and are less protective in the first place.

Of course, not all creative people were so well nurtured by their parents. Writers in particular often have suffered a hostile early environment, which they later overcame. In fact, they often seem to need to write in order to continue their recovery. Nevertheless, there was usually some nurturing person who helped them survive.

When parents encourage adventurousness, the child develops a **flexible** personality. This has a number of ramifications. In his book *The Open and Closed Mind*, Milton Rokeach (1960) reviewed research on this subject, and found that individuals with a more flexible personality tend to be less rigid, less neurotic, and less anxious than most. Most important, they are also less authoritarian. (This concept is close to Rank's personality theory, presented in chapter 3.)

The Product: Transformed

The third product criterion, which typically results from the efforts of the open-minded, flexible person, is **transformation**. This involves the capacity to reformulate a situation or field. Jackson and Messick suggest that some products "combine elements in ways that defy tradition and that yield a new perspective" (p. 312). Such products have "the power to transform the constraints of reality" (p. 313).

In any field of human endeavor, there are **constraints,** rules within which an effort must be confined. The world's greatest artistic and scientific achievements have rarely involved breaking the rules. Rather, they have somehow caused us to understand the rules in imaginative new ways. If these achievers were to disregard traditional constraints completely, we would scarcely be able to fathom their intent.

For example, much of Beethoven's music may be considered transformational; Beethoven was able to produce new forms without disregarding the stringent constraints placed on the composition of what we now call classical music. The natural response one has to a transformation is a high sense of **stimulation.**

The Fourth Characteristic

The Person: Reflective and Spontaneous/Poetic

The remaining cognitive trait suggested by this theory is the combination of **reflection** and **spontaneity**. *Reflection* indicates a slow, cautious approach to problem solving; *spontaneity* refers to an electric, risk-taking leap of faith. Here we are talking about the speed of the thought process, as opposed to the level of awareness seen in the dichotomy between analysis and intuition. The creative act often starts with a spontaneous spark, followed by careful reflection on the implications of the idea.

Sometimes, however, the process occurs in reverse, as in the case of the intervention of Fuchsian functions (a complex mathematical technique). The great French mathematician Henri Poincaré tells of spending months considering the problem of the functions. Tiring of his labors, he decided to take a trip to the country for a rest. But as he placed his foot on the first step of the bus that was to take him, the entire complex solution came to him in a flash. He was certain he had the answer, though it was to take him six more months, in those precomputer days, to develop the proofs that assured the correctness of his idea.

The combination of reflective and spontaneous thinking is precisely what the creative poet must have. It is in the nature of the poetic personality to be able to switch at will back and forth between these two cognitive styles. Jackson and Messick use the term *poetic* in its most generic sense, in that all great achievements are a kind of poetry. They seem simultaneously to unravel complications carefully and to leap to the heart of the matter.

The Product: Condensed

Thus the fourth criterion for the creative product is **condensation**. Always in such a product, complex information is unified and expressed in a highly condensed form. A simple purity results that nevertheless has an enormous **summary power**. This is true not only in the arts, but also in the sciences. For example, a number of physicists have described Einstein's famous formula, $E = mc^2$, derived from the theory of relativity, as poetic.

When a product demonstrates great condensation, a single encounter with it is never enough. The desire to **savor** it again and again seems natural. We want to relish the experience repeatedly, whether the experience is as abstract as a surrealistic painting or as substantial as a magnificiently prepared meal.

In Conclusion

Although Jackson and Messick's model offers many implications for research (especially in the area of the judgment of products), and though it has been cited frequently in other publications, little empirical study of it has been completed. Nevertheless, it has great summary power and gives the best single overview of the creative process. In the chapters that follow, many of the concepts included in this model, as well as others that I believe to be vital, will be considered in much greater detail. In the next chapter, the personal qualities of the creative person will be examined.

2

Eight Personal Qualities of the Creative Mind

Chapter Highlights:

Personality Measurement
Tolerance of Ambiguity
    Stimulus Freedom
    Functional Freedom
    Flexibility
    Risk Taking
    Preference for Disorder
    Delay of Gratification
    Androgyny
A Summary List of Creative Personality Traits

Key Terms and Concepts

Androgyny
Asking questions test
Asymmetry
Complexity
Constructs
Defense mechanisms

Delay of gratification
Flexibility
Functional fixity
Functional freedom
Internal reliability
Interscorer reliability

Preference for disorder	Test-retest reliability
Risk taking	Tolerance of ambiguity
Sex role identification	Two-string test
Stimulus freedom	Validity

Important Person:

Sandra Bem

How Kuriosity Killed the Kat

This is the story about a very curious cat named Kat. One day Kat was wandering in the woods where he came upon a big house made of fish. Without thinking he ate much of that house. The next morning when he woke up he had grown considerably larger. Even as he walked down the street he was getting bigger. Finally he got bigger than any building ever made. He walked up to the Empire State building in N.Y.C. and accidentally crushed it. The people had to think of a way to stop him so they made this great iron box which made the cat curious. He finally got inside it but it was too heavy to get him out of again. There he lived for the rest of his life. But he was still curious until his death, which was 6,820,000 years later. They buried him in the state of Rhode Island, and I mean the whole state.

—Ralph Titus, a seventh-grade student

Some people reading this little story might consider it merely cute; others would notice the restless imagination darting from place to place, the bold exaggeration, the disdain for the trite. These are early signs that this boy's mind has great creative possibilities. He has developed differently from his less imaginative peers. In this chapter, the eight essential personal qualities of creative individuals are examined. A list of other traits that may also be involved is presented at the end of the chapter. But before examining the personal traits, let us briefly consider how scientists go about measuring them.

Personality Measurement

When they first read about personality measurement, some students are surprised. They find it hard to believe that psychologists try to measure something so changeable and individual as a personality trait. They find it hard to accept statements such as "Jim is high in exhibitionism," or "Ann scored in the twentieth percentile in self-image." Certainly it is reasonable to ask how answering questions about a person's self-perception or making up little stories about the meaning of some picture (most personality "tests" use one of these approaches) can yield a true picture of that person's psyche.

Three questions must be asked of any personality measure to determine whether it is acceptable.

1. Is it reliable? Does it measure a trait consistently for a significant number of people? If it doesn't, then we cannot be sure that the trait it alleges to measure even exists. A measure of a personality trait is considered reliable if those taking it:

Get consistent scores over several administrations of the measure (**test-retest reliability**).

Get about the same score on one part of the measure as they do on another. For example, they get a similar score on the first half as on the second, or for even numbered questions as for odd (**internal reliability**).

Get about the same score no matter who is scoring the measure (**interscorer reliability**).

2. Is it valid? That is, does the measure accurately portray the trait that it claims to be measuring? This is a more difficult question. It must be admitted that all personality traits are really only concepts. They are **constructs,** that is, generalizations about some set of thoughts, feelings, attitudes, and behaviors that someone, usually a social scientist, alleges exist in some population of people. A number of techniques are used to determine the **validity** of a personality instrument.

3. Most important, is it useful? Ultimately, the question about a personality test score is whether it serves some socially useful purpose.

Does knowing a person's score or level on some trait help us to predict what that person is likely to do or not do in some set of circumstances? Does having that information make us more able to control that person's situation in a way that will prove helpful to him or her? Does having that information make us more likely to understand that person's behavior, or better able to understand human functioning in general? Thus the mark of a personality test (or of a personality theory, such as the one presented in this chapter, for that matter) is whether it can attain its own goal.

A number of reliable, valid, and highly useful personality measures exist. However, because of these measures' potential for causing harm to the individual's life, their selection and interpretation should be kept in the hands of highly trained specialists.

Tolerance of Ambiguity

Scholars do not know whether personal qualities can be direct causes of creativity, but it does seem clear that they are intimately involved in the process. The best evidence indicates that one trait above all, **tolerance of ambiguity,** is vital to the creative process and that seven others contribute both to the existence of this trait and to its role in promoting creativity. Figure 2–1 illustrates these relationships.

An ambiguous situation is one in which you have no framework to help direct your decisions and actions. Relevant facts are missing, the rules are unclear, the right procedures unavailable (MacKinnon 1978). For a five-year-old, the first day of kindergarten would be an example. For the forty-three-year-old, the reunion of his or her high school graduating class would be another.

People react differently to ambiguous situations. A situation that causes mild concern and heightened interest in some individuals may cause great tension and the desire to flee in others. The ability to remain open-minded in the face of ambiguity (and sometimes really to enjoy it) is a hallmark of the creative personality (Barron 1968, Sarnoff and Cole 1983, Torrance 1979). As Getzels (1975) puts it, "From this point of view, the core of creativity is not in the unconscious or regression to primary process thought, even in the service

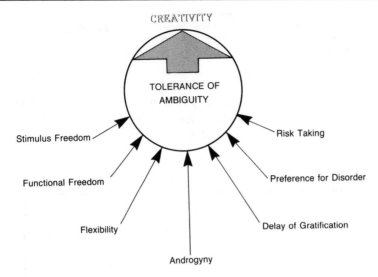

Figure 2–1. PERSONAL QUALITIES AND CREATIVITY

of the ego. It is not in withdrawal from the world; it is in openness to the world" (p. 334).

Imagine a continuum of emotionality going from low to high. Along this continuum extends the degree of familiarity/strangeness the average person perceives in a situation at a particular moment. The face of a brother, for instance, would seem very familiar, a flying saucer very strange. Along this continuum also extend the emotional reactions to the situation, from boredom to terror (see figure 2–2).

This continuum represents the relationship as it exists for the average person and for the creative. For the creative person, each of the emotional responses occur at a higher point (more to the right) on the continuum. Thus, for the creative person, a greater degree of strangeness or ambiguity is needed to cause fear or terror. This in turn fosters the ability to react creatively.

What else do we know about the personal qualities of such a person? Seven other personality traits have been seen to make significant contributions to tolerance of ambiguity (see figure 2–1). But before we proceed to the first of these traits, you might want to try your imagination on the Story-writing Test.

	Very familiar	Somewhat familiar	Somewhat strange	Very strange
Average person	Boredom	Interest	Excitement	Fear Terror
Creative person	Boredom	Interest	Excitement	Fear Terror

Figure 2–2. RELATIONSHIP BETWEEN LEVEL OF FAMILIARITY AND EMOTIONAL RESPONSE FOR AVERAGE AND CREATIVE PERSONS

Figure 2–3. THE STORY-WRITING TEST

Make up a story about the picture shown in figure 2–3. Be as descriptive and imaginative as you can. Think of a story that no one else would and take up to eight minutes to complete it.

Stimulus Freedom

In one of my studies of creativity, 1,200 junior and senior high school students from three different states took the Story-writing Test. Amazingly, about 900 of the stories were almost exactly alike! Can you guess what the common story was? It went like this:

Once upon a time there was a cat named Tom. He was very curious. One day he was looking around and spied a suspicious looking box.

He heard a scratching noise coming from it. He lifted up one side and there he saw a mouse named Jerry. Jerry was a fat little mouse and looked delicious. Without thinking, he made a grab for Jerry. The box crashed down on him and broke his head (skull, neck, back, etc.)! That was how curiosity killed the cat!

The other 300 stories were infinitely more variable. The story by Ralph Titus that introduced this chapter was one of them. And here is one more, written by an eighth grader.

Joe, the chipmunk, was chasing a butterfly. He was starving.

The sky overhead was streaked with clouds, the sun when it shone barely filtered through the trees, the burnt floor of the forest made the day seem completely gloomy. Joe wondered how he was going to get any food. He thought of last night—the men, the monsters. Some had four sharp claws, others had huge round eyes and pointed teeth. Joe was so scared!

Suddenly a bear jumped out of the bushes and was after him. He ran to a stream and started swimming. He was safe—only for a little, but . . . [the story stops here because time ran out.]

What is the major difference between the group of common stories and these others that are so much more flamboyant? The writers of the first group of stories were almost always constrained by the lines that surround the picture.

If you were to reread the instructions for this exercise, you would note that they do not include a rule against going outside the square boundaries of the picture. Nevertheless, the first group of writers all acted as though there had been such a rule. Under those circumstances, there isn't much to write about. The picture was purposely made extremely simple, in order to see whether the writer's imagination could embellish it (Torrance, Peterson, and Davis 1963).

The writers of the creative stories frequently used the small square in the picture merely as a departure point from which they could travel to other, more exotic places. Many saw it as a window or a door through which they could exit the picture frame. Others (like Ralph Titus) stretched their imaginations mightily in describing the square (for instance, a house made of fish). And a small number (as in the last story) simply disregarded the square altogether.

The trait illustrated by this activity is known as **stimulus freedom**. It has two aspects. When the stated rules of a situation interfere with the creative ideas of people who have stimulus freedom, those people are likely to bend the rules to their needs. More important, they do not assume that rules exist when the situation is ambiguous (Getzels 1975, I. Taylor 1975, Torrance 1979). The stimulus-bound person follows rules religiously, and when faced with ambiguity is likely to assume nonexistent directions in order to alleviate the fear of being wrong. This fear is undoubtedly one of the most effective inhibitors of creativity.

The ability to solve the ubiquitous "nine-dot problem" presented in figure 2–4 illustrates this trait. In this problem, all nine dots must be connected with four straight lines, without letting the pen or pencil leave the paper. The solution appears in figure 2–5.

Torrance (1979) describes the relevance of this problem to stimulus freedom thus:

> This is symbolic of the problem of first- and second-order changes. Most people assume that the nine dots contain a rectangle and that the solution must be found within the rectangle, a self-imposed condition. One's failure does not lie in the impossibility of the task, but in the attempted solutions. A person will continue to fail as long as he attempts only first-order change possibilities. Solutions become easy once one breaks away from the image of the rectangle and looks outside of the nine dots. The solution is a second-order change which involves leaving the "field" (the rectangle). The analogy between this and many real life family, business, and educational situations is obvious (pp. 178–79).

The analogy of the Story-writing Test above should also be obvious.

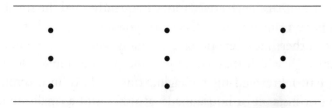

Figure 2–4. THE NINE-DOT PROBLEM

Breaking free from assumptions about a specific situation is only half of the problem. It is also necessary sometimes to disengage from the mind-set of one's surroundings. Famous creators have been known to go to extremes to achieve this. Levey (cited in Parnes and Harding 1962) describes some methods:

> In order to produce a state of inspiration, Schiller kept rotten apples in his desk; Shelley and Rousseau remained bareheaded in the sunshine; Bossuet worked in a cold room with his head wrapped in furs; Milton, Descartes, Leibniz and Rossini lay stretched out; Tycho Brahe and Leibniz secluded themselves for very long periods, Thoreau built his hermitage, Proust worked in a cork-lined room, Carlyle in a noise-proof chamber, and Balzac wore a monkish working garb; Gretry and Schiller immersed their feet in ice-cold water; Guido Reni could paint, and de Musset could write poetry, only when dressed in magnificent style; Mozart, following exercise; Lamennais, in a room of shadowy darkness, and D'Annunzio, Farnol and Frost only at night. The aesthetician, Baumgarten, advised poets seeking inspiration to ride on horseback, to drink wine in moderation, and, provided they were chaste, to look at beautiful women (p. 87).

Functional Freedom

How can the man in figure 2–6 reach the second string in order to tie the two strings together? Each string is almost 9 feet long. They are permanently attached to the ceiling of the room 14 feet apart. To help him solve this problem, the man may use either a mousetrap or a wooden spring-type clothespin. Neither of these is long enough so that he could use it to reach the other string. The explanation follows in figure 2–7.

Either a clothespin or a rat trap may be used to solve the problem: one or the other can be easily attached to one of the strings, then swung away from the other. The other string is grasped, and the first string caught as it swings back. Now they may be tied together readily.

Many people are unable to reach this solution because they cannot imagine clothespins or rat traps being used for other than their usual purposes (Duncker 1945, MacKinnon 1978, Torrance 1979). This is

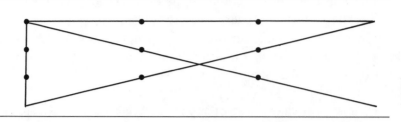

Figure 2-5. SOLUTION TO THE NINE-DOT PROBLEM

Figure 2-6. THE TWO-STRING TEST

called **functional fixity,** and it frequently blocks creative ideas. Its opposite is **functional freedom.**

A case in point: a graduate student in psychology studied the problem and said, "I've got it! The answer is the rat trap. You catch a bunch of rats until you get one that isn't seriously hurt. You make a pet of it, then train it to be a 'trapeze' rat. It will then jump up on one of the strings and swing it until it is able to swing over to you while you are holding the other string!" (See figure 2-8.) This is a good example of **functional fixity:** a rat trap can only be used to capture rats. This solution might work, but it is much more complicated than simply using the trap as a weight.

One young nun who was trying to solve the problem decided that the rat trap and clothespin were being used as ruses. Lifting the apron of her habit (the long, formal dress nuns used to wear), she seized the oversized rosary beads hanging from her belt and swung them over her head while holding one of the strings. The beads caught on the other string, and beaming with satisfaction, she tied the two strings together while those watching applauded! (See figure 2–9.)

This is a creative method for solving the problem if you happen to be a nun, but it wouldn't work for most of us.

A PARABLE

Once upon a time a disciple traveled thousands of miles to meet a master. Having finally arrived, he slept, washed himself, and carefully prepared himself for the long-awaited encounter. When the appointed time came, he was anxious to ask as many questions as possible.

Upon meeting with the disciple, the master quietly prepared some hot tea. He offered the refreshment to the disciple, who accepted by extending his cup. The master began to pour and continued until the boiling tea began to overflow onto the disciple's lap. In great consternation, the disciple waved his other hand and cried out, "Master, you must stop pouring!"

The master looked up and said, "Your mind is like your cup. It is so full of questions that there is no room for answers. You must first empty your mind if we are to start our discourse."

As this parable teaches, life is a process of growing functional fixity—the more we learn of how things work, the more we tend to accept the patterns as unalterable. The Two-string Test is a simple illustration of the ways rigidity can creep into thinking patterns. Researchers have used it as a technique for exploring the creative abilities of thousands of people (Maier 1931).

It is necessary here to distinguish between problem solving and creativity. Problem solving may range all the way from the second

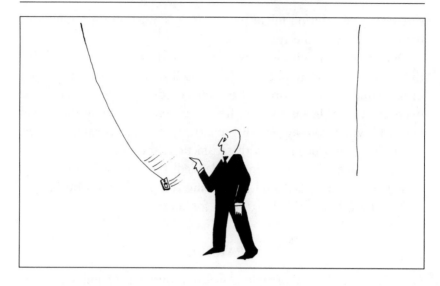

Figure 2-7. SOLUTION TO THE TWO-STRING TEST

grader's solution to a simple arithmetic problem to Einstein's development of the theory of relativity. Only at the highly imaginative and original levels may problem solving be considered creative. Nevertheless, it is clear that functional fixity interferes with problem solving at all levels.

Figure 2-8. THE ACROBATIC RAT

Figure 2-9. THE NUN'S SOLUTION

Flexibility

One of the most interesting findings in the study of creative development has to do with **flexibility**. Before explaining this concept more fully, you may wish to take the Asking Questions Test.

Figure 2–10. THE ASKING QUESTIONS TEST

List all of the questions you can think of to ask about the drawing in figure 2–10. Do not ask questions that can be answered just by looking at the drawing. Try to ask questions no one else would think of. Time limit: five minutes.

Flexibility, the ability to see the *whole* of the situation, has been seen in many studies as a critical element in the creative act (MacKinnon 1975, 1978, C. Taylor 1964a, Torrance 1979). Seeing all of the components in a problem, and not just fixating on one of the parts, is much more likely to produce a creative solution. In high-pressure situations, such as taking a test, most people seem to latch on to the first decent idea they get and push it as far as they can. For example, a common response to the Asking Questions Test is to ask six or seven questions about the clown's hat or shoes. This is in accordance with the directions, but it is not nearly as imaginative as the same number of divergent questions.

The scoring of this test of flexibility involves counting the number of questions asked that fall into separate categories (Torrance and Templeton 1963). Examples of some of the types of categories they use (but not the real ones) are listed below.

Some categories for scoring the Asking Questions Test:

1. Characters not in the picture
2. Costume in general

3. Family and home of the clown
4. The clown's hat
5. Magical talents
6. The clown's pants
7. Physical occurrences not in the water

Risk Taking

In the Ring Toss Game seen in figure 2–11, the farther the peg is from the tosser, the greater the number of points scored for a successful toss. The pins become equally harder to hit the farther away they are from the tossing line. At which of the pegs do you think you would most likely aim?

This child's game is a simple illustration of the fourth characteristic of creative people, **risk taking** (Atkinson 1964). People who aim at the number one position take a very limited risk, and even if they ring the pin all ten times, their maximum possible score is 10 (1 point per pin). Those who aim at the tenth pin have only one-tenth the chance of scoring, so even though the tenth pin is worth 10 points, their most likely score is also 10 (one success × 10 points). Those willing to take a moderate risk would probably aim at the fifth pin. Here the likely score would be 25 (five successes × 5 points).

These figures obviously only hold for this particular game, but they are probably representative of the real world. Those who take tiny

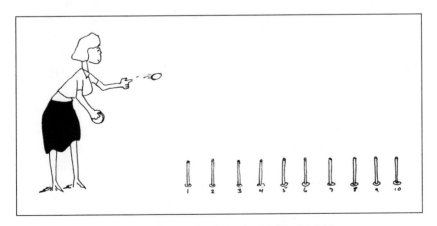

Figure 2–11. THE RING TOSS GAME

risks or huge risks are less likely to be successful in their endeavors than are those who take moderate risks. Interestingly, research indicates that the proclivity for taking moderate risks is highly associated with tolerance of ambiguity.

Preference for Disorder

If you decide to take the Barron-Welsh Figure Preference Test (see figure 2–12), don't try to figure out what it is measuring. Just choose one of each of the pairs that you truly like.

"Correct" answers to the Figure Preference Test:

1. A	3. B	5. B	7. A	9. B
2. B	4. A	6. B	8. A	10. B

Can you see why the answers to the Figure Preference Test are considered correct, in terms of tolerance of ambiguity and creativity? What are the two elements that characterize the differences between each of the pairs of pictures?

They are **complexity** and **asymmetry**. Creative people regularly prefer these kinds of pictures to those that are simple and symmetrical. The underlying variable, says psychologist Frank Barron, is a **preference for disorder,** because it is ultimately more interesting to creative persons than is order. That is not to say that all artists live in disorderly garrets, or that all scientists refuse to comb their hair, but rather that highly creative people enjoy the challenge of bringing order out of disorder, their own order (Barron 1968, Barron and Welsh 1952, MacKinnon 1975, 1978, Welsh 1959).

Why should disorder be more interesting? MacKinnon (1978) explains it well:

It is clear that creative persons are especially disposed to admit complexity and even disorder into their perceptions without being made anxious by the resulting chaos. It is not so much that they like disorder per se, but that they prefer the richness of the disordered to the stark barrenness of the simple. They appear to be challenged by disordered multiplicity, which arouses in them a strong need which in them is

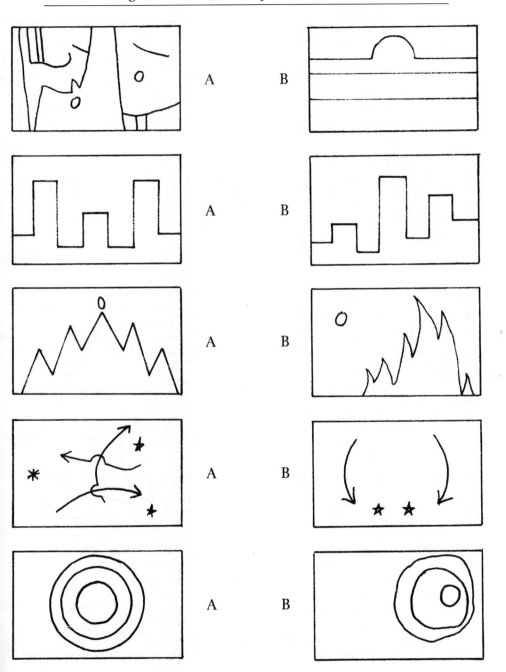

Figure 2-12. THE BARRON-WELSH FIGURE PREFERENCE TEST

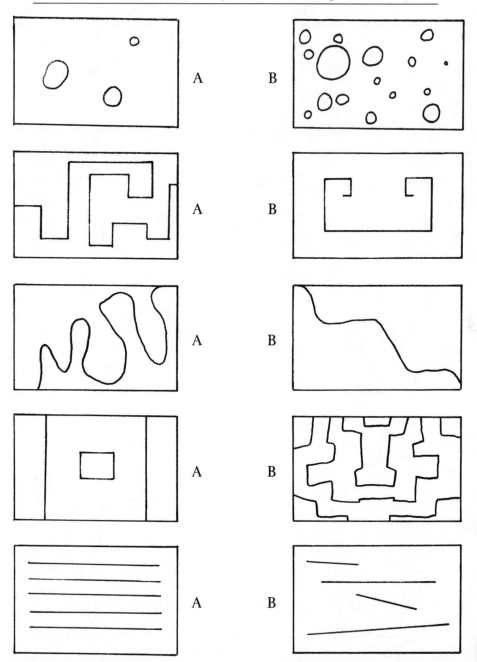

Figure 2-12 (*Continued*)

serviced by a superior capacity to achieve the most difficult and far-reaching ordering of the richness that they are willing to experience (p. 62).

Delay of Gratification

The willingness to endure the stress of prolonged effort so as to reap higher pleasures is the fifth trait that contributes to tolerance of ambiguity. In psychological circles, it is referred to as **delay of gratification.** This is what makes some people save money in order to make a major purchase. It is also what makes some creative people spend years on a project without recognition or reward.

As Thomas Edison said, "Creativity is one part inspiration and 99 parts perspiration." He demonstrated his faith in this statement through the way in which he invented the light bulb. Early in his work, he got the idea of passing electricity through a filament placed in a vacuum in a glass sphere. Nevertheless, he had to conduct 2,004 experiments, using different materials for the filament, before he discovered that carbonized thread would not burn out quickly.

Androgyny

Unfortunately, history has recognized a marked difference between the achievements of males and females. Until the second half of this century, this was routinely explained as a result of the difference between male and female brains: for the most part, female brains were thought simply to lack the "creative gene." Only in recent decades have social scientists suggested that the apparent lack of female creative productivity over the centuries may be less the result of sex than of sex role.

SEX ROLE IDENTIFICATION QUESTIONNAIRE

You might want to try this questionnaire—if so, try not to think what the "right" answers for your gender should be. Simply put a letter *A* in front of the statement number if you agree with a statement, and a *B* in front of statements with which you disagree.

_____ 1. If I get too much change in a store, I always give it back.

_____ 2. I think I would like the work of an interior decorator.

_____ 3. I am somewhat afraid of the dark.

_____ 4. I become irritated when I see someone spit on the sidewalk.

_____ 5. In school, I was sometimes sent to the principal for bad behavior.

_____ 6. I like to hunt.

_____ 7. A windstorm usually scares me.

_____ 8. I prefer a shower to a bath.

_____ 9. I always tried to get the best grades I could.

_____ 10. I think I would enjoy the work of a building contractor.

_____ 11. I like to boast about my achievements now and then.

_____ 12. I would never feel right if I thought I was not doing my share of the work of any group to which I belonged.

_____ 13. I get excited rather easily.

_____ 14. I am apt to hide my feelings about some things to the point that people may hurt me without knowing it.

_____ 15. When someone talks against certain nationalities, I usually speak against such talk even if it makes me unpopular.

_____ 16. I think I would like racing a car.

_____ 17. The thought of being in an automobile accident is very frightening to me.

_____ 18. I must admit I feel sort of scared when I go to a strange place.

_____ 19. I think I would enjoy being a nurse.

_____ 20. Sometimes I just feel like picking a fight with someone.

_____ 21. I believe I have a certain talent for understanding other people, and for sympathizing with their problems.

_____ 22. I prefer adventure stories to romantic stories.

_____ 23. I like to look at "men's" magazines.

_____ 24. I think I would enjoy being a dress designer.

Sorting out what is genetically different between the sexes from permanent differences that are learned is a complicated matter. Furthermore, it is becoming increasingly clear that **sex role identification,** which is learned first in families and then reinforced by school and work experience, plays a large part in a person's belief about whether or not she or he can be creative.

An excellent example of this may be seen in a study that was done on first graders (Torrance 1963b, 1979). Their creative abilities were measured by asking them to suggest how three toys could be improved so that they would be more fun to play with. The toys were a fire truck (considered a male toy), a nurse's kit (considered a girl's toy), and a stuffed dog (considered neutral at this age). The responses were scored according to fluency (total number of ideas), flexibility (the number of ideas that were qualitatively different from each other), and originality (the number of ideas that no one else in the group had thought of).

The average scores broke down as would be expected: boys' scores in each of the category types were higher than girls' for the fire truck; girls' were similarly superior to boys' for the nurse's kit; and the two sexes did about equally well with the stuffed dog.

Torrance administered the same test two years later, when the children were about to enter the third grade. The change was striking: the boys earned scores superior to those of the girls on all of the toys, even including the nurse's kit. A number of explanations are possible. Perhaps girls simply become less creative with age. This seems unlikely, though, especially over such a short period of time. Torrance concluded that sex role identification was the cause. He suggests that elementary school teachers (most of whom are female) teach young girls that they "should not question the *status quo.*" As he puts it, "You often hear teachers say, 'I need some strong boys to help me.'" Girls are more likely to be praised for being 'lady-like.'"

This study suggests that parents may not discourage creative imagination in girls but that elementary school teachers probably do. There is other evidence that sex role identification is a significant factor in creative ability. Before considering it, take a closer look at what this concept means. Here is the scoring for the sex role identification questionnaire.

The sex role identification test measures the degree to which individuals identify with (feel a close association with) their own sex. If you are female, give yourself 1 point for each answer below that is the same as yours. If you are a male, give yourself 1 point for every answer that is the same as yours.

1. A	7. A	13. A	19. A
2. A	8. B	14. A	20. B
3. A	9. A	15. B	21. A
4. A	10. B	16. B	22. B
5. B	11. B	17. A	23. B
6. B	12. A	18. A	24. A

A major study of the relationship between sex role identification and creativity used a questionnaire like this (Roe 1946, 1975). It found that people who have an ordinary level of creative ability tend to score rather low if they are males (at about 6) and high if they are females (at about 18). (Males who get really low scores I call "macho men," and women who get really high scores I refer to as "Scarlett O'Haras.") However, highly creative males were found to be much closer to the center of this continuum (at about 10). This was also true of highly creative females (they averaged about 14). Figure 2–13 illustrates this relationship. Notice that these highly creative people did not reverse their sex roles; they did not score like the members of the opposite sex. They were just closer to the center of the range.

Why should this be so? Roe's conclusion was that high creativity requires individuals to have some of the qualities of the opposite sex. Creative males need to have that characteristic usually associated with

1	2	3	4	5	6	7	8	9	10	11	12	13	14	15	16	17	18	19	20	21	22	23	24

T
y Macho Creative Creative Scarlett
p Man Man Woman O'Hara
e
Average Score

Figure 2–13. THE SEX ROLE IDENTIFICATION SCALE

females, sensitivity to the feelings of others, in order to get in touch with their creative urges. Females, on the other hand, need the characteristic more typically associated with males, assertiveness, in order to promote their ideas in a critical world. To use Ghiselin's (1952) phrase, there is a "purity of motive" in these individuals that transcends the more ordinary gender roles.

In his extensive study of highly creative male architects (1978), MacKinnon also reached this conclusion:

> The evidence is clear. The more creative a person is the more he reveals an openness to his own feelings and emotions, a sensitive intellect and understanding self-awareness, and wide-ranging interests including many which in the American culture are thought of as feminine. In the realm of sexual identification and interest, our creative subjects appear to give more expression to the feminine side of their nature than do less creative persons. In the language of the Swiss psychologist, Carl G. Jung (1956), creative persons are not so completely identified with their masculine persona roles as to blind themselves to or to deny expression to the more feminine traits of the anima [Jung's term for the unconscious female nature] (p. 61).

In their study of creative women mathematicians, Helson and Crutchfield (1970) did not find that these women were as high on measures of masculine "orientation and interests" but did discover that they were like the creative men in most other personality traits. Helson asked "how a woman could so suppress her feminine nature to be a mathematician without suppressing her originality also," and concluded that "part of the answer seems to be that the women mathematicians are introverts, whose 'natures' are not the modal American type" (meaning a typical American woman) (p. 248).

The questionnaire presented earlier is only one of many tests of sex role identification. Inventing one is easy: simply ask a large number of questions that might be answered differently by people of both sexes, and choose those questions that clearly differentiate between the two.

Recently, a new aspect of sex role identification has been identified. Known as **androgyny,** it too has ramifications for creative thinking. The word is made up of the Greek for male, *andro,* and for female, *gyne.* It refers to those persons who have higher than average male *and* female elements in their personalities. More specifically, such persons are more likely to behave in a way appropriate to a situation, regardless of their gender. For example, when someone forces his way into a line at the movies, the traditional female role calls for a woman to look disapproving but to say nothing. The androgynous female would tell the offender in no uncertain terms to go to the end of the line. When a baby left unattended in a carriage starts to cry, the traditional male response would be to try to find some woman to take care of its needs. The androgynous male would pick up the infant and attempt to comfort it.

Androgyny is not seen merely as the midpoint between the two poles of masculinity and femininity. Rather, it is at a higher level of sex role identification than is either of the more traditional roles. Figure 2–14 illustrates this relationship.

Researcher Sandra Bem (1975) conducted an experiment that illustrates the relationship between androgyny and creativity. First, she measured the subjects' level of androgyny by a sex role test that she devised. Then she administered a test that offered choices of pairs of activities, one of the pair being of the type usually performed by a male and the other by a female, listing a pay level next to each activity. In some cases the male activity (for example, oiling hinges in a door factory) paid more, and sometimes the female activity (preparing baby bottles in a hospital) was more highly paid.

It came as no surprise that those rated low in androgyny were much more likely to choose the activities that related to their own sex, even though half the time these were lower paying. In a second phase of the experiment, each subject was asked to perform three male tasks, three female tasks, and three neutral tasks. Those subjects

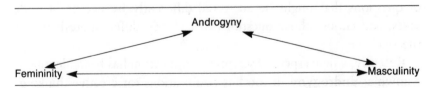

Figure 2–14. THREE LEVELS OF SEX ROLE RELATIONSHIPS

who identified highly with their own sex felt much worse than did the androgynous subjects about performing a task that was not traditionally done by their sex. The low-androgyny individuals said they "felt less attractive and likeable, more nervous and peculiar, less masculine or feminine, and didn't enjoy the experience."

Bem concluded that rigid sex roles are costly to the personality (it is really a form of functional fixity). Such rigidity frequently causes conflict and requires great expenditure of energy to deal with the stress brought about by the conflicts. Often **defense mechanisms** (see next chapter) are called into play to avoid awareness of the conflicts. Bem concluded that the androgynous role is far more functional because it fosters the search for the truly appropriate course of action. This is also more likely to cultivate creativity.

A Summary List of Creative Personality Traits

These eight personal qualities are indicated by research to be strongly involved in creativity. Numerous other traits, however, probably also play a relevant role. Here is a summary list of these traits.

According to reliable research, it may be said that creative persons

Are more sensitive to the existence of problems.

Have a somewhat greater tendency toward emotional disturbance, but also have more self-control for dealing with this tendency.

Are able to be both analytical and intuitive in their thinking.

Are able to think both convergently—solving problems that have only one correct answer—and divergently—solving problems that have many possible answers.

Demonstrate greater determination and perseverance.

Have higher than average intelligence but do not often measure in the "genius" range.

Are more open to experience and less defensive about accepting new information.

See themselves as responsible for most of what happens to them.

Enjoy being playful and childlike; have the ability to toy with the environment.

Engage more frequently in solitary activities, especially as children.

Are more likely to question the status quo.

Are more independent of the judgment of others.

Are less afraid of their own impulses and hidden emotions.

Like to do their own planning, make their own decisions, and need the least training and experience in self-guidance.

Do not like to work with others, and prefer their own judgment of their work to the judgment of others. They therefore seldom ask other students or their teachers for opinions.

Take a hopeful outlook when presented with complex, difficult tasks.

Have the most ideas when a chance to express individual opinion is presented. These ideas frequently evoke the ridicule of others.

Are most likely to stand their ground in the face of criticism.

Are the most resourceful when unusual circumstances arise.

Are not necessarily the "best" students.

Show an imaginative use of many different words.

Are more original. Their ideas are qualitatively different from everyone else's.

Of course not every highly creative person will be seen to possess all of these traits. Nevertheless, the more a person possesses (or tries to achieve) these personal qualities, the more his or her creativity is likely to blossom.

3

Theories about the Formation of Creative Personality Traits

Chapter Highlights:

The Psychoanalytic Theories
    Freud's Theory
    Kris's Theory
    Jung's Theory
    Rank's Theory
    Adler's Theory
    Hammer's Theory

The Humanistic Theories
    Maslow's Theory
    Rogers's Theory
    Fromm's Theory

Which School of Thought Is Best?

Key Terms and Concepts

Acquiescing personality
Collective unconscious
Compensatory theory
Creative personality
Defense mechanisms

Endocept
Fully functioning person
Hierarchy of needs
Neurotic personality
Peak experience

Regression   Sublimation
Self-transcendence

Important People

Alfred Adler   Ernst Kris
Sigmund Freud   Abraham Maslow
Erich Fromm   Otto Rank
Emanuel Hammer   Carl Rogers
Carl Jung

We have studied variations infinitely less than we have studied deviations. This is probably because variations get along so well without us. But if the neurotic deviations are interesting, the variations are fascinating.

— E.F. Hammer (1961)

The eight qualities examined in the last chapter give us one perspective on the creative person. They give us a picture of some major influences on the thinking of such persons but do not describe how they got to be that way. In this chapter, we will examine the most significant theories that explain the formation of creative personality traits.

There must be as many as fifty theories to explain the creative personality. The best of them fall rather decisively into one of two schools of thought: the psychoanalytic and the humanistic.

The Psychoanalytic Theories

In general, psychoanalytic theorists see creativity as the result of overcoming some problem, usually one that began in childhood. The creative person is viewed as someone who has had a traumatic experience, which he or she dealt with by allowing conscious and unconscious ideas to mingle into an innovative resolution of the trauma. The creative act is seen as transforming an unhealthy psychic state into a healthy one.

Freud's Theory

Some psychologists have argued that creative ability is a personality trait that becomes fixed in the first five years of life. The chief proponent of this view was Sigmund Freud (1856–1939). He was fascinated by the concept of creativity, his own as well as others', and wrote a number of books and papers on the subject (1933, 1948, 1951, 1953), the most famous of which is *On Creativity and the Unconscious* (1959). Freud's explanation of the creative process depends heavily on his ideas about **defense mechanisms,** which are unconscious attempts to prevent awareness of unpleasant or unacceptable ideas. Because defense mechanisms prevent an accurate perception of the world and because they use up psychic energy, they usually interfere with creative productivity. Definitions of those occurring most commonly are provided in table 3–1.

It should be noted that introjection (number 6) is a type of identification (number 5). Further, projection (number 8) is related to, but is significantly different from, reaction formation (number 9).

Freud believed that although most defense mechanisms interfere with the creative act, the mechanism he called **sublimation** is actually the primary cause of creativity. Freud strongly believed that people are only motivated to be creative when they cannot directly fulfill their sexual needs.

This link between unconscious sexual needs and creativity begins in the early years of life. Although many people do not think of children as having sexual needs, Freud argued that at the age of four it is typical for children to develop a physical desire for the parent of the opposite sex. Since this need is virtually never met, sublimation sets in and the beginning of a fertile imagination is born. As he put it:

> Should we not look for the first traces of imaginative activity as early as in childhood? The child's best-loved and most intense occupation is with his play or games. Might we not say that every child at play

Table 3–1
COMMON DEFENSE MECHANISMS

Defense Mechanism	Definition
1. Repression	Unconsciously forgetting experiences that are unpleasant to remember.
2. Compensation	Attempting to make up for an unconsciously perceived inadequacy by excelling at something else.
3. Sublimation	When unable to fulfill your sex drives, making up for it by being creative in some artistic way (for example, becoming a great violinist).
4. Rationalization	Coming to believe that a condition that was contrary to your desires is actually what you had wanted all along (for example, sour grapes—"I'm glad I missed the trip; it would have been boring anyway.").
5. Identification	Adopting the standards and values of someone you wish you were like.
6. Introjection	Adopting the standards and values of someone with whom you are afraid to disagree.
7. Regression	Reverting to behaviors that were previously successful when current behavior is unsuccessful (for example, crying about getting a low grade in school with the unconscious hope that the teacher will change the grade).
8. Projection	Ascribing to another person the feelings you actually have about him or her.
9. Reaction formation	Adopting feelings toward another person that are the opposite of your real feelings toward that person.
10. Displacement	When afraid to express your feelings toward one person (for example, anger at your boss), expressing them to someone less powerful (you yell at your son, for instance).
11. Compartmentalization	Having two mutually incompatible beliefs at the same time (for example, "Even though Joe is black, he's so nice, he's the same as a white man").

Source: Dacey 1986.

behaves like a creative writer, in that he creates a world of his own or, rather, rearranges the things of his world in a new way that pleases him? (1959, p. 81)

Freud traced many specific artistic works to the artist's sublimation. For example, he suggested that Leonardo da Vinci's many paintings of the Madonna resulted from a sublimated longing for sexual fulfillment with a mother figure, since he lost his own mother early in his life. Freud argued that all cultural achievement was the result of sublimation. So strongly did he believe this that when he turned forty-one and found his own creative drive to be waning, he decided to curtail all sexual activity with his wife in order to maintain his ability to contribute to psychoanalytic theory.

Kris's Theory

Ernst Kris (1900–57) asserted that another defense mechanism, **regression,** is also often involved in the creative act. He stated that when a person is able to regress to a childlike frame of mind, the barriers between the conscious and unconscious mind are weakened and the unconscious material is more readily available to awareness (1952, 1965a). This material frequently contains the germs of creative insights.

Kris describes this process in vivid psychoanalytic terms:

The barrier between the id and the ego has temporarily become permeable. Impulses reach preconsciousness more easily than under other conditions, and their translation into formed expression can proceed painlessly. Forces previously used for repression are being used by the ego for another purpose. All energy seems to be vested in the process of coming to consciousness; hence the similarity between inspirational experiences and those of a hallucinatory kind, a similarity once more clearest in its difference (1965b, p. 36).

Arieti (1966) has termed this type of thought an **endocept** (from the Greek *endo,* meaning inside). An endocept is a thought that is amorphous, so unformed that it cannot be expressed to others. It is contrasted with the concept, which is a more mature form of cognition and which has less of an emotional component. Arieti describes it thus: "The endocept is a primitive organization of past experiences, perceptions, memory traces, and images of things and movements. These previous experiences, which are repressed and not brought back to consciousness, continue to have an indirect influence" (p. 54).

Creative people are those best able to retrieve material in their unconscious minds. An "early history of traumatization" probably plays an unusually great part in this, Kris surmised. The audience (the reader of a poem, for example) exactly reverses this process. First there is a cognitive recognition of what the artist is trying to express, followed by an emotional, unconscious experience of the artist's feelings and experiences. The task of the audience is to *recreate* the artist's creation.

As adults, we are never more childlike, Kris believed, than when we are making love. In this act, we touch the wellsprings of our lives. We sometimes talk baby talk, tickle each other, and say silly things. Kris believed that most of us are only able to return to childhood, briefly, during love making.

Creative people are those rare birds who are uninhibited enough to be childlike in their thinking about things other than sex. They can maintain a playful attitude about the most serious concerns of life. In doing so, they are able to look at problems in a fresh, innovative way, to "regress in the service of the ego." To others, they may seem to be regressing into a "second childhood," but if they are also intelligent, creativity may result.

How can this process be fostered? Kris admitted that we just don't know. "When as psychoanalysts we study the artist's personality we are subject to the limitations imposed by the therapeutic situation. Hence most of the statements of psychoanalysts seem to focus on relevant but not on specific factors" (1965b, p. 41).

Jung's Theory

Carl Jung (1875–1961) was a close associate of Freud, who also believed that the unconscious plays a vital role in high-level creativity. He acknowledged that the individual's experiences, and especially those having to do with sex, are important, but he believed that great ideas come from a deeper source (1933, 1956).

Jung suggested that each person's unconscious mind is formed by a personal past. In addition, the vague memories of the experiences of the whole human race are stored there. Like other animals, we can unconsciously "remember" the most influential understandings of our forebears. It is from this **collective unconscious** that the greatest inventions, theories, art, and other new achievements are drawn. This process is what lends continuity to human existence.

"The artist is not a person endowed with free will who seeks his own ends," Jung said, "but one who allows art to realize its purpose through him" (1966, p. 201). How reminiscent of the Greek concept of the muse visiting the poet! The creative personality, then, is that which is most capable of communing with both types of unconscious thought.

Rank's Theory

A student of Freud's, Otto Rank (1884–1939) hypothesized that people are born without a will of their own. The will is a slowly developing function of the ego (1945, 1965). Babies in a nursery behave rather similarly; we can see little evidence of individual will. Very soon, however, children start to differentiate themselves from each other in what they want. They begin to develop a will of their own.

Parents respond to this developing will in one of three ways. Rank estimated that 75–80 percent of all parents find themselves threatened by it. They see it as their job to control the child, so whenever the child says, "I want to do this," they say, "No!" Furthermore, there's a natural tendency to say *no* in a way that sounds critical of the child's motives. The implication is "And you shouldn't have asked in the first place."

Often young children conclude, "Not only was my desire wrong, but I am not a good person. My will is bad. My will gets me into trouble. This could cost me the love of my parents." So they rather quickly learn to become **acquiescors**. That is the description Rank assigned to most of us.

Most of us are not aware of it, but research indicates that there is a high correlation between what we decide and what the authority figures in our lives want. For example, people tend to be of the same religion, political party, and socioeconomic level as their parents.

Rank said that this acquiescence to parental will results because we are afraid that if we deviate from their beliefs too much, we're going to be all alone.

Another type of parent is inconsistent. Sometimes a child's request meets with the parent's approval, and sometimes the same request is refused and criticized. The child is uncertain about what will happen. This person Rank call the **neurotic,** the personality type that results from inconsistent parenting. Such persons often develop phobias that they hope may protect them. Like acquiescors, they cannot be innovative.

For the smallest group of children, the parental response is almost always supportive. In effect, the parent says, "I will not oppose what you want unless you are endangering your own safety or the rights and safety of other people. Other than that, I will say yes and back you up on it." This is not permissive, because such parents do encourage appropriate behavior. However, the children get the impression that what they think and want is really important. Children raised this way tend to develop what Rank calls a **creative personality.** Because they feel their desires are worthy, they dare to be "a minority of one" and thus are the only people who have a chance of being truly creative. Because personality formation happens within the first five years of life, Rank believed that no one who was not "backed up" by her or his parents in early childhood has any chance of being creative.

Adler's Theory

Alfred Adler (1870–1937) contributed the **compensatory theory** of creativity (1917). He departed from the Freudian adherence to the concept of defense mechanisms by arguing that the creative act is primarily an attempt to compensate for some perceived inferiority. Most often, the perception of being inferior begins in childhood.

Adler originally explained the compensation in organic terms (deafness, a club foot, and so forth). He later came to view the deficit as being either physical or psychological. Disagreeing with Freud and Jung, he argued that compensation for the perceived inferiority stems from conscious, rather than unconscious, efforts. He "posited an innate pattern of behavior striving for positive growth and self-actualization" and saw creativity as "supreme usefulness, and those who are more creative are more useful for purposes of serving a social function" (cited in Taylor and Getzels 1975, p. 6).

Hammer's Theory

On the basis of his research with adolescent artists, Emanuel Hammer (1926–   ) offers an updated version of Adler's view (1984). He used projective techniques (the *Rorschach Test*, the *Thematic Apperception Test*, the *H-T-P Drawing Test*, and the *Unpleasant Concept Test*) in reaching his conclusions. These instruments were administered to two groups of college art students, one categorized as highly creative, and one as "merely facile."

As compared with the second group, the creative students demonstrate a number of unusual traits. The creative students

1. Were "emotionally reserved persons who tend to step back from situations in which one readily exchanges feelings with others" (p. 104)
2. Were more likely to observe than to participate
3. Suffered unhappy feelings because they felt that others reject them
4. Were more likely to resort to fantasy in their daily lives
5. Were much more in touch with "deep, personal, intimate regions" within themselves
6. Converted their retreat from others "into an emphasis upon self-directedness, independence, criticality, and individuality (p. 105)
7. "Put forth an effort to accomplish what matters to [them], no matter how hard the effort" (p. 107)
8. Were masochistic, but with a strong tendency to be exhibition-istic about the pain that this causes
9. Were able to "harmonize all the manifold ingredients into an effective integration" (p. 109)

Hammer also addressed the old question of whether "creativity is next to madness." He found that his young artists definitely manifest emotional disturbance, and cites numerous cases of famous persons for whom this was true. He describes the writings of W.H. Auden and Edmund Wilson on their "wounds," and refers to Sophocles' work *Philoctetes*, a story about a warrior who has a foul wound but is neverthessless sought out by others because of his superior qualities. Hammer concurs with MacKinnon—in his findings on architects (see chapter 2—that most highly creative artists are compensating for deep emotional conflicts, and asserts that "the crucial personality ingredient is a willingness first to face, then to shape, to mold, to work the painful material within rather than to merely moan. In [the creative artist] we see the height man can reach in achieving a triumph of health over illness" (p. 115).

The Humanistic Theories

Unlike most of the psychoanalytic theories, the humanist theories see creativity as a result of a high degree of psychological health. They give a much smaller role to unconscious drives and compensation for deficits in the personality, and much more credit to positive, self-fulfilling tendencies. They also see creativity as developing throughout life, rather than as being restricted to the first five years. The idea that creativity can be cultivated throughout the life span has had its strongest proponent in psychologist Abraham Maslow, who was well known for his opposition to the psychoanalytic point of view.

Maslow's Theory

Abraham Maslow (1908–70) believed that human beings have six basic instincts, which manifest themselves as needs. These needs must be met in a sequential order, with the most primitive needs present at birth, and the higher-order needs developing as maturation proceeds (1954, 1962). The six instinctual needs are described in table 3–2.

The sequence of this **hierarchy of needs** is clear: no one is likely to be self-actualizing while suffering from severe hunger pains. Maslow sees the first four as "deficiency" needs, because it is possible to satisfy them to the point that they are no longer deficient. When we feel hungry, it is possible to eat enough so that the need is fulfilled.

Table 3–2

MASLOW'S HIERARCHY OF NEEDS

Type of Need	*Level of Need*	
1. Physiological needs. These are the needs we have for basic creature comforts: food, water, warmth, air, sex.	Deficiency	Low
2. Safety needs. We must feel we are free from threat to our lives. Safety needs include our desires for familiarity, regularity, and a secure home.	Deficiency	
3. Belongingness and love needs. All people want to feel that they belong somewhere and that at least one other person feels a sense of love and caring for them.	Deficiency	
4. Esteem needs. We need to feel that we are worthwhile and capable, and that the society we live in values our contribution to it.	Deficiency	
5. Self-actualization needs. We also need to be in touch with those resources that lie deep within us. These include imagination and creativity, our ability to experience great joy, and to make total use of our potential. Maslow suggests that we carry not only our past inside us, but also our future, in the sense that the direction of our growth lies within us and needs to be fulfilled.	Being	
6. Aesthetic needs. Very few people actually are aware of having an aesthetic need, which is the need to make an important contribution to mankind. It is the desire to have a deep understanding of the world around us and the purpose of life. This need exists on a high level, and only a few (for example, Abraham Lincoln, Albert Einstein, Margaret Mead) experience it.	Being	High

Source: Adapted from Maslow, 1962.

The highest two he calls "being" needs, because nurturing them makes them even greater, which in turn enriches our being. For example, learning to understand and appreciate music increases the desire to learn more about it. It is an instinctual tendency in humans to attempt to satisfy the deficiency needs in order to attend to the more highly rewarding being needs.

Maslow believed that psychoanalysts like Freud and Adler over-emphasized the deficiency needs; they saw motivation as a drive to eliminate the lower-level needs. Psychoanalysts generally have this bias, he believed, because most of their experience is as doctors who treat ill people. Especially in the industrialized countries, most people have few problems meeting their lower-level needs and so do spend at least some of their time trying to achieve self-actualization.

The process of self-actualization is closely analogous to creativity. Free of neurosis, self-actualizing people are able to concentrate on essentials. They are likely to achieve an occasional **peak experience** – a momentary flash of insight that brings with it great joy and gratitude for being alive. The peak experience is self-forgetful, a moment of unselfish ecstasy.

Rogers's Theory

Carl Rogers (1902–87) identified three inner conditions of the creative person:

1. An openness to experience that prohibits rigidity
2. The ability to evaluate situations according to one's own personal standards
3. The ability to experiment and to accept the unstable

Any person who possesses these three traits is also likely to be endowed with excellent psychological health (1959, 1961). As a result, such a person may be said to be "**fully functioning,** the type of person from whom creative products and creative living naturally emerge" (1959, p. 34).

Fromm's Theory

Erich Fromm (1900–80) argued that creativity is largely a matter of having the right set of attitudes (1941, 1959). He described five relevant attitudes that can be fostered at any point in life:

1. The capacity to be puzzled or surprised
2. The ability to concentrate

3. An objective knowledge of self
4. The ability to accept conflict and tension resulting from polarity
5. The willingness to let go of security, such as parental support

Fromm saw creativity as stemming from the basic human need to rise above one's instinctive nature (in this he is similar to Maslow). This need in turn orients the individual toward productivity and away from self-centeredness. As Fromm put it: "In the act of creation humans transcend themselves as creatures, raise themselves beyond the passivity and accidentalness of their existence into the realm of purposefulness and freedom" (1955, p. 29).

The essence of this concept of **self-transcendence** is derived from Fromm's religious belief. He felt that there are two ways to experience the existence of God: the transcendental and the immanent. The transcendental God is perceived as knowing and controlling everything, even to the fall of the merest sparrow. Fromm allowed that this perception may be correct but that he saw little evidence of it. Far clearer to him was the concept of God that is manifested within us, the immanent God. We experience this aspect of godliness when we have what Maslow called a peak experience, the great joy that results from a flash of insight into a problem or, even better, into ourselves. We are in touch with the immanent manifestation of God, Fromm believed, when we do or feel something that seems somehow greater than ourselves. We are, momentarily, greater than ourselves. We are in communication with the wellsprings of our very essence, and it is inevitably an ecstatic feeling. In this sense, immanent godliness and creativity are synonymous!

Which School of Thought Is Best?

Although these two sets of theories—the psychoanalytic and the humanistic—offer radically different explanations of the creative personality, I doubt whether it makes much sense to argue which of them is right and which is wrong. For one thing, they remain in such a speculative state that nothing but an endless argument is likely to result. On the other hand, it does make sense to discuss which is more likely to generate new hypotheses and thus new knowledge about this subject.

The psychoanalytic emphasis on the unconscious mind and on compensation for a difficult childhood certainly is relevant in the lives of many highly productive people. In their excellent study entitled *300 Eminent Personalities* (1978), Mildred, Victor, and Ted Goertzel found this point of view to be especially descriptive of writers, most of whom had had a difficult childhood. The ability to overcome adversity has surely motivated many creative efforts throughout history. (This finding, by the way, appears to contradict Rank's position that the "neurotic" personality never results in creativity.)

Virtually all psychoanalytic writers also emphasize the first years of life as a critical period, at the end of which creative ability becomes fixed. However, most agree that intense psychoanalysis sometimes enables people to overcome this early fixation. One assumption of the psychoanalytic position (with the exception of Carl Jung) is that creative people tend to suffer from emotional disturbance; in fact, some have gone so far as to assert that "creativity is next to madness." In his study (1978) of one hundred architects who were among "the most creative in the U.S.," MacKinnon found that indeed they did have a higher than average level of psychopathology but that they also had an unusually great ability to deal effectively with it.

Although no psychoanalytic theorist would suggest that creative people tend to be mentally ill, an emphasis on a healthy ability to handle life's problems is far more representative of the humanistic school of thought. This school draws its name from its belief that humans determine their own fates, not divine, cosmic, or other forces. This is not to say that humanism is atheistic but that self-reliance is a natural human trait. Humanists see creativity as more conscious, cognitive, and intentional than do the psychoanalysts. The humanistic concept is that creativity is born through a striving for the highest possibilities in life, rather than as a defense against neurosis.

Psychiatrist R.D. Laing suggests that creative people may seem strange, not because they are unbalanced, but because they see the truth so clearly. They lack the ordinary defense mechanisms so common in the rest of us, and thus are often deeply pained by the many injustices in the world. Their noble attempts to right these wrongs frequently drive their efforts.

It is my opinion, therefore, that although psychoanalysis extends a number of theoretically rich paths, the more positive, active, self-fulfilling concepts of the humanists are more likely to produce fruitful insights into this mysterious process.

4

Brain Physiology

Chapter Highlights:

Lateral Dominance in the Brain
Left and Right Brain Dominance
A Brief History of the Discovery of Laterality
The Concept of Dominance
The Bicameral Mind
Recent Research
Laterality and the Whole Brain
Left-handedness and Creativity
Sociobiology of the Brain

Key Terms and Concepts

Apraxia
Bicameral mind
Cerebral localization
Cognitive phenotype
Eureka phenomenon
Genotype
Hemisphericality
Incubation

The *Ingenuity Test*
The innovation hierarchy
   of Findlay and Lumsden
Lateral dominance
Linking thesis
Minimal brain damage
Phrenology
Sociobiology of the brain

Important People:

Paul Broca   Julian Jaynes
John Flanagan   Arthur Koestler
Franz Gall

T his chapter considers two facets of the physiology of the brain which are alleged to have major effects on creative thinking: **lateral dominance** and the **sociobiology of the brain.**

Lateral Dominance in the Brain

The cerebral cortex (that convoluted, 1-inch-thick layer on the top of the brain in which thinking, sensation, and perception occur) is divided into two halves, or hemispheres. In most people, one side is dominant over the other. The vast majority of us are right-handed, and thus we tend to be dominated by the left lateral (side) of the brain. Left-handers tend to be dominated by the right side of their brains. This was first learned when it was noticed that damage to one side of the brain usually impairs the functioning of the opposite side of the body. This relationship is known as lateral dominance (and sometimes as **hemisphericality**). See figure 4–1.

Before going into the relationships between lateral dominance and creativity, here are several questions from another well-known test of creativity (ingenuity), developed by John C. Flanagan (1958). I urge you to give it a try. The means of scoring it and an explanation of why it is considered a valid and reliable test of creativity, together with the implications for lateral dominance, will be presented later in this chapter.

THE INGENUITY TEST[a]

Below are several sample items from a test of your ability to do a special type of work. This ability is important for some types of work

---

[a]Excerpted from *Flanagan Aptitude Classification Tests: Ingenuity,* Form A by John C. Flanagan. Copyright © 1957 by John C. Flanagan. Reprinted by permission of the publisher, Science Research Associates, Inc.

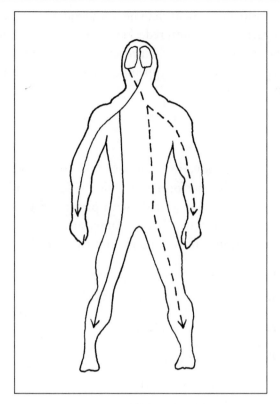

Figure 4–1. LATERAL DOMINANCE

and not very important to others. After each test item, there are five words or phrases with some of the letters blocked out. You are to select the one that best matches your answer if the letters were filled in.

1. In the process of writing a report, several hundred reference books were used. It was decided that a list of the authors and the titles of the books would be included at the end of the report for bibliographic references. In order to speed up the alphabetizing process for this bibliography, it was decided that each reference would be listed on a small

a. n _ _ s. b. t _ _ r. c. r _ _ d. d. c _ _ d. e. s _ _ e.

2. Bob Johnson, a draftsman, keeps a compass lying loose in a desk drawer, along with a lot of other equipment he needs frequently.

Since he has more equipment than he has adequate room for, the desk drawer compartment is cluttered. Therefore, he has often pricked a finger on the compass point when reaching for a pencil or something else. To keep this from ever happening again, he embeds the compass point in an

a. a_ _ _ _l.   b. e_ _ _ _r.   c. i_ _ _ _d.   d. a_ _ _ _t.

e. e_ _ _ _e.

3. A corporation advertises its new high-fidelity phonograph as having "distortion-free performance which reduces rumble to an inaudible minimum." In the ad it shows a picture of a chicken and an egg to illustrate its claims. These claims are briefly stated in the accompanying slogan which contains the two words

a. Faithful l_ _ _ _ _ _ _ _ _t.

b. Faithful t_ _ _ _ _ _ _ _ _d.

c. Faithful r_ _ _ _ _ _ _ _ _n.

d. Faithful n_ _ _ _ _ _ _ _ _e.

e. Faithful s_ _ _ _ _ _ _ _ _l.

4. It is possible to add vertical lines to the pages of a notebook or to rule blank paper quickly and easily by using a handmade stamp and a regular stamp pad. This solution makes it possible to vary the thickness of the lines by changing the tension of the material used. This special stamp is made from a block of wood, several thumbtacks, and three or four narrow

a. r_ _ _ _r b_ _ _s.   b. h_ _ _ _t n_ _ _s.

c. t_ _ _ _k s_ _ _s.   d. l_ _ _ _e h_ _ _s.

e. o_ _ _ _d u_ _ _s.

5. A contractor was asked to build a two-bedroom house so that maximum use could be made of wall and cupboard space and so that housework could be kept to a minimum. The contractor eliminated a great deal of extra work by building in a double-duty linen closet. This was made accessible from both bedrooms by placing one set of

linen drawers between the two rooms. For each drawer, each room had a separate set of

a. t_ _ _ _ _s.   b. g_ _ _ _ _s.   c. p_ _ _ _ _ _s.

d. h_ _ _ _ _s.   e. r_ _ _ _ _s.

6. A man tells a friend of his who is a paint manufacturer he is going to paint the walls of a playroom white, with small irregularly spaced and irregularly shaped red dots all over. The manufacturer claims he can make a special paint which will do the entire job with a single application. He says he would make a white water-base paint and would force into it globules of red paint which would remain

a. u_ _ _ _ _ _ _t because of their r_d b_ _e.

b. s_ _ _ _ _ _ _d because of their o_l b_ _e.

c. u_ _ _ _ _ _ _d because of their d_y d_ _e.

d. d_ _ _ _ _ _ _d because of their r_d t_ _e.

e. p_ _ _ _ _ _ _s because of their h_o b_ _e.

7. On an aircraft instrument panel it is very important to know whether certain of the auxiliary electrical systems are working at all times. To keep the pilot informed, a light was installed that was lit when one of the systems was out of order. The light was out when they were all working satisfactorily. This caused trouble because the light bulb burned out and the pilot did not know when the system was out of order. Since it is important that the pilot always know when one of the systems fails, it was decided to change the circuit so that the old interpretation of the signal light was now

a. c_ _ _ _ _ _d.   b. o_ _ _ _ _ _n.   c. f_ _ _ _ _ _t.

d. r_ _ _ _ _ _d.   e. t_ _ _ _ _ _r.

Answers to the Ingenuity Test:

1.	d. card	5.	d. handles
2.	b. eraser	6.	b. suspended because of
3.	c. reproduction		their oil base
4.	a. rubber bands	7.	d. reversed

Left and Right Brain Dominance

Soon after a child is born, its undifferentiated movements develop into a pattern of preference for one hand, eye, and foot over the other. Because almost everyone has a preferred side, the brain may therefore be said to be dominated by the hemisphere of the opposite side. In recent years, it has been learned (Springer and Deutsch 1981) that although each hemisphere has functions that overlap with the other, the left side is primarily concerned with language, and the right is more involved in nonverbal functions such as dance and music. There is some evidence, and much speculation, that the right half also has primary responsibility for creative thinking. The speculation has far outrun the evidence, however, leading to what has been called "dichotomania," splitting up all kinds of mental functions and assigning them to one of the two hemispheres. A list of the most commonly seen dichotomies is given in table 4–1.

Although there is some evidence for each of these dichotomies, most may be more the result of the imaginative guesses of creative theorists than of hard research.

The *Ingenuity Test* is quite unusual, in that like the *Remote Associates Test* given in the next chapter, it claims to have right answers. As explained in greater detail in chapter 5, creativity often combines two aspects of mental functioning: being imaginative, but also being right. A number of those who have investigated lateral dominance have suggested that these two functions tend to occur in opposite sides of the brain. Accuracy (called "convergent thinking" in the next chapter), and originality (referred to as "divergent thinking") appear to be opposite cognitive processes. It is hypothesized that convergent thinking is a left-side function and that originality is a right-side function.

At this time, no strong evidence for this view exists, but if it turns out that this is so, the *Ingenuity Test* may well be a test that succeeds in measuring ability to combine the two kinds of thinking. It appears to do so in two steps:

- You must think divergently, casting about for several possible answers that could fit the problem.

Table 4–1
MENTAL DICHOTOMIES

Left Hemisphere	*Right Hemisphere*
Intellect	Intuition
Convergent	Divergent
Intellectual	Sensuous, emotional
Imaginative	Deductive
Rational	Metaphoric, intuitive
Horizontal	Vertical
Discrete	Continuous
Concrete	Abstract
Realistic	Impulsive
Directed	Free
Differential	Existential
Sequential	Multiple
Historical	Timeless
Analytical	Synthetic, holistic
Explicit	Implicit, tacit
Objective	Subjective
Successive	Simultaneous

Source: Springer and Deutsch 1981, p. 186.

• At the same time, you must think convergently, checking your word or phrase to see if it will fit the options the test's author gives as possible answers. It seems probable that this process would call for frequent switching between the two hemispheres of the brain.

The remaining sections of this chapter will sort out the facts from the fantasy regarding the relationship between laterality and creativity. Let us start by taking a brief look at the history of this illusive concept.

A Brief History of the Discovery of Laterality

It should be no surprise that our knowledge of the way the human brain works is quite recent in the history of medical research. Less than two hundred years ago, no one was sure that the various areas of the brain had different functions. The first person to suggest this was a German anatomist, Franz Gall, early in the nineteenth century. His research led him to believe that speech is located in the frontal lobes, those sections of each hemisphere located toward the front of the head. This is the theory of **cerebral localization.** Unfortunately, most scientists dismissed his report because he also argued that the shape of the skull reflects personality traits, and so it would be possible to study those traits by examining bumps on the head. This approach became known as **phrenology** and has long since been discredited.

Although most doctors branded Gall a quack, he did have some followers. The French professor of medicine Jean Bouillard offered a large sum of money to anyone who could produce a patient with damage to the frontal lobes who had no loss of speech. Knowledge of the landscape of the brain was so primitive in those times, however, that for some years the question remained unresolved.

In 1861 the stalemate ended dramatically. A young French surgeon, Paul Broca, learned of cerebral localization at a meeting of the Society of Anthropology and was reminded of a patient of his who had long suffered from speech impairment and some right-side paralysis. Two days after the meeting, the man died. Broca quickly got permission to autopsy his brain and found what he was looking for: a region of tissue damage (a lesion) on the left frontal lobe. Some months later a similar situation occurred, with the same results. Broca brought this patient's brain with him to the next society meeting and created a furor. Many were impressed, but those who dismissed localization accused him of lying.

Interestingly, although everyone noted that in both cases the lesions were frontal, no one seemed to see the *left side* link. Only after eight more autopsies did Broca publicly announce this finding. Again he was embroiled in controversy. Gustav Dax now claimed that his father, Marc, had already put forth this idea in a paper presented to the society back in 1836 and that Broca had purposely refrained from mentioning it in order to get credit for the discovery. No one at the society could remember hearing the paper read, nor could a copy be produced. Historians have never been able to untangle the claims, but today Broca is credited with the breakthrough.

The Concept of Dominance

The idea that one side of the brain could more powerfully direct mental processes in some persons, and the other side in other persons, was put forth even later. The idea came about mostly because it was learned that equal amounts of lesion in the brain do not result in equal amounts of disruption. By 1868 John Hughlings Jackson, the eminent British neurologist, was guessing that one side may "lead" the other. Increasingly, there was evidence that the interactions between halves are complex, and different in different people. It was learned that areas involved in speaking are not the same as areas given to understanding the speech of others. The discovery of **apraxia,** the inability to perform physical functions such as combing one's hair, led to many new hypotheses.

Eventually, it was accepted that most people are right-handed because their left brains are dominant. It was concluded that the right brain had few important functions, serving mainly as a backup to the more powerful left. Not until the 1930s did some scientists begin to suspect that the influence of culture, with its emphasis on logic and language, has made the left side so important. New functions of the right side, especially of the nonverbal sort, were uncovered, as work in the electrical stimulation of spots in the brain was pioneered by Wilder Penfield and his associates (1959).

Probably the greatest spur to our understanding of hemispheric functions has come from the research on reactions to having the brain "split" by the cutting of the corpus callosum, the thick bundle of nerves that connects the two halves. Research was conducted on animals in the 1950s, and on humans who had had the operation for various reasons in the 1960s, largely by Roger Sperry and his associates (Franco and Sperry 1977, Levy-Agresti and Sperry 1968, Levy, Travarthen, and Sperry 1972, Myers and Sperry 1958, Saul and Sperry 1968, Sperry 1966, 1968, 1974, Zaidel and Sperry 1974). It was found that although the brain still functions rather well, many mental functions are impaired to some extent. Still more was learned about the mysterious right brain. And of greatest importance is the possibility that those who are dominated by their right hemisphere may use more of their total brain and may have more interaction between sides than do those in the majority, the left-brain dominated.

No one knows for sure why this should be so, but one fascinating speculation takes us back 3,000 years.

The Bicameral Mind

Princeton psychologist Julian Jaynes (1976) has suggested that as recently as 3,000 years ago, humans were little more than automatons who had only a vague sense of self. They did of course have language, but they divided its function into two clearly separate types. Internal thoughts they believed to be the voice of a god telling them how to behave. They then could externalize these ideas of the gods into speech and writing. They had a **bicameral mind,** one split into two chambers.

Jaynes gives many examples to support his theory. For instance, the writings of Homer are filled with characters who achieve great feats under the orders of the gods. These persons never decide on a strategy; they simply do what they are told. He suggests that the authors of the Bible, who believed they were merely writing down the speech of God, may be another example.

Gradually, however, as speech, writing, and other mental operations such as mathematics and physics became more complex, reliance on the left hemisphere also grew. The "auditory hallucinations" dwindled except in those of low intelligence, the bicameral mind slowly broke down, and the gods became mute.

In their place came consciousness. According to Jaynes, self-awareness is the product of the growth of a concept of internal "I-ness." This in turn results from increases in reliance on linguistic processes. In modern-day humans, awareness of self has taken on great importance; witness the popular reference to the 1970s as the "me generation." Jaynes (and many others) argue, however, that conscious thought plays much less of a mental role than we assume. He states that "consciousness is learned on the basis of language and taught to others. It is a cultural invention rather than a biological necessity" (1976).

One well-known theorist who would have agreed with this position is Sigmund Freud. He characterized the unconscious mind (though not the right brain specifically) as having a weak concept of time and space and as being largely involved with images rather than words. He saw the unconscious as being limited to a more primitive language that is likely to be used in dreams and in so-called Freudian slips (Freud 1924). He also was adamant that creativity almost always stems from original ideas, often first produced in symbolic form, in this nebulous world of the unconscious mind. His student Ernst Kris (1965) argued that only people who are able to "regress in the service of their egos" into this more childlike mental space are likely to be creatively productive. Of course Kris recognized the important role of the conscious mind in providing logic and discipline to the process but insisted that these can come only later in the creative act (see chapter 3).

David Galin (1974) suggests that brain research, especially that on split-brained patients, offers strong evidence for Freudian theory. Galin believes that many psychopathological problems are caused by breakdowns in communication between hemispheres. That is why, for example, a parent may say that an action is being taken out of love for a child, when all the other evidence points to that parent's feeling very antagonistic toward the child.

In his strikingly insightful book *The Act of Creation* (1964), Arthur Koestler explored the role of the unconscious in a wide range of creative acts. He found strong evidence for **incubation,** a process in which the thinker "takes a vacation" from trying to solve a problem and later finds that a full-blown solution to the problem occurs in a flash. This abrupt insight is also known as the **Eureka phenomenon,** after a story from Greek folklore. As the story goes, Archimedes was required by the king on pain of death to determine whether a gift of a crown was solid gold or not. Unable to find an answer he tried to relax himself (he was naturally quite nervous because of the death threat!) by taking a bath. He noticed that the water in the tub rose proportionately to the amount he immersed himself and realized he had discovered a means of determining the composition of the crown. Overjoyed, he is said to have run through the streets of the town naked, crying the Greek word, "Eureka!", which means "I have found it!"

Koestler argued that creative ideas are most often the result of joining together unrelated concepts in new and productive ways. The conscious mind, relying as it does on logical rules and precise verbal formats, is frequently precluded from achieving this. Because it is more spontaneous and intuitive, the unconscious is more likely to produce such fortuitous associations. But the unconscious mind can only work on a problem when the conscious mind is not doing so. For this reason, Koestler believed, so many creative ideas have resulted only when the problem has been "put on the back burner." No one knowledgeable in this field would maintain that all conscious functioning takes place in the left brain and that all unconscious thought takes place in the right brain. Nevertheless, there appears to be good reason to suspect that there is a tendency in this direction.

Recent Research

Citing the finding of the Soviet neuropsychologist Luria (1973) that electrically weak neural stimuli can evoke strong responses, Arieti (1966) states that the brain hemispheres of some people are unusually capable of intercommunication as a result of very weak neural charges. Because of this condition, such people are able to come up with remote but highly interesting associations that evade the rest of us (see chapter 5 for more on this). On the basis of his own research, he concludes that

> in the creative person, too, a weak stimulus, such as a characteristic of an object, may become a strong one when used as a metaphor. A weak stimulus such as a falling apple may evoke the concept of the force of gravity. . . . The apple and the moon not only have the common quality of being attracted by the earth; they are part of the class of gravitational bodies, a new engram [a thought represented in neural connections] appearing for the first time in the mind of Newton. In these cases of creativity the old meanings, by being interconnected and interpreted, form a new meaningfulness (pp. 397, 398).

If it is the case that it normally takes stronger impulses to make connections between hemispheres than within them, then those persons whose neurons can be stimulated by weaker impulses would have a creative advantage over those who need stronger ones. Of course this also assumes that interconnections between hemispheres are the more likely to yield imaginative thoughts.

Among the more promising research efforts of late have been those examining how two groups of subjects, one low in creativity and one high, perform on measures of hemispheric preference. Recent efforts have focused on a variety of measures: lateral eye movement, EEG rates, visual field tasks, dichotic listening tasks, and self-report instruments.

Lateral eye movements refer to shifts in the gaze, either to the left or right, that occur when people engage in reflective thinking. A substantial body of evidence suggests that reflective thinking involving the left hemisphere produces right lateral eye movements, while thinking engaging the right hemisphere results in left lateral eye movements (Bakan 1969, Kinsbourne 1972, Kocel et al. 1972).

Falcone and Loder (1984) found that subjects scoring high on Guilford's Uses Test tended to gaze to the left more often and longer while taking that test than did subjects who scored low. They found no difference in the direction of lateral eye gaze when subjects were taking Mednick's Remote Associates Test (see chapter 5 for more on these tests). The authors explain the different results as a product of the different natures of the two tests. While the Uses Test is clearly a matter of divergent thinking and visual imagery, the Remote Associates Test initially involves divergent processes, but then requires convergent thinking in order to recognize the particular overlapping associations. Falcone and Loder believe that their findings support the idea that persons dominated by the right side of their brains are more creative.

Brain lateralization can be directly measured by comparisons of electroencephalogram (EEG) readings of the two sides of the brain during activity. If the right side of the brain gains dominance during creative thinking, then it is reasonable to expect that EEG measurements will indicate this. Martindale et al. (1984) did find that highly creative subjects, as assessed by a variety of measures, do exhibit greater right than left hemisphere EEG activity during creative performance than do subjects who are ranked lower in creativity. This pattern of activity was not found during the performance of a noncreative task.

Katz (1983) had subjects who had been classified into two groups of high and low creativity perform a number of tasks known to engage one hemisphere over the other. In addition to lateral eye movement, the subjects performed visual field and dichotic listening tasks. Visual field tasks are those in which items are presented to only the left or right visual field, and subjects then identify them. Dichotic listening tasks involve the simultaneous presentation of two items, either words or melodies, into each ear through headphones; subjects are then asked to recall or recognize the items. In both tasks, superiority in performance in either the right visual field or the right ear indicates greater left hemisphere processing, and vice versa. The author found that by knowing only the scores on the hemispheric tasks, one could predict 75 percent of the time whether a subject could be retroactively classified into a low or high creativity group. Tagano et al. (1983) found a similar relationship between divergent thinking (one aspect of creativity) and hemispheric dominance, as measured by a dichotic listening task.

Torrance (1982) developed a self-report measure of "hemispheric processing style," which he has named "Your Style of Thinking and Learning." He administered the test to college graduate students who were also assessed by a variety of means for their creative style and ability. He found significant correlations among what he calls "low-left hemisphere processing," "high-right hemisphere processing," and creative style. The links among these two types of processing and creative ability were not strong, but there was a tendency for high creative ability to be associated with a diminished use of left hemisphere processing in general.

Unfortunately, this recent research is not conclusive. For every study that establishes a link between creativity and asymmetrical hemisphere processing, one can find another study that says otherwise (see Brittain 1985, Doerr 1980, Dorethy and Reeves 1979, and Rosen et al. 1983). There are many methodological and interpretive problems (an excellent summary of them may be found in Gardner 1982, pp. 278–85), not the least of which is that all these studies rely on tests of creativity that can be seriously challenged.

To overcome this problem, Katz (1986) looked specifically at a high creativity population. He chose highly creative people from the disciplines of architecture, science, and mathematics. In addition to showing high creativity on the basis of standard psychometric tests, these subjects were judged to be highly creative on the basis of objective criteria, such as number of patents earned and number of articles published, and on subjective criteria, such as peer evaluations. The results found that hemisphericality is related to some indices of creativity, that it is not related to general intelligence (also found to be the case in Katz' earlier study (1983) above, and that the different professions use different modes of processing information.

Laterality and the Whole Brain

Hermann (1981) offers a description of the probable relationships between laterality and the whole brain, as they affect creative problem solving:

> If you think through a creative process consisting of interest, preparation, incubation, illumination, verification, and exploitation, then it becomes clear that the process itself has left-brained, right-brained and whole-brained phases to it. If you started with interest being the first stage, then I would speculate that would be whole-brained. Preparation is clearly left-brained. That means doing the rigorous task of defining a problem and specifying it in its essence. Incubation, on the other hand, is clearly right-brained. It involves getting away from the problem and engaging in an activity that permits the effortless, natural processes of the right brain to mull over the complexities of the problem, so as to permit the mind to come up with new combinations that could lead to a solution. The illustration stage is where this kind of "Aha" can occur, which produces one or more possible ideas or potential solutions. The verification stage, then, is the critical left-brained analysis of the idea or potential solution against the specifications of the problem. The final stage could be called "exploitation," which is the putting to use or applying the solution which emerges from the previous stages. Exploitation is probably whole-brained. (p. 13.)

The stages Hermann refers to are discussed in some detail in the next chapter. Given the present state of research, he is right to use the word *speculate*, but his theory offers an intriguing look at hemispheric relationships that might well turn out to describe the way brain processes really happen.

Left-handedness and Creativity

If left-handers are right-dominated, and the right side is all that has just been suggested, they should be more creative. Many famous lefties certainly were—Leonardo da Vinci, Benjamin Franklin, and Michelangelo, to name a few. But is this the case for the general population? Let's examine the facts.

First of all, it should be noted that left-handers have been viewed throughout the ages as unsavory characters, and even perhaps as in league with the devil. In French, the word for left is *gauche*, which means clumsy. The *American Heritage Dictionary* includes among its definitions of *left-handed* "awkward, maladroit [against the right], obliquely derisive, dubious, and insincere, as in left-handed flattery." There are many allusions in the Bible that show a bias against the left. If left-handers are more creatively productive, it certainly has not been recognized historically!

Causes of Left-handedness. Despite early beliefs in the sinister causes of being left-handed (the word *sinister* means left in Latin), scientists today identify two major causes. In some cases genetic inheritance is probably the cause, especially when it occurs in several generations of a family. In other cases, it may come about as a result of **minimal brain damage** to the left hemisphere, probably during the birth process. Because of this damage, the person comes to rely more heavily than usual on the right side of the brain for language as well as for other functions.

Twins appear to be a special case of this. Only about 10 percent of the population is left-handed (this figure used to be 5 percent, which was no doubt due to the practice in many schools of discouraging left-handed writing); twins, however, are left-handed 25 percent of the time. This is true for both monozygotic (identical, single-egg) and dizygotic (fraternal, two-egg) twins. Minimal brain damage has been given as one reason: some mothers of twins have smaller than average pelvises, and so twins are squeezed together and are more likely to suffer slight brain lesions. Another theory argues that in monozygotic twins, there is a mirror-imaging effect in which each twin has opposite features from the other. Included are the whorls in fingerprints and in hair at the top of the head. This might be true, at least in some of the cases, with handedness. This explanation offers no help with dizygotic twins, however.

Handedness and Mental Laterality. When surgeons are about to perform brain surgery, they sometimes preface it with tests of laterality using a sodium amytal procedure. This chemical is capable of anesthetizing one hemisphere at a time, so the doctor can determine where speech and other functions are centralized. For right-handers, speech is nearly always left-brained, and for more than half of left-handers, this is also the case. Thus the early presumption that all left-handed people are right dominant is simply not true. For other mental functions, the situation becomes even more complicated. In fact, researchers must be cautious even about how they determine such an apparently obvious trait as handedness because so many individuals who write with their left hand are really ambidextrous. Only direct observation is reliable.

A further complication, but also a factor that may shed light on this question, is provided by Levy and Reid (1976). They believed that the way people write may be as important in terms of laterality as the hand they use — whether individuals invert their hands when writing (they appear to be writing upside down; this is sometimes called "hooked" writing). Levy and Reid found that inversion is even more related to brain dominance than handedness. Nevertheless, like the other predictors, it certainly is not perfect. This leaves us with the direct question, in general are left-handers more creative than right-handers?

The Creativity Question. From the standpoint of intelligence, there is no question that left-handers have been given a "bum rap." For instance, they suffer a high incidence of retardation and reading disability. Levy (1976) hypothesized that this is because language and visuospatial abilities compete for neural tissue (as may well be the case for left-handers), and that usually language will win. Levy predicted that if given an IQ test, left-handers will not score differently from right-handers on verbal tests but will have a deficit on the performance tests (for example, rearranging figures to match a pattern). She tested a large group on the *Wechsler Adult Intelligence Test* (the standard in the field) and found her hypothesis supported.

What a complicated picture! According to these results, the left-handed are poorer than their counterparts in the very skills in which the right brain is supposed to excel, but they suffer no loss in language. The most important conclusion is as indicated before: there is no benefit in being left-handed when it comes to standard mental tasks, and there probably is some deficit. However, the one plus indicated over and over again is the increased communication between hemispheres that the left-handed seem to have.

Perhaps the first study to look explicitly at the relationship between handedness and actual creative achievement is the research by my colleagues and me, which is described in chapter 10 of this book. This research found that, compared with the national average of 10 percent left-handed, 20 percent of the most creative were left-handed. This is not a definitive answer, but it offers some evidence in favor of the theory linking left-handedness and creativity.

Sociobiology of the Brain

One of the most interesting theories in the field of creativity has recently been published. Known as an "evolutionary theory of discovery and innovation," the research is being led by Scott Findlay and Charles Lumsden of the University of Toronto (1988): "Our system concept is then integrated with current theories of biocultural dynamics, leading to the hypothesis that creative activity is an evolved strategy in which rules of cognitive development act through the joint inheritance of genetic and cultural information" (p. i). They refer to their concept as a **linking thesis**, which they believe generates a number of interesting hypotheses about the relationships between creativity and age, environmental complexity, and the sociocultural environment.

Of primary importance, however, is their hypothesis that creative activity comes about because there are "collections of neurons that are innately predisposed to respond to particular patterns of electrochemical excitation" (p. ii). Creation occurs as a result of the establishment of new linkages among nodes in the existing structure, as a consequence of "a novel sequence of group selection events" (p. ii).

Thus there must be a complex interaction among five aspects of human existence in order for creativity to occur:

1. The **genotype,** which is the genetic constitution of the person
2. Brain development
3. The **cognitive phenotype,** which is the genetically and environmentally determined manner of thinking the person has developed
4. The physical environment
5. The sociocultural environment

Each of these elements is influenced by the others to various degrees. Figure 4–2 depicts the main paths of influence. Findlay and Lumsden divide creativity into three stages: the mental process; the discovery, which may or may not result from the mental process; and the innovation, which may or may not result from the discovery. Each of these stages also may have a retroactive effect on the five elements that caused them to occur in the first place.

For example, an innovation may alter the physical and/or sociocultural environment so that through natural selection, more persons

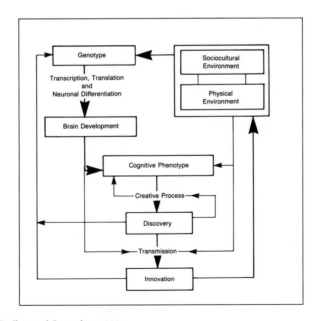

Source: Findlay and Lumsden 1988.

Figure 4–2. THE INNOVATION HIERARCHY

with creatively predisposed genes will be likely to be born and to survive. The interaction of outer and inner forces also accounts for why some periods seem to be conducive to musical innovation, while others promote political change, and still others appear to have fostered no innovation at all.

Findlay and Lumsden's linking theory goes deeply into areas of biology and brain physiology that are beyond the scope of this book (and its author's comprehension). However, the obvious quality of their work and the reactions of other well-known scientists make it seem likely that all of us interested in this field will have to learn more about these subjects.

Research on the main issues reviewed in this chapter has a long way to go in terms of our understanding of the causality of creativity. It would be wonderful if we could point to specific aspects of mental physiology that could automatically lead to facilitation of creative productivity. At present, there are only enticing glimpses of directions we might take. Still, they represent a most encouraging start.

5

The Mental Process

Chapter Highlights:

The Associationist Position
Galton's Theory
James's Theory
Wallas's Theory
Mednick's Theory

The Gestalt Position
Wertheimer's Theory
Kohler's Theory
Gruber's Theory

The Cognitive-Developmental Approach
Cognitive Style
Cognitive Mobility
Piagetian Theory
The Use of Metaphor

Key Terms and Concepts:

Armchair speculation
Associationism
Case study approach
Cognitive mobility

Cognitive style
Ego-control
Ego-resiliency
Empirical investigation

Field dependence/
    independence
Free association
Gestalt
Illumination
Incubation
Mediation

Plenum
Preparation
Recurrence
Serendipity
Similarity
Use of metaphor
Verification

Important People:

Sir Francis Galton
Howard Gardner
Howard Gruber
William James
Wolfgang Kohler

Sarnoff Mednick
Jean Piaget
B.F. Skinner
Graham Wallas
Max Wertheimer

I turned my chair to the fire and dozed. Again the atoms were gamboling before my eyes. This time the smaller groups kept modestly in the background. My mental eye, rendered more acute by repeated visions of this kind, could now distinguish larger structures, of manifold information; long rows, sometimes more closely fitted together; all twining and twisting in snakelike motion. But look! What was that? One of the snakes had seized hold of its own tail, and the form whirled mockingly before my eyes. As if by a flash of lightning, I awoke.

— Hermann Helmholtz,
    nineteenth-century German scientist

As a result of this dream, Helmholtz was able to solve a complex problem on which he was working. Does his phantasmagoric vision reveal the unconscious thought process that takes place during creativity? Is the unconscious mind as important as, or even more so than, the conscious mind in the creative act? Is creativity one mental process or several?

In the late nineteenth century, a central question had evolved among scholars: does the search for knowledge normally proceed elementally (from parts or elements of a problem to the whole), or holistically (from a sense of the whole of the problem to its parts)? Two scientific camps were formed. In this century, they have become known as the associationist and the Gestalt positions. From this academic debate has come the greatest advance in our understanding of the creative act itself. As is often the case in scientific inquiry, the disagreements between the advocates of the two positions are today producing wonderful new insights.

The Associationist Position

> I am trying to tell you that the search for explicative laws in natural facts proceeds in a tortuous fashion. In the face of some inexplicable facts you must try to imagine many general laws, whose connections with your facts escapes you. Then suddenly, in the unexpected connection of a result, a specific situation, and one of those laws, you perceive a line of reasoning that seems more convincing than the others. You try applying it to all similar cases, to use it for making predictions, and you discover that your intuition was right. But until you reach the end you will never know which predicates to introduce into your reasoning and which to omit. I line up so many disjointed elements and I venture some hypotheses. I have to venture many, and many of them are so absurd that I would be ashamed to tell them to you.
>
> — Brother William of Baskerville,
>   a fourteenth-century monk (Umberto Eco 1983).

In this fictional statement, we see an early statement of **associationism**. This is the theory that ideas, especially creative ideas, come not from carefully laid out mental plans but from a series of trial-and-error efforts to solve a problem. However, these efforts are not merely random. They result from the complex associations built up in the mind as the result of living and experiencing the environment. Creativity is seen as the production of unusually appropriate associations.

Harvard psychologist B.F. Skinner (1905–   ) is the most famous representative of this school of thought, and his views on associationism are well known (1948, 1953, 1957, 1968, 1971). He has contributed greatly to the clarification of this theory, but the bases of most of his ideas are hardly new. He borrowed much from a line of philosophers who held that thinking is primarily the assembly of discrete concepts or images to form new ideas.

Plato (in the *Phaedo*) and Aristotle (in the essay "Memory") might be considered the earliest associationists. Aristotle developed the primary laws of association: similarity, contrast, and contiguity. In the seventeenth century, John Locke contributed the concept of the tabula rasa (which means blank tablet)—at birth, the mind contains no thought, and all thinking derives from individual experience. Two centuries later, Herbert Spencer's ideas about the inheritability of association from one generation to the next, though wrong, also proved influential.

These and numerous other thinkers offered their guesses about how the mind perceives the world and creates new thoughts. The first in this long line to have studied mental processes through **empirical investigation** rather than **armchair speculation,** however, was Sir Francis Galton.

Galton's Theory

Sir Francis Galton (1822–1911) was highly respected in nineteenth-century England as a multifaceted scientist. He was a eugenicist, meteorologist, evolutionist, geographer, anthropologist, and statistician, and he probably should be credited as the world's first psychologist. He was a Renaissance man of the first order.

Galton was certain that careful observation could lead to perception of reality. His penchant for measurement was legend (1870). On a trip to Africa, he was struck by the variation in the bodies of the native women. Because of Victorian dress styles, he had no idea that European women also differed greatly. He wanted to record this variation (strictly for scientific purposes, of course) but did not speak the language and was loath to ask a missionary to intercede for him. He was not to be impeded in his search for data, however. Here is how he describes his solution: "I sat at a distance with my sextant (a measuring devise used on ships), and as the ladies turned themselves about, as women always do, to be admired, I surveyed them in every possible way and subsequently measured the distance of the spot where they stood—worked out and tabulated the results at my leisure" (quoted in Pearson 1914, p. 232).

One of his most interesting experiments was his attempt to measure the workings of his own mind. His descriptions of his findings have been insightfully analyzed by Duke University psychologist Herbert Crovitz in his fascinating book *Galton's Walk* (1970). The walk referred to is one taken by Galton down London's Pall Mall, during which he scrupulously recorded each and every thought that crossed his mind. Galton explained his purpose in an article published in *Brain*, July 1879: "My object is to show how the whole of these associated ideas, though they are for the most part exceedingly fleeting and obscure, and barely cross the threshold of our consciousness, may be seized, dragged into daylight, and recorded. I shall then treat the records of some experiments statistically, and shall make out what I can of them" (p. 148).

He was awestruck by his tabulations: "The general impression they left upon me is like that which many of us have experienced when the basement of our house happens to be under thorough sanitary repairs, and we realize for the first time the complex systems of drains and gas- and water-pipes, flues, and so forth, upon which our comfort depends, but which are usually hidden out of sight, and of whose existence, so long as they acted well, we had never troubled ourselves" (1879, p. 162).

His most important conclusion: "The actors on my mental stage were indeed very numerous, but by no means as numerous as I had imagined. They now seemed to be something like the actors in theatres where large processions are represented, who march off one side of the stage, and going round by the back, come again at the other" (p. 162).

At first glance, this conclusion may not seem earth shaking, but Galton had actually discovered two principles that have had enor-

mous impact on our thinking about thinking. The first is his notion
of **recurrence**. This holds that the conscious mind is like a **plenum**.

A plenum is a space totally filled up with objects. An example
would be the ball bearing ring that fits around the wheels of cars.
Little balls fill two concentric rings and roll around in the hub of the
wheel, making the wheel spin much more freely than it would otherwise be. Each ball can only move by taking the place of the ball in
front of it. There is no place else to go. The only possible movement
is cyclical movement. Figure 5–1 illustrates this concept.

Galton argued that this is what happens in the conscious mind. It
is always, at any one point in time, filled up, and thoughts can only
follow each other around. It is good that this is so, because otherwise,
he believed, conscious thought would be random and would have no
order. Orderliness is essential to logical mental processes.

However, if this were the only thing the mind could do, there
could be no new thoughts and therefore no creativity. The second
and probably more important discovery Galton made was that new
input can come into this plenum from another part of the mind. The

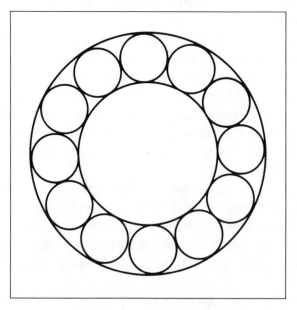

Figure 5–1. A PLENUM

source of this input is the unconscious, the "basement" of the mind. And most important of all, the unconscious can be made conscious through association of thoughts. Thus was discovered the critical notion of **free association.**

The notion was certainly revolutionary. "Ideas in the conscious mind are linked to those in the unconscious mind by threads of similarity." At the turn of the century, Freud and his mentors brought this notion to fruition. They began to realize that ideas hidden from conscious awareness could nevertheless have a powerful effect on a sick person's behavior. Freud's major discovery, at least at that early stage, was that the contents of the unconscious could be revealed by suggesting certain key words to patients. The contents of their unconscious would come forward through their seemingly random associations to those words. Fortunately, others also were able to benefit from Galton's thinking.

James's Theory

William James (1842–1910) was familiar to late nineteenth-century intellectuals as a philosopher, but he was really an avant-garde psychologist. He also believed that creativity was the result both of rich associations and avoidance of commonplace ideas: "I believe that the only difference between a muddle-head and a genius is that between extracting wrong characters and right ones. In other words, a muddle-headed person is a genius spoiled in the making" (1890, p. 352).

In saying this, James made one of the earliest statements about the supremacy of the environment over genetic inheritance in determining ability. Galton, for example, was a strong proponent of the idea that a person could make excellent associations because the capacity was inherited. Galton's *Hereditary Genius* (1870), which emphasized the frequency of creativity within certain well-known families, was a famous argument for this position. James was one of the first to propose that the circumstances of one's upbringing were more important than genes in this regard. In his time, he was virtually alone in putting forth this idea. With Freud, James was unique in thinking that the ability to get in touch with one's unconscious ideas is vital to giving birth to originality. No one has put it better than he:

Most people probably fall several times a day onto a fit of something like this: the eyes are fixed on vacancy, the sounds of the world melt into confused unity, the attention is dispersed so that the whole body is felt, as it were, at once, and the foreground of consciousness is filled, if by anything, by a sort of solemn surrender to the empty passing of time. In the dim background of our mind we know meanwhile what we ought to be doing: getting up, dressing ourselves, answering the person who has spoken to us, trying to make the next step in our reasoning. But somehow we cannot start; the pensée de derrière la tête [literally, thought at the back of the head] fails to pierce the shell of lethargy that wraps our state about. Every moment we expect the spell to break; for we know no reason why it should continue. But it does continue, pulse after pulse, and we float with it, until—also without reason that we can discover—an energy is given, something—we know not what—enables us to gather ourselves together, we wink our eyes, we shake our heads, the background-ideas become effective, and the wheels of life go round again (1890, p. 401).

James clearly recognized the importance to creativity of "thoughts at the back of the mind," but he did not pursue it.

Wallas's Theory

In his *Art of Thought* (1926), Graham Wallas (1885–1932) gave the unconscious a central place in his theory. He delineated four distinct stages in the creative process.

1. Preparation. The problem to be solved is detected in this first stage, and data relevant to it are identified. How should one do this? Some say to learn as much as possible about the problem area. Learn the essence of the nature of the problem, and gather all the basic material that might pertain to it. Others have argued that this kind of familiarization, especially through "book learning," will destroy original thought. As George Bernard Shaw put it, "Reading rots the mind." In his view, knowing a great deal about a field makes the thinker incapable of challenging the rules. Herbert Crovitz offers a most reasonable conclusion:

There are forms as well as content to be learned in preparation. The more varied the problem-solving experiences one has had, the greater the chances of trying a variety of attacks on a problem. It is not that one fails—he can try, try again—it is that he can try different things. As we shall see, and learn to regret deeply, the natural tendency is to keep trying the same old thing when illumination requires more flexibility than that. . . . The "good idea" is the confrontation of the problem by the knowledge that makes a solution rather easy. The "good idea" is a verbalization of what now must be verified; it springs from importing the appropriate knowledge into the problem (1970, p. 80).

Where can this appropriate information come from? Not the conscious mind—it is a plenum that simply revolves around itself. New thoughts must be infused, and they usually come from one's unconscious mind. And how can this be done? Wallas's second stage offers an answer.

2. Incubation. In this stage, continued data gathering or continued mulling over the problem will be counterproductive. It is essential to leave the problem alone. Efforts to solve the problem must be allowed to sink into the unconscious mind. Climb a mountain, clean the garage—do anything other than think about the problem. Albert Einstein was once asked if he thought about physics in images, symbols, or words. He pondered the question and replied that he did none of these—usually he just let it happen in a place in his mind with which he was not in touch, and eventually a solution would come to him. As with a great recipe, there comes a time when all that can be done to mix the ingredients well has been done, and they must be allowed to "cook." This is the *pensée de derrière la tête* to which James refers.

Rudyard Kipling, in describing how he got ideas for his work, put it the most succinctly: "Drift, wait, and obey." This is seldom easy for the problem solver; usually there is a strong drive to get the damned problem solved. Nevertheless, out of frustration, the problem solver will eventually give up, at least temporarily, and then the real search for new ideas can begin. If the second stage is successful, the third stage occurs.

3. Illumination. Suddenly the idea, solution, or new relationship emerges; all the facts "fall into place." Is it insight? Is it some cortical phenomenon? The truthful answer is that no one knows. For some reason, vital new methods, data, or relationships become clear to the thinker. A good guess comes to us from Crovitz: "Consider the *verbalization* of the illumination. The emotional pang of intimation is almost entirely an emotional call that 'something is here!' And then, almost *immediately*, that which is here is given to awareness. But not quite all at once" (1970, p. 86).

Crovitz speaks of the "Oh! There's something now" phenomenon. It is somewhat like the "I've got that person's name on the tip of my tongue" phenomenon. We know that the answer is near but not quite conscious. This leads to a wonderful definition of consciousness: *giving a name or label to a previously unnamed thought*. Is that all the difference there is between conscious and unconscious ideas? It may be! If that is the case, then illumination must be the ability to give a name to a preconscious idea that fits the problem-solving need. All that remains is to figure out how to get the amorphous ideas of the unconscious into the conscious mind for identification and use.

Of course the sense that something is about to emerge does not always signal a solution. Sometimes it only means that some more conscious work is needed. Other times nothing at all comes. These unsuccessful instances tend to be forgotten quickly, which explains why the phenomenon is given so much credence. At any rate, when a feeling of illumination occurs (the so-called Aha or Eureka feeling described in chapter 4), the fourth stage is entered.

4. Verification. The idea is new and appealing. It has exciting possibilities. But does it work? Does it relate the parts into a meaningful whole? Here the idea must be tested against the cold reality of fact. Verification is really the most important aspect of creativity, despite the romantic reputation given to incubation and illumination. Long ago it was suggested that if a million monkeys were taught to type, and if they all were to type for a million hours, one of them would probably type *Macbeth*. The difference between monkeys and humans typing at random is that monkeys would never *know* that they had typed a classic. The ability to recognize when a solution fits a problem is a vital aspect of creativity.

Wallas clearly improved on the theories of his predecessors, but like theirs, his theory is not without its weaknesses. A major one is that incubation, the generator of ideas, is a very passive process. Passivity seems to go against the idea of creating.

Mednick's Theory

Before reading an explanation of this popular theory, you may want to try your hand at the facsimile of the Remote Associates Test, which Mednick designed to test his theory.

THE REMOTE ASSOCIATES TEST

Instructions: In this test you are presented with three words and asked to find a fourth word that is related to the other three. Write this word in the space to the right. For example, what word do you think is related to these three?

cookies   sixteen   heart   _____

The answer in this case is *sweet*. Cookies are sweet; *sweet* is part of the phrase *sweet sixteen* and part of the word *sweetheart*.

Here is another example:

poke   go   molasses   _____

You should have written *slow* in the space provided: *slow poke, go slow, slow as molasses*. As you can see, the fourth word may be related to the other three for various reasons. Now try these:

1. flap   tire   beanstalk   _____
2. mountain   up   school   _____
3. package   cardboard   fist   _____
4. surprise   line   birthday   _____
5. madman   acorn   bolt   _____
6. telephone   high   electric   _____
7. hair   income   fish   _____
8. cream   bulb   heavy   _____
9. up   knife   Bandaid   _____
10. snow   wash   black   _____
11. out   home   jail   _____

12. slugger   belfry   ball   _____

13. stage   game   actor   _____

14. Roman   arithmetic   one   _____

15. cat   color   holes   _____

16. belle   snow   beach   _____

Mednick (1962) believed that creativity is the process by which ideas already in the mind are associated in unusual, original, and useful combinations. Every image or concept we have is associated with other images and concepts. All the associations linked to a particular idea are arranged in a list. Those associations at the top of the list are most closely linked to the idea; as we move down the list, the strength of association becomes weaker and the associated ideas come to mind less quickly. Table 5–2 gives an imaginary example of an idea and the strength of some possible associations. Ten is the highest rating, indicating that the idea "ride" is closely associated with "bike."

If you were asked to say the first thing that comes into your mind when hearing the word *black*, you would probably say "white." White is a strong associate of the concept black. "Shoes" might also come to mind, but this would be lower on the list of associations with black for most people.

When people think about solving a problem, they mentally cast about for an association that might serve as a solution. Most of us accept the first idea that seems to solve the problem. Mednick argues that creative people are those who go farther down the list, searching for more unusual but higher-quality associations to solve their problems. It is these remote associations that produce creative products. The poet Marianne Moore put remote associations together in a pleasing new way when she wrote "the lion's ferocious chrysanthemum head." Although this billowy flower is seldom associated with ferocity, the apparent contradiction is appealing—it makes us see lions in a new and startling way.

Some people have very short lists of ideas that are strongly associated with each other; they can produce only a few associations. These people are often rigid and dogmatic in their beliefs and tend to produce little that is creative. Others have longer lists of less tightly

Table 5–1

SAMPLE ASSOCIATIONS WITH THE CONCEPT "BIKE"

Strength	Association
10	Ride
9	Run
8	Transportation, red
7	Ten-speed
6	Fast
5	
4	The hill on County Road
3	May and Jake
2	
1	Athletic supporter

associated ideas; they are less committed to getting "the one right answer" and are not so threatened by being wrong. They have the flexbility that encourages the mental search for remote associations. Some of their freely associated ideas may be silly, but some produce really creative combinations. Most people fall somewhere between these extremes.

A facsimile of Mednick's Remote Associates Test appeared earlier in this section. This test was designed to measure the ability to associate ideas flexibly and freely. The correct answers are printed here; a discussion of why the test is considered a valid instrument is presented in chapter 7.

Answers to the Remote Associates Test facsimile:

1. jack	5. nut	9. cut	13. play
2. grade, high	6. wire	10. white	14. numeral
3. box	7. net	11. house	15. black
4. party	8. light	12. bat	16. ball

Mednick suggests that "familiarity breeds rigidity": the more we know about a subject, the less likely we are to be creative about it. We willingly accept the laws and principles in a particular area and no longer question them after we have dealt with them for a long time. This may be the reason that theoretical physicists and master chess players are said to have passed their prime after age thirty-five. Einstein, for example, was only nineteen when he discovered his theory of relativity (although he was twenty-six when he finally published it). Unfortunately, only a few are able to resist the growing rigidity of age.

Another aspect of Mednick's theory (1963) has to do with cognitive style. Some people tend to think of the world in visual images— Mednick calls them visualizers. Others tend to use words to symbolize objects—Mednick calls them verbalizers. Since some problems are primarily of the visual type and others are of the verbal type, we can expect to find a strong relationship between problem type and cognitive style. There is considerable research evidence for this view. (Later chapters in this book present methods for facilitating creativity in the cognitive style opposite to an individual's preferred style.)

A final part of Mednick's theory has to do with the way in which a problem is defined. If the definition is narrow, many kinds of associations, some of which might well offer good solutions, are ruled out. As an example of this, Mednick tells about a group that was asked to think of the best way to keep a refrigerator free of frost. Most of the solutions had to do with how to remove frost after it had built up. Only a few thought of preventing frost buildup in the first place. Those who did were able to think of many more possible solutions because of the broader way in which they looked at the problem itself.

How does the mind put together "mutually remote elements in a creatively useful way"? Mednick believes there are three explanations:

1. Serendipity. Elements that rarely occur together in the environment nevertheless occasionally do. The creative person is one who is able to recognize a link between the elements which meets some previously unmet need. The invention of the X-ray and the discoveries of penicillin and radium are familiar examples.

2. Similarity. Sometimes there is a type of similarity between two otherwise remote elements that the creative person recognizes but that others had failed to notice. Marianne Moore's flower-headed lion, mentioned earlier, typifies this type of association.

3. Mediation. Ideas that have nothing in common with each other may have some significant association with a third element. Again, the mediation is only likely to be spotted by a person whose mind is open to such a possibility. The Remote Associates Test is an especially good example of this third approach.

The Gestalt Position

A second group of theorists, known collectively as Gestalt psychologists, argue that creativity is a much more complicated process than merely associating ideas in new and different ways. They believe that the whole of any idea always amounts to more than merely the sum of its parts. Gestalt psychology started at the same time (the late nineteenth century) as associationist psychology and has always been antithetical to it.

Wertheimer's Theory

Max Wertheimer (1880–1943), the founder of Gestaltism, is also associationism's strongest critic (1945). Consider, for instance, this stinging indictment:

> In [the associationists'] aim to get at the elements of thinking they cut to pieces living thinking processes, deal with them blind to structure, assuming that the process is an aggregate, a sum of those elements. In dealing with [creative] processes, they can do nothing but dissect them, and thus show a dead picture stripped of all that is alive in them (1945, p. 12).

The central theme in Wertheimer's view of creative thinking is the formation and alteration of **Gestalts,** which means "mental patterns or forms." The elements of Gestalts have complex relationships and are far more than merely "associated" with each other. Great paintings are made up of elements that are interrelated to the point that "the whole is greater than the sum of the parts."

Wertheimer argues, for example, that creative musicians do not write notes on a paper in hopes of achieving new associations. Rather, they conceive of a half-formed idea of the finished piece of music and then work backward to complete the idea. They develop an overview of the entire structure and then rearrange its parts. Creative solutions are often obtained by seeing an existing Gestalt in a new way. This can happen when we change the position from which we view a scene or problem, or when the personal needs that affect perception change.

Imagine that you are looking into a display window of a clothing store. The brightly colored dresses stand out in the foreground; the pastel curtains behind them are not so prominent, and you don't notice at all that the window dresser has left part of sandwich on the floor. However, suppose you look at that store window when you are extremely hungry. The sandwich will leap into the foreground, and the clothing becomes hardly noticeable.

Wertheimer argued that getting a new point of view on the whole of a problem, rather than rearranging its parts, is more likely to produce creativity. Why is a new point of view so hard to achieve? Many impediments exist. First of all, most people don't like problems, because they "set up strains, stresses, tensions in the thinker." This often produces rigidity.

Jacob Getzels and Mihalyi Csikszentmihalyi (1975) found that the reaction to this first step in creative thinking is the most important distinction between successful and unsuccessful artists. They call it "problem finding." Whereas some artists looked at their empty canvasses as a problem to be solved as succinctly as possible, the more successful enjoyed the ambiguity of the situation and relished wrestling with the many alternatives available.

Kohler's Theory

Another key aspect of Gestalt theory is the concept of instantaneous insight, first researched by Wolfgang Kohler (1887–1967). This concept is the opposite of the trial-and-error chaining of ideas espoused by the associationists.

Kohler's main investigations of insight took place when Kohler was on the African island of Tenerife during World War I. He had gone there to study chimpanzees in 1913 and the next year was unable to leave because of the war. In all, he spent seven years on his studies there (1929).

His classic experiment, described in his wonderful book *The Mentality of Apes* (1925), involved putting bananas out of the reach of caged chimpanzees. He gave the chimps two sticks, both of which were too short individually to reach the bananas but which could be fitted together to make one stick that could reach them. The chimps experimented with the sticks unsuccessfully, even on occasion pushing one stick with the other so that it touched the bananas. Giving up, they would play with the sticks until they noticed that they could be fitted together. This appeared to provide a flash of insight, for they would go immediately to the side of the cage and drag the fruit within reach. This and other research was used to reinforce the Gestaltist contention that learning (and creativity) involves a reorganization or restructuring of mental concepts. (Thus those who adhere to the Gestalt point of view are also sometimes referred to as structuralists.)

Gruber's Theory

A student of Piaget's and a coauthor with Wertheimer (Gruber, Terrell, and Wertheimer 1964), Howard Gruber 1922–) has pioneered, with his students, a **case study approach** in an effort to describe the creative mental process. Gruber laboriously studied the notebooks of the great biologist Charles Darwin to find clues as to the pathways taken by the mind of a genius.

Did he find great flashes of insight striking at unpredictable times? By no means, according to Gardner (1982), who summarizes Gruber's discoveries:

Darwin was seen as a persistent, active, fully engaged person. Counter to the conventional view of creativity as a mystical, irrational process, Darwin experienced no sudden epiphany of inspiration, no wholly novel thoughts or theories. Instead, Darwin marshalled endless lists of thoughts, images, questions, dreams, sketches, comments, arguments, and notes to himself, all of which he continually organized and reorganized. It was all part of a mammoth, painstaking effort to understand the way living processes have yielded the plethora of plant and animal species in the natural world. Key themes were introduced, discussed, and sometimes abandoned only to be revisited at a later time. Pivotal insights were anticipated in earlier scribbles, and occasionally discovered twice. One can even estimate the pace of this creative activity; whereas for normal individuals a mental elimination occurs perhaps once a week, for Darwin, who worked tirelessly on his projects, it seems to have occurred on an almost daily basis (p. 353).

As the result of his reconstruction of Darwin's thinking, Gruber suggested five characteristics of the scientific creative mental process:

1. The person views problems as a whole, and deals with them by analyzing their various interacting subsystems
2. There is a distinct view of the ultimate goal, which guides and motivates the work
3. Each problem is represented by a number of themes or "dominant metaphors." In Darwin's case, some of these were survival, heredity, and natural selection
4. There is a strong empathy for the subject(s) under study
5. Often a distinct sense of loneliness and risk of failure are present, and the fight against discouragement is constant

Both the associationist and Gestaltist schools of thought have a clear-cut theoretical orientation, on the basis of which research has been designed. A newer body of research, and one that is as yet not nearly so organized, is the cognitive-developmental approach.

The Cognitive-Developmental Approach

This approach, which has sprung in a very general way from the theory of cognitive developmentalist Jean Piaget, emphasizes changes in cognition that occur with age. Within this context, these researchers look at creativity from the standpoint of such concepts as **cognitive style, cognitive mobility,** and **use of metaphor.**

Cognitive Style

Cognitive style might be described as a sort of personality trait of one's mental functioning. It pertains not to how well an individual thinks but to the particular way he or she goes about it.

A primary aspect of cognitive style has become known as **field independence/dependence.** Herman Witken and his associates (Witken et al. 1954, 1962), as well as many other researchers have studied the phenomenon for three decades. Field independence refers to the ability to look at a whole picture or problem, break it up into parts, and then attend to the more relevant parts while blocking out the less relevant. Anyone who has ever tried to "find the star in this picture" knows about field independence.

The two principle measures of field independence are the Rod and Frame Test and the Embedded Figures Test. In the former task, a person is placed in a totally darkened room and is then confronted with a luminous rod within a tilted luminous frame. The subject must place the rod in an upright position while disregarding the context of the tilted frame (see figure 5–2).

Likewise, the *Embedded Figures Test* involves recognizing a small but relevant form (a star) within a larger field of meaningless forms (see figure 5–3). The solution to the test can be seen in figure 5–4.

Figure 5–2. THE ROD AND FRAME TEST

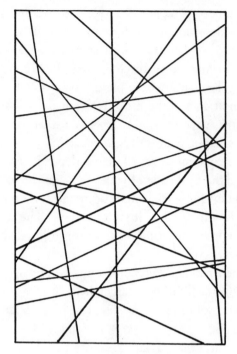

Figure 5-3. THE EMBEDDED FIGURES TEST

Although Witken's early efforts in this area did not attempt to link the concept of field independence to creativity, more and more creativity researchers have turned to this aspect of cognitive style. Gestaltists such as Wertheimer (1945) proposed that a major task of creativity involved the ability to break up a problem-solving task into parts that are not immediately recognizable, and then to reorganize them in new, meaningful ways that solve the problem creatively.

Cognitive Mobility

Another aspect of cognitive style, mobility, comes from Heinz Werner's (1921–) comparative developmental theory. He argued (1957) that development progresses into distinct areas. An infant begins life with a singular, global system, which includes physical movement, emotions, and the senses, all rolled into one process. As the individual develops, the processes begin to separate from one another, new processes such as cognition appear, and more complex and efficient processes emerge, which dominate the earlier ones. The earlier, primitive processes are still available to the individual, however.

For most problem solving, the most efficient capability would be the presence of a highly developed, complex system, along with the ability to call upon the previously developed, more primitive systems. Although he believed in this principle for all psychological processes, Werner believed that psychological "mobility" was especially useful in creativity. Those individuals who are able to move readily between complex and primitive cognitions are more likely to produce valuable ideas. The problem for researchers, then, is to identify the various cognitive styles that emerge within an individual, observe how they relate to one another, and compare this to creative performance.

The early work on field independence and creativity was inconclusive. Spotts and Mackler (1967), using the Embedded Figures Test to assess field independence, and tests developed by Torrance and by Guilford to assess creativity (see chapter 6), found that college males who possess greater field independence also test higher for creativity. Although this relationship was not particularly strong, it was stronger than the relationship between measured field independence and measures of intelligence. Other researchers at the time (Bieri, Bradburn, and Galinsky 1958) also found that field independent individuals showed only slightly more creativity than their field dependent counterparts.

Researchers began to suspect that field-independence alone did not adequately account for creative performance and began to look at how field independence was influenced by Werner's cognitive mobility (Bloomberg 1971). According to this view, a creative person is someone who not only has achieved a high degree of field independence, but who also can flexibly operate a field dependent level when the problem calls for it. The ability to move from one mental process to another is what is meant by cognitive mobility. It recalls some of the research done on brain lateralization (see chapter 4): high creativity might be due not so much to right brain dominance as to an ability to use both hemispheres in an efficient, integrated manner.

Gamble and Kellner (1968) looked at cognitive mobility with a

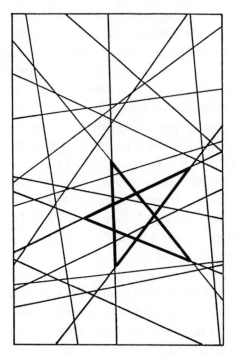

Figure 5–4. SOLUTION TO THE EMBEDDED FIGURES TEST

measure called the Stroop Color-Word Test. In this test, a subject has to identify quickly and accurately ink colors that are spelled out incongruously (for instance, the word *red* printed in green ink, and the right answer is *green*). The authors assumed that recognizing a color is a more primitive process than reading, and that creative people would be able to call upon that more primitive process more readily than would less creative people. In their study, they found that subjects who scored high on the Remote Associates Test also did well on the Stroop Color-Word Test. More recently, Golden (1975) assessed subjects with divergent thinking tasks, teacher ratings of creativity, and a new group version of the Stroop Color-Word Test, and found that highly creative individuals scored significantly higher on the mobility task.

In an interesting study of cognitive mobility that used a projective psychoanalytic technique, Hersch (1962) compared the responses of creative subjects on the Rorschach Test to the responses of noncreative subjects and to schizophrenics. Hersch thought that the creative subjects (so determined by their actual achievements) would not only have more mature responses available than would the noncreative subjects, but would also be more able to use primitive responses, similar to the responses of schizophrenics. A method of categorizing the Rorschach responses into mature or primitive responses on the basis of Werner's theory was used.

The results showed that the creative subjects did have greater availability of both mature and primitive responses than did noncreative subjects. The creative subjects also used more mature responses than did the schizophrenics, and although their primitive responses were similar in some ways, they were also distinctly different. These results strongly confirm Werner's theory.

There have been some attempts to look at how cognitive mobility might work with field independence/dependence to enhance creativity. Some early but incomplete support for such theories was provided by Bloomberg (1971) and Del Gaudio (1976). The evidence appears to indicate that, as Bloomberg put it, "perhaps all creative persons are field independent, but not all field independent persons are creative" (p. 177).

Piagetian Theory

Unfortunately, Jean Piaget himself did not have much to say about creativity, because he had little interest in topics concerning individual differences. A unique ability like creativity does not fit in well with his theory of universal stages. Followers of Piaget have, however, attempted to speculate about creativity within a Piagetian framework. Much of this speculation has centered on the creative potential of formal thought (Piaget's final stage of intellectual development (1966) in which children twelve years old and older begin to consider hypothetical questions based not on reality but on fanciful and abstract possibilities). The child is also able to consider many more factors in combination in order to solve problems.

A number of studies over the years have shown that field independent subjects perform better on some of Piaget's formal operational tasks (Lawson 1976; Neimark 1975, Stone and Day, 1980). Noppe (1985) has looked at formal thought and field independence along with cognitive mobility to see how all three of these variables combine to affect creativity. The idea is that cognitive mobility allows a person to use different kinds of perception in order to extract all the relevant parts of a problem, both big and small. The person then uses convergent formal thought processes to arrive at appropriate solutions. Evidence favoring this view is Noppe's finding that field independence/dependence and formal thought are good predictors of creative ability.

Arlin (1975) has suggested a fifth stage beyond formal operations. She views formal operations as a largely convergent, problem-solving stage, while the new stage is viewed as a divergent problem-finding stage (similar to the idea of Getzels and Csikszentmihalyi presented earlier in this chapter).

Gruber (1981) discusses several possible aspects of a link between formal thought and creativity, and suggests that the great creative discovery of evolution by Darwin is similar to the first creative processes that children discover when they move into adolescence and the formal operation stage. Feldman (1980) also proposes that creativity be viewed as a Piagetian-like transition into a new thought structure.

Lubeck and Biddle (1988) have recently offered an excellent extension of this speculation. They use Piagetian concepts to attempt to resolve two of the major dilemmas posed in creativity theory. First, they point to the continuity controversy between the associationists and the Gestaltists: "(1) the idea that creative insights are built up by associations and prepared for by gradual effort or labor and are followed by periods of elaboration. These descriptions emphasize *continuity* with the past"; versus "(2) the experience of creativity as a sudden insight, a leap ahead or a 'spark,' all of which emphasize *discontinuity* with the past state" (p. 35). Lubeck and Biddle suggest that Piaget's concept (1976) of equilibrium can be used to resolve this dilemma.

Their reasoning goes like this: First a problem is perceived, which forces the thinker into a state of disequilibrium. In fact, as the problem is analyzed, several "minidisequilibria" are caused. The thinker begins searching for ways to return to equilibrium, with much of his or her thinking taking place on an unconscious level. At that level, and to some extent at the conscious level, her thinking follows the associationist model. There is a "progressive equilibration," that is, "a gradual process of self-regulation in attempts to reach self regulated goals" (p. 37). However, the thinker has no experience of satisfaction that the problem is solved until the last piece fits into place. Now he or she experiences the conscious "Aha!" that seems to be an intuitive leap to a new awareness. This part of the process fits well with the Gestalt position. Thus you could say that associationists and the Gestaltists are both right.

The second dilemma that Lubeck and Biddle strive to resolve concerns the Freudian argument that creativity is an effort to *reduce* tension, as contrasted with Barron and Welsh's idea (see chapter 2) that creative people actually seek tension through an attraction to disorder. The relevant Piagetian concept here (Piaget 1952) is functional assimilation. The mind is constantly active, forever setting itself new goals that bring about "external obstacles and inner conflicts" (p. 38). These obstacles and conflicts cause tension, and Freud was right that it is natural to try to get rid of them.

But he was wrong in believing that the goal is merely a return to quiescence. The object is rather a reequilibration to a "new coordination or construction creating a new mental system extending beyond the previous level of organization" (p. 38). It is also natural for the individual to seek incessantly for these new coordinations because he or she realizes instinctively and through learning that he or she will be better off for them. The highly creative person is one who seems to have learned this best.

Piaget (1973) himself summed up these concepts admirably in the title of one of his books, *To Understand Is to Invent.*

The Use of Metaphor

A relatively new concept that is receiving considerable attention is the ability to use and understand metaphors. Common sense suggests a relationship between efficient metaphor use and creativity. Using a metaphor in speech involves calling attention to a similarity between two seemingly dissimilar things. This suggests a process similar to divergent thinking, and there is a growing body of research support for this relationship (Kogan 1983, Jaquish, Block, and Block 1984).

Kogan believes that metaphor use can explain the difference between ordinary divergent thinking and high-quality divergent thinking. A creative person must be able not only to think of many different things from many different categories, but to compare them in unique, qualitatively different ways. Although metaphors are typically first used by older children and adolescents, an outgrowth from this research has been research looking at the symbolic play of very young children and how it relates to creativity (see Kogan 1983 for a good review). The early imaginative play of children is now being viewed as a precursor of later metaphor use and creativity.

An interesting attempt to integrate the work on cognitive styles with the personality characteristics associated with creativity is provided by Block and Block (1980). These researchers proposed earlier that diverse areas of psychology, such as learning, perception, interpersonal behaviors, attitudes, and problem solving, could be viewed within the constructs of **ego-control** and **ego-resiliency**. As the use of the term *ego* suggests, their work could be broadly viewed as an effort to reconcile some aspects of psychoanalytic theory with the more recent behavioral and cognitive research that tends to ignore personality and social context.

Ego-control refers to the extent to which a person can express or contain impulses, feelings, and desires. Ego-overcontrol refers to the ability to control impulse, delay gratification, suppress emotions, and avoid distractions; ego-undercontrol is the opposite. The other construct, ego-resiliency, refers to the ability of a person to modify his or her level of ego-control to meet the demands of the situation. An ego-resilient person can resourcefully adapt to changing circumstances, carefully size up a situation, and make good use of all the problem-solving strategies available to him or her. On the other hand, an ego-brittle person has little flexibility or awareness of the demands of changing situations. When faced with an ambiguous situation and/or increasing stress, such a person tends to become disorganized (see chapter 2).

Block and Block have examined these two constructs in an ongoing longitudinal study of 130 children who have been periodically assessed from age three with a combination of experimental tasks, observer descriptions, and self-report instruments. The aim of this research goes well beyond our concern with creativity, and the Blocks have only infrequently directly discussed the issue (Harrington, Block, and Block 1983), but their results have disclosed interesting links between the cognitive styles discussed earlier and the personality characteristics associated with ego-control and resiliency.

In addition to the relationship between ego-control and delay of gratification, they have found that ego resiliency relates to field independence/dependence and tolerance of ambiguity, as well as to the ability to handle anxiety under stress. Though some of the data more specifically concerned with creativity has not yet been analyzed, this work could provide a significant framework from which to view many of the diverse experimental findings, especially from a developmental perspective.

One of the best sources of the study of the role of metaphor has been the work done by Howard Gardner and his associates at Harvard University's Project Zero. (It was named that because virtually nothing was known of artistic thinking at that time.) His seminal book *Art, Mind, and Brain: A Cognitive Approach to Creativity* (1982) offers many insights into the process.

Gardner has based his research on the theories of three eminent structuralists, Jean Piaget, Noam Chomsky, and Claude Lévi-Strauss. He states that "these thinkers share a belief that the mind operates according to specifiable rules—often unconscious ones—and that these can be ferreted out and made explicit by the systematic examination of human language, action, and problem-solving" (p. 4).

Gardner's main efforts have focused on the relationship between children's art and their understanding of metaphor, both in normal and brain-damaged children. He describes telling a group of youngsters at a seder (the meal Jews eat in memory of the flight of the Hebrews from Egypt) how, after a plague, Pharaoh's "heart was turned to stone." The children interpreted the metaphor variously, but only the older ones could understand the link between the physical universe (hard rocks) and psychological traits (stubborn lack of feeling). Younger children are more apt to apply magical interpretations (God or a witch did it). Gardner believes that the development of the understanding of metaphoric language is as sequential as the stages proposed by Piaget and is closely related to the types of development treated in those theories.

Examining such children's metaphors as a bald man having a "barefoot head" and an elephant being seen as a "gasmask," Gardner and his wife (Gardner and Winner 1982) found clear changes with age in the level of sophistication. Interestingly, there appear to be two opposing features:

1. When you ask children to explain figures of speech, they get better at it steadily as they get older.
2. However, very young children seem to be the best at making up their own metaphors. Furthermore, their own metaphors tend to be one of two types:

> The different patterns of making metaphors may reflect fundamentally different ways of processing information. Children who make their metaphors on visual resemblances may approach experience largely in terms of the physical qualities of objects. On the other hand, children who base their metaphors on action sequences may view the world in terms of the way events unfold over time. We believe that the difference may continue into adulthood, underlying diverse styles in the creation and appreciation of artistic forms (p. 164).

These researchers believe that the spontaneous production of metaphors declines somewhat during the school years. This is probably because the child, having mastered a basic vocabulary, has less need to "stretch the resources of language to express new meanings" (p. 165). In addition, there is greater pressure from teachers and parents to get the right answers, so children become less risk taking in their language. Gardner and Winner point to the *Shakespeare Parallel Text Series*, which offers a translation of the bard's plays into everyday English ("Stand and unfold yourself" becomes "Stand still and tell me who you are"), as a step in the wrong direction. "If, as we have shown, students of this age have the potential to deal with complex metaphors, there is no necessity to rewrite Shakespeare" (p. 167).

It is exciting to think that Gardner and Winner may be offering us the explanation of why some people become scientists and others writers, and that they may have an important key to fostering such talent. Of course, this is not to say that they have the answers to such questions as why children develop one of the two forms of "metaphorizing" (or neither), but their work appears to be a giant step in the right direction.

And so an analysis of cognitive aspects of creativity may be grouped into three schools of thought. These are the associationist, Gestalt, and cognitive-developmental schools. Each of them is significantly different from the other two. Which is right, or perhaps, more right? The theory of one psychologist who may be seen as having sympathies with all three offers what I believe to be an excellent rapprochement. The comprehensive theory of J.P. Guilford, who applies his concept of creative thinking to problem solving, is detailed in the next chapter.

6

Creative Problem Solving

Chapter Highlights:

Guilford's Theory
  Guilford's Model of Creative Problem Solving
The Problem of Filtering
The Problem of Memory
  The Yogic Sponge Position
Problems with Convergent Production
  Functional Fixity
Problems with Divergent Production
  Lateral Thinking
  Discovering Hidden Assumptions
  Brainstorming
  Synectics
  Sociodrama
Some Other Approaches to Creative Problem Solving
  The Reluctantly Creative Student
  Hallman's Obstacles and Aids to Creative Problem
    Solving
  Guidelines for Creative Problem Solving

Key Terms and Concepts:

Authoritarianism	Perceptual blocks
Brainstorming	Personal analogy
Cognition	Psychic censor
Convergent thinking	Sociodrama
Direct analogy	Structure of Intellect
Divergent thinking	Model
Evaluation	Symbolic analogy
Fantasy analogy	Synectics
Field dependence/	Water Jar Test
independence	Worst-case analysis
Ideal	Yogic sponge position
Memory	

Important People:

Edward de Bono	Abraham Luchins
Karl Duncker	Alex Osborn
William J.J. Gordon	Lewis Terman
J.P. Guilford	J. Paul Torrance

———————————

T rue creative genius is rare, but all of us have at least some creative ability. Normally, we use it in trying to solve problems. You might say that the average person's creative problem solving compares to the thinking of the creative genius the way the work of a good auto mechanic compares to that of a famous brain surgeon: both involve insight and imagination, but the level is very different.

In table 6–1 a comparison of seven models of problem solving is presented. There is not a great deal of agreement among them. No

SEVEN MODELS OF THE CREATIVE PROBLEM-SOLVING PROCESS

Stage	Wallas	Dewey	Rossman	Bransford and Stein	Vaigiu	Osborne	Polya
				Theorist			
1.	Preparation	Sensing difficulty Defining difficulty	Problem observed Problem formulated Available information surveyed	Identify problems Define problem	Preparation Definition Frustration	I. Fact finding 1. Problem 2. Preparation	Understanding the problem
2.	Incubation				Incubation		
3.	Illumination	Suggesting possible solutions	Solutions formulated	Explore approaches	Illumination	II. Idea finding 3. Idea production 4. Idea development	Deciding what to do
4.	Verification	Considering consequences	Solutions critically examined	Look at effects		III. Solution finding 5. Evaluation	Carrying out the plan
5.			New ideas formulated				Looking back
6.		Accepting a solution	New ideas accepted and tested			6. Adoption	

two models agree completely on the "right" sequence of steps. Nevertheless, taken as a whole, they offer a comprehensive picture of what some scientists have found when they have tried to recreate how good problem solvers go about it.

But there is an inherent weakness in the method these studies used. Typically, the researchers interviewed a variety of problem solvers and then summarized what they were told. It is possible (and probably likely) that the persons who were interviewed remembered the sequences of the problem-solving efforts as being more orderly than it actually was. They may have "tidied up" the process unconsciously. This is the contention of Guilford (1965), who sees it as much less logical and sequential than do these other theorists. His position is considered next.

Guilford's Theory

J.P. Guilford (1897–　　) was the first to call for a great expansion in research on creativity. He did so in his presidential address to the American Psychological Association (1950), in which he scolded his fellow psychologists for avoiding this complex field. He has himself been one of the foremost constributors to this expansion (1959a and 1959b, 1962, 1967, 1975).

Through the use of a complex statistical technique known as factor analysis, Guilford and his colleagues have attempted to map the intellectual operations of the human mind, with a special interest in its creative functioning. The result has been the creation of a theory he calls the **structure of the intellect.**

In building this theory, Guilford and his associates gave a large variety of mental tests to a large number of people. Some were standard IQ tests; others were more unusual, such as tests of spatial relations and social knowledge. He wanted to see how ability on one type of test interrelates with ability on the other types of tests. From this, he believed he could identify the basic cognitive abilities. (For this, he used a complex statistical procedure called "factor analysis," hence his approach is sometimes known as the factorial theory.)

The results of Guilford's research have fascinated psychologists and educators. His most significant finding is that the intellect is made up of five types of mental operation. (It also includes four types of contents. These are discussed in chapter 10). The mental operations form a central theme in his model of creative problem solving. The five operations of the structure of intellect are:

1. **Cognition,** which means discovery, rediscovery, or recognition
2. **Memory,** which implies retention of what is cognized
3 **Convergent thinking,** which is thinking that results in the right or wrong answer to a question that can have only one right answer ("How much is 2 + 2?")
4. **Divergent thinking,** which is thinking in different directions, or searching for a variety of answers to questions that may have many right answers ("What would happen if it rained up?")
5. **Evaluation,** which is reaching decisions about the accuracy, goodness, or suitability of information

Although all five operations are involved in creative thinking to some extent, Guilford believes that two types of productive thinking are most important: (1) divergent thinking is essential in generating a wide range of ideas, and (2) convergent thinking is then used to identify the most useful or appropriate of the possible solutions that the thinker has produced. On the basis of this theory, Guilford and his colleagues have designed a number of tests of various aspects of creativity.

Guilford's Model of Creative Problem Solving

Guilford's model for creative problem solving is based solidly on his theory of the structure of the intellect. A schematic drawing of his model appears in figure 6–1.

Guilford states that problem-solving behavior begins with some input, either from the outside environment or from within the body—what he calls somatic input. The individual is often not consciously aware that new information is being presented and sometimes is unwilling to let it become conscious. Thus at this first stage a filter exists, which determines whether the input will have any influ-

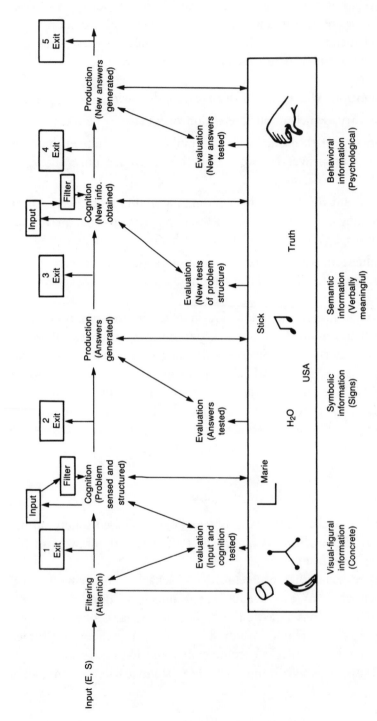

Source: Guilford 1966. Copyright 1966 by McGraw-Hill Book Company. Reproduced with permission.

Figure 6–1. THE GUILFORD MODEL FOR PROBLEM SOLVING

ence on behavior. Exit 1 represents avoidance of the problem altogether. If the process aborts at exit 1, the person is not even aware that a problem exists.

Memory storage affects all steps, beginning with the filter. Evaluation occurs throughout the process as the individual constantly checks and corrects. Once the problem is recognized (a cognitive operation that depends upon memory and evaluation), the search for answers starts.

At exit 2, the person may quit the problem for some conscious reason. For example, he or she may decide something like, "I just don't have time to think about that now," or "I just don't know enough about it. Let someone else deal with it."

If the problem is recognized as one that must be dealt with, exits 1 and 2 are avoided, and specific answers begin to be generated. Here is the place where field independence and cognitive mobility (see chapter 5) have a central function. It should be noted that cognition of the problem (between the two exit choices) usually involves new environmental or somatic input and that a filter here may also prevent awareness of them. Up to this point, Guilford may be seen as leaning toward the developmental and Gestalt approaches to the subject.

At the production stage, convergent or divergent answers (or both) are produced. The associationist view is most evident in divergent thinking, although the capacity to create metaphors is certainly a relevant factor. The ability to dig far down into memory and discover useful remote associations is the essence of divergent thinking.

Exit 3 is the stage at which most people give up. They accept any answer that appears to suffice, because problem solving is viewed as an onerous task. It is often a difficult struggle, one that calls for tenacity and perseverance.

When an individual can withstand the temptation to "cop out" at exit 3, there is the possibility of what Mednick calls higher-quality associations. The Gestaltists and developmentalists would agree that here, new structuring of the problem, through higher-level cognition of its nature, is likely to happen. New and richer inputs add to the deeper understanding of the situation, and if the thinker does not give up at exit 4, the production of uniquely valuable ideas may occur at the second production phase. The problem solver who makes it to exit 5 is clearly the one most likely to offer a truly creative solution!

Guilford's model shows creative problem solving to be even more complex than was previously thought. It points up many junctures at which problem solving can go awry. It appears to offer a reasonable rapprochement between the historically competing theories of associationist, cognitive/developmental, and Gestalt psychology discussed in the previous chapter. Most important, it has exciting ramifications for discovering how we can foster creative thinking. Let us pause for a moment and look at a stimulating example.

There are four variables in Guilford's model that are especially vital to the creative aspect of the process. These are the filter, the memory, and convergent and divergent production. Problems with any of these variables can block problem solving. What follows are discussions of each of these problems, and suggestions for how they may be resolved.

The Problem of Filtering

Mental filters are essential to effective thinking. Without them, we would try to pay attention to every minor stimulus that passes in front of our senses and would never achieve anything. This appears to be one of the problems facing the mentally retarded: they have trouble concentrating on one thing while blocking out irrelevant stimuli from other sources.

However, having an overly rigid filter system can also interfere with successful problem solving. It can prevent us not only from gaining a clear understanding of the parameters of the problem, but also from being aware that it exists. Adams (1986) suggests a number of sources of what he calls **perceptual blocks,** such as:

Fear of taking a risk. Because authority figures such as parents, teachers, and bosses usually reward us only if we get the "right" answer, we learn to be cautious out of fear of disapproval, sarcasm, and ridicule. We develop an intolerance for ambiguity.

No appetite for chaos. Good problem solvers not only have less fear of the unknown, but they also enjoy exploring it. As Barron and Welsh discovered (see chapter 2), they have a preference for disorder, because it affords more interesting possibilities.

Judging rather than generating ideas. Carl Jung (1956) first suggested that people may be divided into those who tend to judge and those who tend to perceive in a nonjudgmental way. Those in the former group are much more likely to filter out perceptions because their unconscious mind indicates that the perception might turn out to be dangerous. According to Adams, those in this group are also more likely to believe in stereotypes that lead to prejudices.

The Problem of Memory

There are three phases in the act of remembering things (Hayes 1981): (1) encoding the information into manageable "chunks," (2) storing it, and (3) retrieving the information when wanted. There are many books and articles on encoding and storing techniques, but from the standpoint of problem solving, retrieval is usually the problem. Tricks to aid in retrieval also abound. An example is going through the alphabet to see whether any letter will jog the memory to produce a person's forgotten name. Wallas's concept of incubation—simply leaving a problem alone for a while—is another. I have found a technique learned in a yoga class to be particularly helpful.

The Yogic Sponge Position

The yogis agree with Freud that the mind is like an iceberg, in that 90 percent of all memory is unconscious. Much of this material is hard to obtain, because the **psychic censor** prevents it from coming to awareness. As was mentioned in the previous section, most of us find it difficult to remember anything that is controversial or damaging to our egos. What is necessary is to relax the strong grip of the psychic censor long enough to allow imaginative ideas to "float to the surface." The sponge position taught in hatha yoga seems to be quite effective in achieving this.

First, try to put a problem you are working on out of your mind and decide you are going to relax your body. This can best be done through a series of stretching exercises, but just twisting and stretching your body around for a while will suffice. Next, lie down on a firm but comfortable surface (a floor with a rug will do, but never a bed or couch). Starting at the toes and proceeding upward through each body part, imagine complete relaxation of tendons and muscles. When you reach the top of your head, imagine a psychic hole in your forehead. Through this hole begins to flow a warm, golden fluid that is capable of soothing all tensions and stresses. Slowly it moves into all your body parts.

In thinking about the movement of this marvelous fluid, your mind becomes blank to all other stimuli. This is hard to achieve at first, but with practice it comes. It helps to have an experienced yoga teacher talk you through it the first few times. After a while, you will have a sense of floating away. Sounds seem to come from a greater and greater distance as you sink into yourself.

In time, you allow yourself (sometimes have to force yourself) to come back to the world. Often at this point you will become aware that you have an idea in mind that might bear on your problem. Without straining to do it, let your mind explore the idea. Frequently you will be surprised to find that you have a whole new point of view on the problem, one that lets you generate new solutions. Sometimes, like a robin with a worm, you will discover a whole chain of thoughts that will lead to creative possibilities. With practice, you will begin to experience your memory as the imaginative sponge it really is.

Problems with Convergent Production

Convergent thinking refers to the ability to select and employ a series of logical steps that lead to the production of a correct answer to a problem for which there is only one answer: 325×739, for example.

The major impediment to effective convergent thinking lies not in the use of a problem-solving paradigm, but in the selection of a good one. The primary cause of this is functional fixity.

Functional Fixity

Karl Duncker (1903–40) started from the rather obvious point that all thought, whether conscious or unconscious, is limited by past learning. He called this functional fixity. This means that as we learn about how things work (all kinds of things, from machines to social interactions), these functions tend to become fixed in our minds, and often we are unable to imagine them being any other way (for example, associate them with anything new). Furthermore, as we attain more education, we tend to see functions as more and more complicated, and we come to expect them to be.

An example of this may be seen in the graduate student's efforts to solve the Two-String Test presented in chapter 2. His solution: catching rats until one lived and could be trained as an acrobat that would swing on the string to him. Rat traps could only be used to catch rats—a clear case of functional fixity.

Fixity can occur not only in terms of the functions of things, but also with problem-solving methods themselves. Abraham Luchins (1952) demonstrated this succinctly with his now famous water jar experiment. Table 6–2 demonstrates this problem, and the reader is urged to try it. In each problem the subject uses the empty water jars indicated in columns A, B, and C to obtain the amount of water in column D.

Table 6–2
THE LUCHINS WATER JAR PROBLEM

	Use These Jars as Measures			*Required Water*
Problem	*A*	*B*	*C*	*D*
1.	3	29	3	20
2.	21	127	3	100
3.	14	163	25	99
4.	18	43	10	5
5.	9	42	6	21
6.	20	59	4	31
7.	23	49	3	20
8.	15	39	3	18
9.	28	76	3	42
10.	18	48	4	22

Source: Luchins, 1942.

By the time you got to the sixth problem, you probably devised a solution that amounts to this formula: $B - A - 2C = D$; you would be right. This formula also works fine for the remaining four problems, and if you are like most people, you went right on using your formula. But for these four problems, there is a much simpler formula; for example, Problems 7 and 9 can be solved by $A - C = D$; problems 8 and 10 can be solved by $A + C = D$. If you noticed this, you are much less likely than the rest of us to suffer from functional fixity.

Duncker observed that most of the time when people solve a problem they are shocked by how simple the solution is and are amazed that they didn't see the solution sooner. His contribution was a way to generate large numbers of simple ideas about how to solve a problem that specifically avoid functional fixity. These ideas may then be evaluated and verified.

Briefly, Duncker used a greatly shortened vocabulary of often used words and combined them in ways designed to force new viewpoints. An example comes from a problem that he designed: "A person has an inoperable tumor in his stomach. There are rays that can destroy the tumor, but they will also destroy surrounding tissue if turned up strong enough to kill the tumor" (1945, p. 26).

He then used the forty-two prepositions from a basic English vocabulary list of 850 words to look at the possible relationship between two rays. Some of the combinations are:

Take a ray about a ray

Take a ray across a ray

Take a ray after a ray

Take a ray against a ray

Take a ray among a ray

Some of the sentences obviously make no sense. One does though— take a ray across a ray—and it offers a solution. Figure 6–2 portrays it. One ray is beamed through the stomach at an intensity just low enough so that it cannot damage tissue. Another ray of the same intensity is beamed from another angle, so that one beam flows across the beam from the other ray at the location of the tumor. There, and only there, the tissue is destroyed.

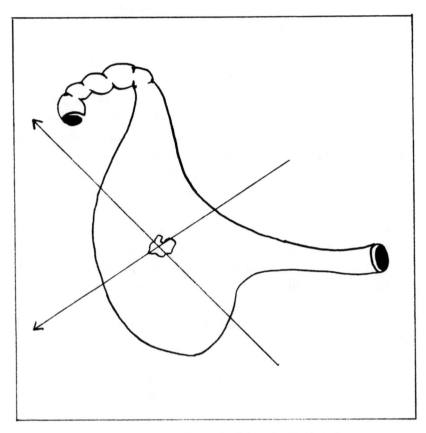

Figure 6-2. DUNCKER'S TUMOR PROBLEM

Variations on Dunker's problem-solving scheme are numerous. One comes from a friend of mine who places slips of paper with aspects of a problem written on them in a bowl. He then draws them out two at a time to see whether the random combinations give him any new insights into how to tackle his problem!

Problems with Divergent Production

Divergent thinking is the ability to produce numerous answers to a problem for which more than one answer may be correct: what would happen if it rained up, for example. Many suggestions have been made as to how divergent production may be fostered. Several of the best are described below.

Lateral Thinking

In his book *New Think* (1971) Edward de Bono makes a distinction between vertical thinking (which means mental operations that move in a straight line back and forth between lower- and higher-level concepts) and lateral thinking (which means looking for alternate ways of defining or interpreting a problem). He states, "Vertical thinking digs the same hole deeper; lateral thinking is concerned with digging a hole in another place" (p. 15).

Vertical thinking plays an essential role in creative thinking, but if the hole is in the wrong place, then no amount of logic is going to put it in the right place. No matter how obvious this may seem to every digger, it is still easier to go on digging in the same place than to start all over again in a new place.

De Bono contrasts vertical and lateral thinking (1970, 1971, 1984) in several ways:

Vertical thinking is selective, lateral thinking is generative. Whereas vertical thinking is aimed at finding the right solution by following one path, lateral thinking is more concerned with richness than with rightness and thus is likely to generate numerous pathways of thought.

Vertical thinking is analytical, lateral thinking is provocative. The lateral thinker seeks information not for its own sake but for its ability to provoke or even shock. It does not even have to be true, so long as it is effective.

Lateral thinking welcomes intrusions by "irrelevant" information. New thinking patterns are seldom structured from within; some outside influence is usually necessary. De Bono suggests that the more seemingly irrelevant an idea is, the greater the possibility that it will effectively alter the existing thought pattern.

Vertical thinking is sequential, lateral thinking can make mental jumps. Vertical thinking proceeds through a series of steps, with each step emerging from the preceding step. Lateral thinking, on the other hand, feels free to make "psychic leaps." The thinker can jump around, using conscious and unconscious material, and does not worry about the logic of his thinking, because he knows he can come back later to reorganize his ideas and fill in the details.

Vertical thinking is "high probability," lateral thinking is "low probability." Vertical thinking is more likely to give you a good answer, but you will need lateral thinking for a great one, though the odds for getting such a superlative idea are also lower.

Discovering Hidden Assumptions

Bransford and Stein (1984) believe that searching for inconsistencies can free up creative thinking. They point to the discoveries of Copernicus, who constantly examined the assumptions implicit in his theory, as examples of this skill. They argue that "you do not have to be a scientist to search for inconsistencies that can signal the need to examine basic assumptions. For example, after generating a possible idea or suggestion, an effective strategy is to search for alternatives that are reasonable yet contradict or are inconsistent with the idea you are considering. Consider the proverb 'He who hesitates is lost.' This is undoubtedly good advice, but so is, 'Haste makes waste'" (p. 95).

Bransford and Stein also suggest another technique for spotting erroneous assumptions: the **worst-case analysis.** When you have formulated a potential solution to a problem, try to imagine that the worst possible result occurs. For example, you are considering taking a job, and you make a list of all the negative things that could happen to you if the job does not work out. This could lead you to ask questions about the job that would not have occurred to you otherwise. You might discover some preventive measures that would be helpful too.

Another strategy suggested by these authors is to ask others to critique our ideas. "Others ask for criticism and then get defensive when people actually provide some," say Bransford and Stein. "It takes some courage to seek and use criticism. Nevertheless, it is important to use this strategy because it is one of the most powerful" (p. 99). This is one of the best ways to overcome "functional fixity," described in chapter 2. We get used to thinking of things, concepts, relationships as having only one function, and it is hard to imagine anything else. The criticism of others may help us to realize alternatives.

Analogies have also played a key role in the evolution of science and technology. For example, Benjamin Franklin noticed that a pointed object would draw a much stronger spark than a blunt object when both were in the vicinity of an electrified body. However, he originally thought this an unimportant observation. Until he recognized the analogy between clouds and electrified bodies he did not realize that pointed rods of iron could be used to protect buildings and ships from damage by lightning. Similarly, the printing press was developed in part from the analogies Gutenberg saw in the wine press and the punches used for making coins. Another illustration of the key role analogies can play in facilitating great discoveries was provided in the reflections of August Wilhelm Kekule twenty-five years after he published his model for the structure of the benzene molecule.

In chapter 5, Wallas's concept of incubation was introduced. This can be useful in uncovering hidden assumptions. Often when attempting to solve a problem we get stuck in a rut and keep coming up with the same unacceptable answer. What is needed is a fresh appraisal of the problem. Incubation may mean just leaving the problem alone for a few hours or days, or even months. However, it is also possible to take only a short break, perhaps twenty minutes, while clearing the mind of everything. The yogic technique can be of great use here.

One final piece of advice from Bransford and Stein involves their *ideal* approach to problem solving:

> An awareness of the processes that underlie problem solving becomes most valuable when you are having difficulty. If you are observant, you can often catch yourself failing to (1) *Identify* potential problems, (2) *Define* them appropriately, (3) *Explore* a variety of possible approaches, (4) *Act on your ideas, or (5) Look* at the effects of your actions. By becoming aware of these possible sources of difficulty you have a much better chance of approaching problems in optimal ways. . . .
>
> By identifying the attitudes that inhibit success and defining their

causes we can begin to explore strategies that may overcome our earlier failures. In addition, by actively using appropriate strategies, we can build self-confidence by giving ourselves the opportunity to observe success. The tendency to avoid new areas becomes especially strong when others are performing well while we experience considerable difficulty. A common way to define such difficulties is simply to assume we are inept or slow and others are talented. An alternate perspective is that everyone experiences difficulty when first learning about a new area: there is too much new information to attend to at once. If you stick with the task, however, you will find that it becomes easier and easier to perform (pp. 121, 123).

Brainstorming

First developed by Alex Osborn, an executive of a major New York advertising firm, **brainstorming** is a technique designed to help small groups produce high-quality ideas. It is based on the concept that producing ideas should be kept quite separate from the evaluation of their worth (Osborn 1963). It was developed because Osborn had observed that most conferences, which are based on the principles of debate, seldom hatch creative solutions. In such meetings, criticism of the participants' thoughts plays a large role.

Brainstorming sessions are guided by a different set of rules:

There may be no criticism of ideas. Often a leader is chosen whose job it is to ring a bell if any criticism occurs.

Participants strive to avoid editing their own ideas, consciously or unconsciously.

Wild, funny, or even silly ideas are welcome. They frequently spawn high-quality thoughts.

Production of a large quantity of suggestions is encouraged.

Building on the contributions of others is also welcome.

Suggestions are tape-recorded or jotted down by a group secretary.

Only when the group feels it has exhausted all the possibilities are the suggestions evaluated (now convergent production takes the place of divergent production).

The following example illustrates how brainstorming works.

THE OREGON COMMUNICATIONS PROBLEM

Some years ago, the story goes, telephone company executives met to address a major problem in the state of Oregon. The two major population centers are on the eastern and western sides of the state, separated by the steep-sided Cascade Mountains. In winter, the telephone lines connecting the centers became laden with snow and ice, and frequently snap. They can be repaired only at a high cost in terms of people and equipment.

The group decided to use the brainstorming approach. At first, suggestions were rather mundane: bury all the wires in the ground, use radio waves (satellites had not yet been invented), and so on. But the group pressed on, and soon the ideas became more imaginative (if not more practical): move all the people from one side of the state to the other, cover the whole state with a giant plastic bowl, wrap the wires in fur coats, attach the wires to "shakers," and (my favorite) trap all the pigeons living in San Francisco building eaves and train them to sit on Oregon's wires, thus "killling two birds at once"!

Then someone proposed heating pads (connected to an electrical source by long extension cords) strapped to the bellies of airplanes: the planes would fly low over the wires and melt the ice before it became too heavy. This got a few laughs, but it also inspired the idea that was finally accepted: helicopters generate a good deal of heat and blow it straight down; have *them* fly up and down the lines. This method undoubtedly saved lives of telephone line repair crews and over $8 million a year.

Several variations on brainstorming have been developed. The stop-and-go method calls for short sessions of idea generation, alternated with brief idea evaluation sessions. This helps participants stay on the right track. The Phillips 66 method is used with large groups. After the presentation of a problem, subgroups of five or six are formed, which then brainstorm solutions. After a stated period of time, the leader of each subgroup reports on the group's best ideas to the large group. In the reverse method, the problem is stated in reverse form. For example, all the ways to prevent a group from effectively solving problems are described. This method often promotes suggestions that illuminate the real problem.

Researchers (Hudgins 1960, Stein 1975) have demonstrated that this technique is superior to individual efforts in solving many types, but for problems such as those involving arithmetic. Apparently the difference depends on whether the individuals have all the information they need. When they do not, a group can pool its knowledge to produce higher quality thoughts.

A more recent extension of brainstorming is known as **synectics**.

Synectics

The word *synectics* is coined from two Greek words meaning the joining together of different and apparently irrelevant elements. The developer of this technique, William Gordon (1961), has made many contributions to education and management science. He is a proponent of "making the strange familiar," and "making the familiar strange." The method is the opposite of those described above, in that he emphasizes the *dissociation* between things. The role of metaphor (see chapter 5) is vital in his approach.

Gordon also deemphasizes the roles of inspiration and being a "genius," believing that all people can greatly improve their creative abilities if they understand the underlying psychological processes. This assumption is directly counter to the view that maintains that any analysis of the creative process by the individual will hinder or even stop the process. Another theoretical assumption of synectics is that the emotional, irrational components of the creative process are more important than the intellectual, rational components and that it is these emotional, irrational components that must be understood in order to increase creative ability.

A synectics problem-stating-and-solving group typically consists of six individuals from different backgrounds, such as physics, engineering, biology, geology, marketing, and chemistry. They spend part of their time dissecting invention problems and part of their time implementing solutions through such means as building working models, conducting experiments and investigating market potentials.

The two important steps of the synectics process are (1) "making the strange familiar" and (2) making the familiar strange." The first step refers to breaking down a problem until it is understood. The second step involves true creativity, where the trick is to look at an old problem in a new way:

> To make the familiar strange is to distort, invert, or transpose the everyday ways of looking and responding which render the world a secure and familiar place. . . . It is the conscious attempt to achieve a new look at the same old world, people, ideas, feelings, and things. In the "familiar world" objects are always right-side up; the child who bends and peers at the world from between his legs is experimenting with the familiar made strange (Gordon 1961).

A synectics problem-solving session uses four primary mechanisms for making the familiar strange and each is metaphorical in character. They are personal analogy, direct analogy, symbolic analogy, and fantasy analogy.

1. **Personal analogy** refers to a personal identification with the elements of a problem. The process is similar to empathy, except that the problem solver can identify with inanimate problems such as the movement of subatomic particles or a piece of music rather than just with other people's feelings.

2. **Direct analogy** refers to just that, a direct comparison of parallel facts, knowledge, or technology. A good example of direct analogy is Alexander Graham Bell's first telephone, which was designed upon observations he made of the way the human ear worked.

3. **Symbolic analogy** uses objective and impersonal images to describe the problem. The image that is conjured up may not be realistic or technologically possible but is esthetically satisfying. It captures the essence of a relationship between a problem and a poetic response. The response is more immediate than with other mechanisms.

4. **Fantasy analogy** in synectics takes Freud's view that artistic creativity is the fulfillment of a wish and extends it to technical invention as well. This mechanism typically begins with the problem-solving group's asking itself the question, "In our wildest fantasies, how do we want this solution to work?" Possible solutions are then translated into more practical terms and reevaluated.

According to synectics theory, no successful, creative problem solving is possible without the presence of some combination of these mechanisms. They are intended as psychological tools with which we can consciously tap the subconscious. The leader of the group plays an important role in directing the discussion so as to incorporate these mechanisms into the process. All of the mechanisms depend to some degree on conscious self-deceit, whereby the problem solver is aware that a possible analogy or solution violates the laws of reality but is willing to suspend those laws temporarily.

Another aspect of synectics is the policy of sometimes stating a problem only in the most general terms. Here are two examples:

• One group was asked to think of all possible ways to store things. Among other ideas they thought of the "merry-go-round" system at a laundry, where clothing is hooked on a part of a chain drive, and the clerk gets a particular garment by turning on the drive's motor and waiting for the garment to come by. The real problem was how to park cars more effectively. Now, hooking the front of a car on a chain drive and pulling it away might not be very practical, but it offers a very original idea that might stimulate others.

• An equally original but far more successful example involved crushed glass that results from compacting old cars. The metal can be used in making new cars; the glass cannot. Earlier efforts by other groups, which were asked to deal directly with the glass problems, only produced costly solutions like dumping it in the ocean. The synectics group was first asked, "What are all the ways to deal with waste products?" They suggested using the waste to make something else. Next the group was told of the broken glass problem and asked to think of uses for it. Here direct analogy came in. Someone said that the crushed glass reminded him of crystals of sugar. He suggested that as with cotton candy, the glass could be melted and, through centrifugal force, sprayed against the inner walls of a spinning cylinder to produce sheets of spun glass. The wonderful result was fiberglass!

Sociodrama

Sociodrama is a group problem-solving process with a twist. First developed by Moreno (1946) and more recently adapted by Torrance and others (1975), sociodrama is used to solve a group or social problem by dramatic methods. Essentially, the ideas underlying the group problem-solving approaches discussed earlier are placed in a deliberately contrived, dramatic context. The individuals involved, from preschoolers to adults, gather and decide on a problem, place it within a dramatic setting, assign roles, and then improvise a play.

Torrance (1976) believes that "playing a role permits a person to go beyond himself and shed some of the inhibitions that stifle the production of alternative solutions. Playing a role gives a person a kind of license to think, say, and do things he would not otherwise do." Because of its imaginative nature, sociodrama has been used to solve future as well as present-day problems and conflicts.

The leader or "director" of the group has the task of guiding the sociodrama session toward possible solutions in an objective way, trying not to influence the outcome. The leader may use a variety of production techniques before, during, and after a sociodrama session. The leader may also provide props, music, lights, decorations, and so on, all in an effort to create the right atmosphere so that the "actors" will identify with their characters and setting. But underneath all the frills, the steps in a sociodrama session are very similar to other group problem-solving methods:

Step 1: *Defining the problem.* The leader of the group must guide the discussion toward defining the problem that will be the topic of the sociodrama session. In this initial stage, all responses are accepted; no judgments are allowed.

Step 2: *Establishing a conflict situation.* From the various initial responses, the group must agree on a clear and objective statement of the problem or conflict situation. Again, judgment is deferred, and no direction for resolution is given.

Step 3: *Casting characters.* Assigning roles should be a sensitive and careful step. Participation should be voluntary, but the leader should encourage experimentation. The same role should be played by different members of the group in order to elicit different points of view.

Step 4: *Warming up the participants.* The actors should be given a chance to think about and discuss their roles and the setting. Additional observers (all members of the group don't have to participate in every session) should be encouraged to consider possible directions the play could take. The observers could be asked to identify with certain points of view.

Step 5: *Acting out the situation.* During the actual acting out of the drama, the skill and experience of the leader becomes important. The "director" must employ a variety of production techniques to evoke constructive dialogue and possible solutions from the actors. The director should be especially sensitive to areas of conflict among group members. However, the leader must also be careful not to direct the play toward any particular outcome.

Step 6: *Cutting the action.* Another important role of the leader is to stop the play when necessary. This could be when a successful resolution appears or when the actors become blocked or too distressed. The leader may see an opportunity to restructure a new setting in which to act on the same problem.

Step 7: *Discussing and analyzing the results.* What happens during this stage is left up to the group. The primary tasks are to redefine the problem and to state clearly the possible solutions arising from the sociodrama session.

Step 8: *Further testing and/or implementation of ideas for new behavior.* Again, the exact nature of this step is left up to the group, and there are a variety of possible directions. Proposed solutions that have been generated in the initial sociodrama session could be tested in new sessions. Alternatively, such proposed solutions could be generalized to situations outside of the specific context of the sociodrama session. Ultimately, the solutions are evaluated during this step.

Torrance believes that sociodrama can promote a holistic consciousness arising from the right hemisphere of the brain. Specifically, he believes that certain production techniques can be employed by the director of a session to induce states of consciousness such as heightened awareness, rapture, regression, meditation, reverie, and so forth. For example, when the soliloquy technique is used, one or more actors may be asked, particularly after a heated exchange, to turn and soliloquize their emotions and feelings about what just happened in the play. Not only may the soliloquy bring out some original idea not mentioned in the dialogue of the play, but the time out may also provide an opportunity for incubation to occur, which will allow new ideas to come forth once the play resumes.

In the double technique, one actor in a conflict situation is joined by another actor who takes on the same role, an "other self." This other self then tries to spur the actor toward deeper levels of expanded consciousness. A variation is the multiple double technique, in which more than two actors play the same role, with each playing a different mood or perspective. One person could play the "good" side of an actor in a conflict situation and another could be the "bad" side. Some other commonly used techniques are role reversal, future projection, a dance technique, and a dream/fantasy technique.

Some Other Approaches to Creative Problem Solving

It should be noted that not everyone believes that using creativity to solve problems is a good idea. Take, for example, the story of the "reluctantly creative student." It is told by a professor at his college.

The Reluctantly Creative Student

Some time ago, I received a call from a colleague who asked if I would be the referee on the grading of an examination question. It seemed that he was about to give a student a zero for his answer to a physics question, while the student claimed he should receive a perfect score and would do so if the system were not set up against him. The instructor and the student agreed to submit this to an impartial arbiter, and I was selected.

I went to my colleague's office and read the examination question, which was: "Show how it is possible to determine the height of a tall building with the aid of a barometer."

The student's answer was "Take the barometer to the top of the building, attach a long rope to it, lower the barometer to the street, and then bring it up, measuring the length of the rope. The length of the rope is the height of the building."

Now, this is a very interesting answer, but should the student get credit for it? I pointed out that the student really had a strong case for full credit, since he had answered the question completely and correctly. On the other hand, if full credit were given it could well contribute to a high grade for the student in his physics course. A high grade is supposed to certify that the student knows some physics, but the answer to the question did not confirm this. With this in mind, I suggested that the student have another try at answering the question. I was not surprised that my colleagues agreed to this, but I was surprised that the student did.

Acting in terms of the agreement, I gave the student six minutes to answer the question, with the warning that the answer should show some knowledge of physics. At the end of five minutes, he had not written anything. I asked if he wished to give up, since I had another class to take care of, but he said no, he was not giving up. He had many answers to this problem; he was just thinking of the best one. I excused myself for interrupting him, and asked him to please go on. In the next minute, he dashed off his answer, which was: "Take the barometer to the top of the building and lean over the edge of the roof. Drop the barometer, timing its fall with a stopwatch. Then using the formula $S = 1/2\ at\ 2$, calculate the height of the building."

At this point, I asked my colleague if he would give up. He conceded, and I gave the student almost full credit. In leaving my colleague's office, I recalled that the student had said he had other answers to the problem, so I asked him what they were. "Oh, yes," said the student. "There are many ways of getting the height of a tall building with the aid of a barometer. For example, you could take the barometer out on a sunny day and measure the height of the barometer, the length of its shadow, and the length of the shadow of the building, and by the use of simple proportion, determine the height of the building.

"Fine," I said. "And the others?"

"Yes," said the student. "There is a very basic measurement method that you will like. In this method, you take the barometer and begin to walk up the stairs. As you climb the stairs, you mark off the length of the barometer along the wall. You then count the number of marks, and this will give you the height of the building in barometer units. A very direct method."

"Of course, if you want a more sophisticated method, you can tie the barometer to the end of a string, swing it as a pendulum, and determine the value of g, the height of the building can, in principle, be calculated."

Finally he concluded, "If you don't limit me to physics solutions to this problem, there are many other answers, such as taking the barometer to the basement and knocking on the superintendent's door. When the superintendent answers, you speak to him as follows: 'Dear Mr. Superintendent, here I have a very fine barometer. If you will tell me the height of this building, I will give you this barometer.'"

At this point, I asked the student if he really didn't know the answer to the problem. He admitted he did, but that he was so fed up with college instructors trying to teach him to think and to use creative thinking, instead of showing him the structure of the subject matter, that he decided to take off on what he regarded mostly as a sham.

But creative problem solving is *not* a sham, whatever the student may think. Parents and teachers who show the young how to do it are performing a crucial service to our society.

Hallman's Obstacles and Aids to Creative Problem Solving

Hallman (1966) has suggested four obstacles and seven aids to creative problem solving:

Pressure to conform. Probably the major inhibitor, this involves standardized routines and inflexible rules. Authoritarian parents and teachers who place emphasis on following orders are responsible for the demise of a great deal of creative talent.

Ridicule of unusual ideas. This destroys one's feelings of worth, and makes one defensive and compulsive.

An excessive quest for success and the rewards it brings. In most cases, this means trying to meet the standards and demands of others in order to obtain the rewards they have to give. In the long run, this distorts one's view of reality, and robs one of the strength of character required in a creative act.

Intolerance of a playful attitude. Innovation calls for playing around with ideas, a willingness to fantasize and make-believe, and a healthy disrespect for accepted concepts. Here the creative person is seen as childlike and silly and his activity as wasteful, but these are only appearances. As Hallman remarks, "Creativity is profound fun."

Parents and teachers can teach children to be more creative, but not with traditional authoritarian methods. Hallman urges the following aids:

Provide for self-initiated learning. Most teachers find it hard to encourage children to initiate and direct their own learning. After all, this is certainly not the way most of them were taught. Teachers fear that if children are given greater freedom to explore reality on their own, the students will learn wrong things, and/or will not learn the right things in the proper sequence. We must put less emphasis on learning "the right facts" and more on learning how to learn. Even if our children do temporarily mislearn a few things, in the long run the practice in experimentation and imagination will be greatly to their benefit.

Encourage pupils to overlearn. Only when a child makes himself fully familiar with a particular situation can he detach himself enough to get an original view of it.

Defer judgment. The teacher encourages the child to make wild guesses, to juggle improbable relationships, to take intellectual risks, to take a chance on appearing ridiculous. He or she does not block unusual ideas by overstating what is required, or by providing correct answers too quickly.

Promote intellectual flexibility. Children are encouraged to shift their point of view, to dream up new ideas for things, to imagine as many possible solutions to a particular problem as possible.

Encourage self-evaluation. When a person comes up with a creative idea, at this time he is always a minority of one. History is replete with examples of ideas that were rejected for years before people began to realize their worth. Therefore, the creative person must be one who knows his or her own mind and is relatively independent of the judgment of others. In order to become a good judge of his or her own thinking, the child must be given ample opportunity to practice such judgments.

Use lots of open-ended questions. One extensive study showed that 90 percent of the time the average teacher asks questions to which there can be only one right answer, which the teacher already knows. Questions that pique curiosity and allow many possible right answers are asked only 10 percent of the time.

Assist the child to cope with frustration and failure. Thomas Edison tried more than two thousand combinations of metal before he found just the right kind for the electric element in his first light bulb (Hallman 1967).

Guidelines for Creative Problem Solving

Here are some suggestions that should make you a more creative problem solver:

Avoid the "filtering out" process that blocks problems from awareness. Become more sensitive to problems by practicing looking for them.

Never accept the first solution you think of. Generate a number of possible solutions, then select the best from among them.

Be aware of your own defensiveness concerning the problem. When we feel threatened by a problem, we are less likely to think of creative solutions to it.

Get feedback on the solution you decide on from others who are less personally involved.

Try to think of what solutions someone else might think of to your problem.

Give your ideas a chance to incubate. Successful problem solvers report that they frequently put a problem away for a while, and later on the solution comes to them full-blown. It is clear that they have been thinking about it on a subconscious level, which is often superior to a conscious, more logical approach.

Sometimes ideas seem to fork, like the branches on a tree; one idea produces two more, each of which produces two more, and so on. It is often useful to diagram your thinking, so that you can follow each possible branch to its completion.

Be self-confident. Many ideas die because their formulator thinks they might be silly. Females are especially vulnerable here, according to research.

7

Assessing Creative Potential

Chapter Highlights:

Reasons for the Measurement of Creativity
    Enrichment
    Remediation
    Vocational Counseling
    Instructional Evaluation
    Studying Developmental Patterns over the Life Span

Instruments for Measuring Creative Potential
    Tests That Purport to Measure Creativity Directly
    Tests That Measure Elements of Creativity
    Tests That Measure Personality Traits Associated
        with Creativity
    Nontest Assessment of Creative Potential

Searching for "Supra-rational" Creativity

Key Terms and Concepts:

The Asking Questions Test
The Bem Sex Role
   Inventory
The Creativity
   Questionnaire

The Criterion problem
The dimensionality
   problem
Direct observation of
   creative performance

Experiential listings

The Figure Preference Test

Good student syndrome

The Idea-generation Test

The Ingenuity Test

Precocity

Prodigiousness

The Purdue Test

The Remote Associates
  Test

The Sex Role Identity
  Test

The Story-telling Test

Supra-rational creativity

The Two-String Test

The Water Jar Test

Important Person:

E.P. Torrance

I n the preceding chapters of this book, discussion of the traits of creative people has been intermingled with tests that evaluate creative ability. This chapter concentrates on the reasons for measuring creativity and the various types of measures currently available.

Reasons for the Measurement of Creativity

Of the several reasons for measuring creative potential, five appear to be preeminent: enrichment, remediation, vocational guidance, the evaluation of educational programs, and studying creative development across the life span.

Enrichment

The chief purpose for the invention of creativity tests has been the identification of the gifted. Because creative ability is so precious, it behooves society, and especially parents and educators, to provide an enriched environment for those who possess high ability. However, this use of tests has been quite controversial since its inception in the 1950s.

In fact, the concept of "giftedness" is itself controversial, mostly because of the different meanings it takes. Historically, it meant having high intelligence, and intelligence tests have been the primary means of selecting the gifted. Traditionally, the intellectually gifted have been allowed to skip grades and have been enrolled in "advanced placement" classes that give them more and harder work to do. Yet little evidence exists that such treatment leads to extraordinary performance on the part of these graduates.

For example, Lewis Terman (1927–1959) reported a groundbreaking longitudinal study of the lives of 1,528 Californian youngsters with IQs of 140 and above (they were called "geniuses") (Terman, 1925). He found that although these students achieved at a higher than average level, virtually none of them became famous for the quality of their accomplishments. This might be called the **good student syndrome**: in their efforts to do well in school and in life, they appear to have lacked or lost the adventurous imagination required to achieve great success.

Another problem with emphasizing intelligence is that it tends to underemphasize specific talent, the second definition of giftedness. Thus programs for the gifted have recently begun to include the talented, those who show promise in fields such as dancing and music. Such talents can also be assessed with considerable accuracy.

Intelligence and talent have in common the notion of **precocity**. A precocious child is one who is able to do things that are ordinarily done only by those who are older. This advantage may or may not be maintained throughout the life span, but in any case, it says little about the person's capacity for achieving *original* productivity. This latter capacity we call **prodigiousness**. The child prodigy is one whose achievements "are so extraordinary and rare as to inspire wonder" (the *American Heritage Dictionary*). Mozart's early symphonies were not just an excellent accomplishment for a child; they were so good that orchestras still play them as a regular part of their programs.

Prodigious children are invariably creative, while precocious mathematicians or ice skaters may not be. Conversely, prodigious children may not score above average on IQ tests. In fact, some famously prodigious people were suspected of mental retardation in their early years (see chapter 1).

A number of educational theorists have suggested that high creative ability should be included as a criterion for selection for the gifted programs, but at present, this view is not popular in most U.S. school systems. The major reasons given for their exclusion is the lack of confidence in tests of creativity. More will be said about this below.

Remediation

A second use of assessment is the identification of those who are unusually low in creative ability. These children tend to suffer a deficit in imagination, which may have come about for a wide variety of reasons. Since imagination is essential to problem solving and to a number of other human traits, it makes as much sense to attempt remediation in this area as it does to try to help those poor in math or reading ability.

Unfortunately, remedial programs in creativity are exceedingly rare. This is partly because of our lack of knowledge of how to go about this task (see appendix). It is probably also due to the rarefaction of the trait: because many people see it as an inherited trait of the elite, rather than a learnable capacity, few schools have attempted to establish remedial programs.

Vocational Counseling

The use of creativity assessment in helping students choose educational tracks and career paths is in its infancy today. Nevertheless it seems obvious that information about this ability would be useful in advising students about pursuing educational and vocational goals that may require the presence of creativity.

Instructional Evaluation

In the 1960s, a worldwide interest arose in developing programs that would facilitate creative thinking. New instructional techniques were designed for all subject areas, especially in language arts. Separate courses were even designed to "teach creativity."

No doubt excesses occurred. Some teachers refrained from criticizing students' spelling and grammar in the belief that to do so would discourage imagination. A popular book of the time, *Up the Down Staircase* (Kaufman 1966), chronicled the case of a student who, when a teacher corrected the grammar of a highly emotional paper she had written, tried to kill herself by jumping out of a school window. Other teachers encouraged original views of history and science, while failing to cover essential facts.

Still other teachers were undoubtedly successful in promoting creative growth. However, the steady decline in the nation's average SAT scores that also occurred in the 1960s and 1970s was attributed almost solely to these teaching efforts, and the nation turned against "creativity teaching." We now know that other factors such as excessive TV watching, the absence of homework supervision, and an increase in the number of lower-ability students taking the test also contributed greatly to the decline, but the knowledge came too late to save the successful approaches.

Unfortunately, a lack of evaluation of results made it impossible to identify the effective programs. Thus, for good or bad, the programs and instructional techniques for cultivating creativity were, for the most part, simply discarded as the country went "back to basics."

Now there is a resurgence of these efforts in the classroom. However, administrators and school committees who are overseeing this resurgence are insisting on much more and much better evaluation of its results.

Studying Developmental Patterns over the Life Span

Psychologists are interested in the developmental patterns of creativity for two reasons: they want to know what the normal growth and decline are like for various types of people; and they want to discover whether there are peak periods during which creativity may best be cultivated (see chapter 9).

This research presents a special problem: To compare age groups (or racial groups, the two genders, and so on), it is necessary to use the same, or at least comparable, tests. However, few tests are equally appropriate for all groups. For example, one of Torrance's (1974a and 1975b) tests uses tin cans as test objects, and another uses stuffed toys. As Romaniuk and Romaniuk (1981) explain,

> When using the same types of tasks and applying them to the issue of equivalence, a creative problem-solving task which is considered to be fun and challenging may be tapping the creativity of some examinees while the same task, considered boring and unchallenging to a different age or cohort group, may be tapping a psychological construct other than creativity. In the specific case of improving a toy monkey, older and younger examinees may differ in their views concerning the appropriateness of the task in measuring what each considers to be creative (p. 373).

Jaquish and Ripple (1980a, 1980b) were successful in studying the divergent thinking abilities (one aspect of creativity) in a group ranging in age from ten to eighty-four. They used an adaptation of Cunnington and Crutchfield's Sounds and Images Test, which involves playing a tape recording of four "weird" sounds and asking examinees to use their imagination to suggest many causes of the sounds. This study in detailed in chapter 9.

Let us turn now to an examination of the methods of assessment.

Instruments for Measuring Creative Potential

We can assess creative potential by several approaches: measurement of it directly; indirect measurement, by evaluating elements that make up the trait; measurement of personality traits closely associated with the trait; and nontest measures of several kinds. A fifth approach, judging the actual products of creative efforts, is the subject of the next chapter.

Tests That Purport to Measure Creativity Directly

There have been a number of attempts to design a basic test of creativity. To date, only one such test has had any success: the Remote Associates Test, compiled by Sarnoff Mednick (1962), a facsimile of which appears in chapter 5.

The theory that supports Mednick's test was presented in chapter 5. It states that those people who have many ideas associated in their minds and who have relatively loose associations among these ideas are most likely to be creative.

The Remote Associates Test was designed to identify those for whom this is so. It does so by presenting thirty sets of three words that are known to have weak (remote) ties with each other in the minds of most people. Furthermore, the close association of each set of three words with a fourth word is also known. The typical associations among the words used in the test have been established through the responses of thousands of people. For example, when you say "rat" to most people, they are quite unlikely to respond with "blue" or "cottage." On the other hand, a large number of people associate each of these three words with the word *cheese*.

In designing this test, Mednick chose many sets of words that are remote from each other but associated to a fourth word, and then asked individuals known to be highly creative in guessing the fourth word when presented with the sets of three. He picked the thirty sets on which these people scored best and made them into a test that he then tried out on many other creative people.

The results were gratifying. The test appears to make sharp distinctions between a wide variety of highly creative and ordinarily creative groups. For architects, science and math teachers, college professors in several fields, and graduate psychology students, the test proved adept at distinguishing between those rated high and low in creative ability (Mednick 1962).

It is possible to disagree with Mednick's choice of correct answers (who could believe that a creativity test could have only one right answer!) or to believe that other answers are just as good. However, "the proof is in the pudding"—the test appears to do well what it was designed for, identifying quickly, simply, and accurately those who have high potential.

It should be noted that potential is not the same as actual achievement—those with promise do not always fulfill it. Perhaps Mednick's test is only good at finding those who are already productive but not so good at predicting ability. To be sure of this, it is necessary to test children with the RAT and then wait some years to see if in fact they are genuinely creative as adults. This has not been done. Although the final word on the RAT will have to await further research, for now it is one of the most interesting of the available tests.

Tests That Measure Elements of Creativity

One thing we know for certain is that creativity is multidimensional—that is, it is made up of several clearly identifiable elements. Many of the best studies have used test batteries of two or more of these elements, believing that if a person scores high on these tests, it is likely that she or he is creative. Some of the most tested elements are considered here.

Originality.

The Story-writing Test. The story-writing Test, which appears in chapter 2, was used there to demonstrate stimulus freedom. It may also be scored as a test of originality. Torrance et al. (1963) developed a scoring format that included twenty-two factors. Eleven of these were selected and adapted for scoring this test for the study of creativity completed for this book (see chapter 10). This latter scoring scheme is presented here.

When scoring imaginative stories, the eleven qualities listed below should be considered separately. If the whole story being judged manifests the quality clearly, a score of 2 is given for that quality. If the quality is definitely not there, a score of 0 is assigned. When it is hard to say if the quality is manifested, or if it comes through clearly but weakly, a 1 is given. The eleven scores for the eleven qualities are summed for a total score. Therefore, story ratings may range from totals of 0 to 22. (Adapted from Torrance et al. 1963).

Characteristics:

1. *Picturesque wording.* Writing may be said to be picturesque if it is strikingly graphic, colorful, and descriptively objective.
2. *Vividness.* This quality is shown through liveliness and intensity. There is a penetrating strength and force.

3. *Original setting.* The setting or theme of the story is unusual and original, as compared with the more ordinary ones written by persons of similar age and training. Caution must be taken for settings that appear original but are really only adaptations of TV plots, comic strips, and so forth.

4. *Individuality of style.* There is a specialness about the wording and grammar that sets the author apart from the others.

5. *Becomingness.* There is a sense that the author so well identifies with the characters of the story that she or he is "becoming" a member of the cast. The writer knows the characters so well that their personalities are clearly developed (to the extent that this can reasonably be done, in the case of short stories).

6. *Perceptive sensitivity.* The writer not only knows the characters, but there is also considerable insight and empathy for their feelings and dilemmas.

7. *Imagination.* Inventiveness, fantasy, unique situations, original actions – all are indications that this trait is present. There is a clear-cut departure from the norm.

8. *Finding the essence.* All the words and phrases seem appropriate and essential to the plot of the story. There is not much "fluff."

9. *Flexibility.* The writer avoids such clichés as "lived happily ever after" and "once upon a time." The style is fresh and vigorous, even excitingly different.

10. *Communication of emotion.* A distinct mood or feeling is established: cheerfulness, gloominess, suspense, rejoicing, and so on.

11. *Coherent unity.* Diverse elements are brought into harmony and unity. The story clearly "hangs together."

The Uses for a Brick Test. In a five-minute period write down all the different kinds of uses you can think of for a brick. The scoring for this test of your hypothetical creative ability is described below. You will be scored not only for the number of uses you think of, but also on how different they are from each other and on their originality. For example, using a brick to build a house is acceptable, but using a brick to catch worms (you leave a brick on the ground, and when you come back two weeks later to pick it up, there will be worms under it) is a much more original idea. Try this now.

The Uses for a Brick Test is usually scored for fluency and flexibility, as well as originality. For fluency, simply add up the total number of your ideas. For flexibility, total all the suggestions that are truly different, categorically, from all the others. For example if you said "Make a wall, a fence, a house, a beehive, and so on," you can take only one point, because they are all examples of building (more on the concept of flexibility appears later). Two points may be awarded for each original idea, that is, for each suggestion you honestly believe is substantially different from those most people would have thought of. Using bricks to build a beehive would probably be an example.

Of course it is hard, and probably impossible, for you to score yourself objectively on this test. However, with hundreds or even thousands of responses to this test, scoring flexibility and originality become much more objective. And that is what is usually done with the scoring guides for popular tests of originality.

The Purdue Test. A third example of an originality test is usually used in an industrial setting: the Purdue Test. A facsimile of it is reproduced in figure 7–1, and a discussion of its scoring follows.

The Purdue Test is scored in just the same way as is the Uses for a Brick Test: one point for each answer given (fluency); one point for each answer that is truly different from the others (flexibility); and up to two points for each answer that is significantly different from the answers others give (originality).

Ingenuity. The Ingenuity Test appears in chapter 4. It is possible that because this test requires some degree of both convergent and divergent thinking, it may be tapping the extent of coordination between the two halves of the brain.

Functional Freedom. Maier's Two-String Test (chapter 2), the Luchins Water Jar Test (chapter 6), and Duncker's Idea-generation Problems (chapter 6) all attempt to measure functional freedom. This is the capacity to avoid rigid thinking and authoritarian attitudes that prevent fresh new approaches to problem solving.

DIRECTIONS

The purpose of this test is to find out how fluent, flexible, and original you are in your thinking.   There are three sections of the test with a different type item in each section.   An example of each type is below.

LIST AS MANY POSSIBLE
USES AS YOU CAN FOR
THIS OBJECT

LIST AS MANY POSSIBLE USES AS YOU CAN FOR
THESE TWO OBJECTS WHEN THEY ARE USED
TOGETHER

WHAT IS THIS ?   LIST AS MANY
POSSIBILITIES AS
YOU CAN

There is a total of 20 items and you have two minutes for each item.

Make your responses as brief as possible and put them on the lines beneath each item.

Copyright 1957 by Purdue Research Foundation, Printed in U.S.A. Distributed by the University Book Store, 360 State St., W. Lafayette, Indiana

Figure 7–1. THE PURDUE TEST

Tests That Measure Personality Traits Associated with Creativity

At least fifty personal qualities are alleged to be associated with creativity, and some kind of test has been designed to measure most of them. Four traits have been more clearly established than the others. They were discussed in chapter 2, and will be briefly reviewed here.

Flexibility. The Asking Questions Test, a part of the Torrance Test of Creative Thinking by E.P. Torrance (1966a, 1966b, 1972), was used to measure flexibility. It was presented and described in chapter 2.

Risk Taking. The simple game of ring toss was used to demonstrate the effects of risk taking on creativity, although there are many other possibilities. This task was discussed in chapter 2.

Preference for Disorder. A facsimile of the Barron-Welsh (1952) Figure Preference Test, illustrated preference for disorder. It was considered in chapter 2.

Sex Role Identity. Sex role identity was measured and discussed in chapter 2 by a simple sex role test. A more sophisticated instrument has been devised by Sandra Bem (1975). It is known as the Bem Sex Role Inventory.

Nontest Assessment of Creative Potential

Using paper-and-pencil tests to assess creativity always suffers from a number of problems. The major problem, known as the **dimensionality problem,** is that the test may measure only some (or none) of the factors in creativity. A second problem is that the test may be attempting to measure valid dimensions but is an inadequate criterion of them; there is insufficient external validation (such as looking at the subject's actual creative achievements) of the items used on the test. This is the **criterion problem.** Other measurement difficulties of testing include the following: the test situation is often stress provoking; the test taker may be having an off day; the effects of time limits, the wording of instructions, and the stimuli used have different meanings for different individuals (Lundsteen 1980, Speedie et al. 1976, Renzulli 1976).[a]

In an effort to circumvent these problems, a number of alternative approaches have been devised.

Checklists and Questionnaires. These instruments are based on research on the characteristics typically possessed by creative people. They include questions like "How many and what kinds of collections have

[a]The Creative Education Foundation (Franklin Street, Buffalo, N.Y. 14207) and the Center for Creative Learning (P.O. Box 619, Honeoye, N.Y. 14471, [716] 367–3560) are also excellent sources of literature on this and other topics.

you had in your lifetime?" and "Would you rather lead an archaeo-logical dig or read about one?" Here is an example of a creativity questionnaire.

Below are a number of pairs of statements that people might make about themselves. You should pick the statement in each pair that is most like you. Sometimes both statements may be like you, and sometimes neither may be. Even when it is hard to choose, try to pick that statement that is just a little truer for you.

1. A. I like to do what is expected of me, and avoid doing things that others would think are unusual or "weird."
   B. I like to come and go whenever I please.
2. A. I like to depend only on myself when deciding what to do.
   B. When I admire someone, I like to tell him or her so.
3. A. I like things in my life to remain stable.
   B. I often criticize people in authority when I think they're wrong.
4. A. I usually say what I think about things.
   B. I usually follow instructions and do what is expected of me.
5. A. I like to be appreciated and given credit by those in charge of me.
   B. Because I am the best judge of my own action, I almost never ask others for their opinions of what I am doing.
6. A. In my daydreams, I am likely to imagine being saved from great danger by someone I admire.
   B. In my daydreams, I am likely to imagine myself writing a book that offers solutions to the world's problems.

This questionnaire no doubt appears obvious, but when used in its full form with fourth graders it correlates highly with other measures of creative ability (by the way, the "correct" answers to this sample (those that favor creativity) are: 1-B, 2-A, 3-B, 4-A, 5-B, and 6-B). A variety of questionnaires, designed for a wide range of ages, is available.

Experiential Listings. This technique evaluates what individuals say they have done in the past. A number of studies have found a high correlation between such "self-reports" and future creative achievement. Of several formats, the simplest requires the individual to write a brief autobiography, which is then rated for quality and quantity of creative behavior.

A more formal method, developed by Bull (1960), is called The State of Past Creative Activities. The instructions are: "List any creative activities in which you are or have been engaged during the past 1–3 years. These may include artistic, literary, or scientific activities (for example, taking part in a play, sketching, contributing to a journal, paper, or magazine, constructing original scientific apparatus, exhibiting paintings, etc.). Please give details of the activity or product, including any public exhibition of the product" (p. 34).

Each activity is rated according to a set of criteria. Then the individual is rated overall from 1 to 9 according to a second set of criteria. A variation on asking people about their creative experiences is to request them to present a portfolio of their work, or some representation of it, such as a set of photos. The portfolio may then be rated as above.

Direct Observation of Creative Performance. This is probably the most obvious but the least developed method of assessment. Watching how people react in a situation seems the most valid technique, but it is time consuming and can be too subjective.

Perhaps the most common use of this approach is in the classroom, where teachers trained in observation rank their students after having observed them in a wide variety of circumstances (Treffinger, Ripple, and Dacey 1968). Organizations like the military have also used this approach, especially in the espionage branches. Here prospective spies are put in difficult situations, and the imagination and success of their reactions are rated.

Personnel specialists in business and government are also beginning to employ this method. Walkup (1967) recommends that the interviewee be asked to attempt the solution of a problem of which he or she has no special knowledge. One of his favorites is to ask how the person would go about measuring the velocity of a rifle bullet over the first 15 feet of travel. He says,

> It is interesting to observe how different types of people think aloud about this problem. Surprisingly, many simply refuse to tackle the problem at all. When pressed, they end up saying that if they were faced with this problem

in real life, their only course would be to search the literature and find out how it was solved in the past. Other applicants make a few feeble attempts such as suggesting the use of a stop watch, presumably because this is the only way they have seen velocities measured (p. 12).

Creative applicants usually come up with four or five ideas that are reasonably practical, even if the details have not been worked out.

Walkup also proposes that a job applicant be interviewed by a person known to be creative, who is told to discuss her or his own ideas for half an hour. If at the end of that time, you can't pry the two of them apart, you can be pretty sure of the applicant's potential.

Searching for "Supra-rational" Creativity

One of the best-known researchers in the field of creativity is psychologist E.P. Torrance. In an article written with Laura Hall (cited in Torrance, 1979), the concept of **supra-rational creativity** is explained. As opposed to the normal step-by-step ability to solve problems imaginatively, this higher type of creativity involves unusual levels of insight, intuition, and even revelation. Whereas the first type may be measured by written tests, this extraordinary type cannot. As these two authors put it:

The altered states of consciousness which produce supra-rational creativity may be analogous to the vacuum state of the quantum field. Quantum physics tells us that the vacuum state is a state of least excitation of all matter and energy and that any form of existence can be created from it given the appropriate initial conditions. The vacuum state contains all the rules, all the laws of nature for all the phenomena of the universe. The supra-rational mode of creative thinking may be simply the process of individual creativity gaining access to "cosmic creativity," a "vacuum state of consciousness" which allows instant revelation, intuition, and insight. Functioning from a supra-rational level of creativity would allow the individual to transcend the limits of a rational linear process and explore the virtually limitless field of the further reaches of creative potential (p. 17).

How may we know when a person is operating at the supra-rational level? Torrance and Hall review studies that have attempted to answer this question and list several characteristics as indicating its presence. Supra-rationally creative people:

Are able to withstand being thought of as abnormal and eccentric

Have a rich fantasy life and do a great deal of daydreaming

Are capable of synasthesia (that is, tasting color, seeing sounds)

Have unusual brain wave patterns, especially during creative activity

Become highly excited when confronted with novelty

Sometimes appear able to perform "miracles"—acts that cause wonder and astonishment and are inexplicable by normal standards

Have extraordinary empathy and superawareness of the needs of others

Possess unusual charisma

Produce strong, rich, and accurate images of the future

Experience numerous peak experiences (great joy resulting from striking discoveries)

Integrate numerous polar opposites (for example, feminine-masculine; serious-playful) in their personalities

Because of the above trait, are highly capable of resolving collision-type conflicts between others—they are great peacemakers.

Obviously not all of these characteristics must be present in order to conclude that a person is supra-rationally creative, but the more that are present, the more this special trait may be said to be present. It is clear that no battery of tests currently available would be able to evaluate this list of characteristics. Only direct observation of behavior is likely to identify this loftiest level of creativity.

8

Judging Creative Output

Chapter Highlights:

The Besemer and Treffinger Model
    Novelty
    Resolution
    Elaboration and Synthesis
Refining the Model

Key Terms and Concepts:

Bipolar	Organic
Complex	Original
Creative Product Analysis	Resolution
Matrix	Surprising
Elaboration and synthesis	Understandable
Elegant	Unipolar
Germinal	Useful
Inventivlevel	Valuable
Logical	Well crafted
Novelty	

Important People:

Susan Besemer   Karen O'Quin

Abraham Maslow   Donald Treffinger

Y ou might think that judging actual creative products would be much easier than judging potential, because the product is available to the judge. However, history is replete with misjudgments of the merits of products. Sadly, the treatment accorded the ideas of Galileo about the earth circling the sun was not unusual: he was threatened with torture by church officials until he denied his discoveries. Even expert judges, specialists in a particular area, may disagree radically, as we see in newspaper and magazine reviews of plays, books, music, art, and films.

A number of researchers have been struggling with the problem of product evaluation in recent years (Amabile 1982b, Briskman 1980, Ekvall and Parnes 1984, MacKinnon 1978, Rogers 1983, Taylor and Sandler 1972, Ward and Cox 1974). One of the earliest efforts (Mac-Pherson 1963) involved the concept of **inventivlevel,** which is an integral part of U.S. patent law.

U.S. patent law considers the following elements in granting patents to inventors:

1. Qualified, intellectual activity should have preceded the invention

2. The idea should clearly overcome special difficulties

3. The amount of experimentation carried on before achievement of the novelty is considered relevant

4. A history of failure is also considered relevant

5. The product should be useful and should provide a stride forward

6. A product is deemed particularly creative if persons engaged in that branch of activity had shown prior skepticism about the likelihood of the inventor's line of inquiry

7. The product should fulfill a previously unfulfilled desire (Mac-Pherson 1963)

This definition was helpful but not nearly specific enough for scientific measurement. What is needed is an agreed-upon set of criteria by which creative products and hence creative ability may be judged. As with products themselves, many different notions about the right criteria exist. In their excellent review of this literature, covering more than ninety publications on the topic, Besemer and Treffinger (1981) identified 125 proposed criteria!

These researchers developed a theory that does a superior job of summarizing and interrelating these ideas. Therefore, this chapter will present the comprehensive theory in some detail, as well as the improvements made on it through reliability and validity studies by Besemer and O'Quin (1986, 1987).

It should be noted that the word *product* is used in this chapter in the most general sense. It is not restricted to commercial products (for example, a new kind of corn flakes) but instead covers a wide variety of things or ideas (a new concept of creativity, for instance).

The Besemer and Treffinger Model

Although the words and phrases used to describe creative products vary widely, Besemer and Treffinger suggested that most may be classified into one of three general categories. The three are: (1) **novelty**, (2) **resolution**, and (3) **elaboration and synthesis**. Each of these categories is made up of a number of attributes. This model has been named the **Creative Product Analysis Matrix**, or CPAM, by the authors.

Besemer and O'Quin (1987) have carried out a number of studies in an effort to confirm the theory. First, Besemer designed a judging instrument based on the model. Called the CPAM Adjective Checklist, it contained 110 adjectives and adjectival phrases chosen to represent the categories mentioned above. The checklist was administered to four groups of male and female subjects, for a variety of products. The results of these administrations were evaluated by a number of appropriate statistical techniques. It was found that the reliabilities (the results of the various testings were consistent) were acceptably high. The match between the results and what the CPAM model predicted, however, varied, and caused the researchers to revise the checklist further.

The main problem discovered by these studies involved the way in which the questions were worded. Subjects were asked to rate each product on the basis of each of the 110 adjectives on a 4-point scale, from (1) "does not describe the object at all," to (4) "describes the object extremely well." These are known as **unipolar** items because they are rated from low to high—that is, they have one pole. Apparently subjects had differing understandings of the adjectives used.

In Besemer and O'Quin's second published study (1986)[a], the revised checklist was again administered, using different products. The purpose of this study was to evaluate their revision of the CPAM model. A major revision in this study was to use **bipolar** test items. In this work, choices were made on a continuum. For example, items read:

interesting-1-2-3-4-5-6-7-boring
refined-1-2-3-4-5-6-7-crude
useful-1-2-3-4-5-6-7-useless

The researchers also eliminated terms that were found to be ambiguous (an example would be *pedantic*) and that were too negative. This time, the statistical results came closer to those predicted by the model. The factor analysis strongly supported the concepts of novelty and resolution but did not support the third category, elaboration and synthesis, as well. At present, the model includes these three categories and eleven subcategories. Table 8–1 presents the current model.

Let us look closer at the definitions of these three categories and the eleven criteria of which they are composed.

---

[a]This study is dated 1986, but it actually reports research done after the research reported in the 1987 publication. That is because the journal reporting the study results in 1986 went into print before the other monograph.

Table 8–1

CATEGORIES AND CRITERIA OF THE CREATIVE PRODUCT

Categories		
Novelty	*Resolution*	*Elaboration and Synthesis*
Criteria:		
Original	Valuable	Organic
Surprising	Logical	Elegant
Germinal	Useful	Complex
		Understandable
		Well-crafted

Source: Besemer and O'Quin 1986.

Novelty

Besemer and Treffinger (1981) describe novelty as "the extent of newness of the product: in terms of the number and extent of new processes, new techniques, new materials, new concepts included; in terms of the newness of the product both in and out of the field; in terms of the effects of the product on future creative products" (p. 164).

The novel product is **original** in that it is very rarely seen among products made by people with similar experience and training. It is also **surprising**—before any evaluation is made, the mind registers a sense of being startled or even shocked. Finally, it is **germinal** in that it is likely to suggest other highly original products. Examples of these criteria are presented in table 8–2.

Resolution

Resolution refers to the degree to which a product fulfills the needs of the problem situation. Three of the eleven criteria are subsumed under this dimension. These require that the product be: **valuable,** according to observers, because it fulfills needs; **logical,** by following the established rules that are understood to exist within a particular

Table 8–2
EXAMPLES OF NOVELTY

Criterion	Low Level	Medium Level	High Level
Original	Carbon paper	Microfilm	Photocopy paper
Surprising	Rockwell's art	Da Vinci's art	Dali's art
Germinal	Buggy whip	Phonograph	Silicon chip

Source: Adapted from Besemer and Treffinger 1981.

Table 8–3
EXAMPLES OF RESOLUTION

Criterion Level	Low Level	Medium Level	High Level
Valuable	Cough drops	Aspirin	Pacemaker
Logical	Blank verse	Haiku	Sonnet
Useful	Button	Snap	Zipper

Source: Adapted from Besemer and Treffinger 1981.

discipline; and **useful** in that it has well-recognized practical applications to its field. Illustrative examples for this dimension are presented in table 8–3.

Elaboration and Synthesis

This dimension refers to the "degree to which the product combines unlike elements into a refined, developed, coherent whole" (p. 164). Subsumed here are the remaining five criteria. The product should be: **organic,** in that it has a central core of meaning around which the whole of the product is organized; **elegant,** in such a way that it may be considered refined and understated; **complex,** in that a variety of elements are combined at one or more levels; **understandable,** because it presents itself in a clearly communicated manner; and **well crafted,** in that it is obvious that it has been worked and reworked with care. Examples for this dimension are presented in table 8–4.

Besemer and Treffinger state that it is not necessary for the product

Table 8-4

EXAMPLES OF ELABORATION AND SYNTHESIS

Criterion	Low Level	Medium Level	High Level
Organic	Toddler's painting	Paint by number	"Mona Lisa"
Elegant	Adding machine	Programmable calculator	Computer
Complex	House	Neighborhood	City
Understandable	Schoenberg's music	Beethoven's music	Tchaikovsky's music
Well-crafted	Backyard	Park	Formal garden

Source: Adapted from Besemer and Treffinger 1981.

to excel on all criteria. Thus, being moderately high on all the criteria is comparable to being very high on several and low on several others. As an example, table 8-5 lists my opinions of the levels of creativity of the invention of Alexander Graham Bell's telephone for the eleven criteria.

It may be seen from this example that any product may vary greatly in terms of these criteria. As Abraham Maslow (1972) summed it up, "A first-rate soup is more creative than a second-rate symphony."

Table 8-5

CRITERION RATINGS FOR THE INVENTION OF BELL'S TELEPHONE

Criteria	Level
Original	High
Surprising	High
Germinal	High
Valuable	High
Logical	High
Useful	High
Organic	High
Elegant	Low
Complex	Medium
Understandable	High
Well-crafted	Low

Refining the Model

Besemer, Treffinger, and O'Quin readily admit that there are still problems inherent in their theory. For example, if the "usefulness" criterion is rigorously enforced, most works of fine art would probably be excluded from the definition.

A second problem has to do with the novelty dimension. The question is whether the product must be new to the whole society or only to the creator. If the former, then almost no production by children may be considered creative. However, most experts in the field are in accord that "there is nothing new under the sun," and that therefore novelty must always be judged from the standpoint of the creator's previous experience. The value of the product is, of course, another matter and one that must be judged from the standpoint of the culture or subculture in which is was produced.

Besemer and O'Quin (1986) have suggested a number of avenues of research that they intend to pursue:

1. Experimenting with reducing the number of adjectives that are essential to a reliable, valid rating scale. Obviously, the fewer the items, the shorter the time required to administer the instrument.

2. Testing the instrument with a greater variety of products and subjects to see if the "fit" between the CPAM model and the test results change.

3. Comparing the results of ratings by expert judges with those of amateurs.

4. Developing a subscale to measure humorousness.

Besemer and O'Quin summarize their rationale for trying to measure the quality of creative products: "We do not want to kill the Muse by overscrutinizing her, but magic as an answer in science is less than satisfactory. Perhaps it is in the area of product analysis that the arts and sciences may join forces. In doing so we may enable ordinary folk to make their products more creative by attending to established standards of judgment" (1987, p. 398).

How Creativity Develops

9

Creative Growth across the Life Span

Chapter Highlights:

The Normal Course of Creative Growth

Dacey's Peak Periods Theory, I
    Period One: Birth to Five Years
    Period Two: Eleven to Fifteen Years

Development of Creativity across the Adult Life Span
    Psychohistorical Studies of Creative Achievement
    Cross-sectional Studies of Creative Productivity

Dacey's Peak Periods Theory, II
    Period Three: Eighteen to Twenty Years
    Period Four: Twenty-eight to Thirty Years
    Period Five: Thirty-seven to Forty-five Years
    Period Six: Sixty to Sixty-five Years

Key Terms and Concepts:

Anima

Animus

Critical period hypothesis

Cross-sectional approach

Dacey's theory
Decremental model
Humanist school of
    creative development
Longitudinal approach
Macroneuron
Microneuron

Midcourse correction
Midlife crisis
Polarities
Psychohistorical approach
Psychoanalytical school of
    creative development

Important People:

Wayne Dennis
Roger Gould
Gail Jaquish
Herbert Lehman
Daniel Levinson

Bernice Neugarten
Richard Ripple
Bertrand Russell
Dean Simonton

When are efforts to cultivate creativity most likely to be effective? This question inevitably evokes several others:

> What is the normal course of growth in creativity? Is it a steady process of change, or are there usually specific periods of life during which change is greatest? Is there a tendency toward growth throughout life, or does creativity tend to decrease after a certain age?

> Can creative growth be nurtured at any age? Is there an age after which such efforts are most likely to fail? Are there peak periods during which people are most open to efforts to foster their creative abilities?

The Normal Course of Creative Growth

Given the number of studies in the files, there has been surprisingly little theorizing about the development of creativity across the life span (as Baltes, Reese, and Lipsett, [1980] point out, attention to life span development in general was limited before 1970). A search of the literature produced only one theoretical article, that of Lesner and Hillman (1983). They suggest three stages of change:

1. From birth to eleven years old: "creative internal enrichment." The child "learns basic life skills and develops his or her own distinctive personality" (p. 108).
2. From twelve to sixty years old: "creative external enrichment." This stage is marked by "a very gradual transition that reflects the underlying concurrent transition from the self-centered orientation seen in the first stage to a more outward, socially aware, multifocused orientation which develops gradually as one matures" (p. 109).
3. From sixty to death: "creative self-evaluation." This stage features "a return to a narcissistic orientation that focuses on creative self-evaluation; it entails a process of assessment and taking stock of one's life in preparation for eventual death" (p. 110).

Empirical study of the course of creative output across the life span has also been scant. This type of research is normally done by one of three methods: (1) studying the biographies of the highly creative to see when they were most and least productive (the **psycho-historical approach**); (2) studying the productivity of groups of people of different ages (the **cross-sectional approach**); and (3) studying the achievements of a group of people from their youth to their death (the **longitudinal approach**).

The major studies (Lehman 1953, 1962, 1966, Dennis 1956, 1966, Simonton 1975, 1976, 1977a, 1977b) have been of the first type. These studies have produced the **decremental model** (Schaie 1977). This model holds that creative change is curvilinear—that is, ability increases through childhood, youth, and early adulthood, then levels out in middle adulthood, and decreases with advancing age.

But is aging the cause of the decline? Kogan (1973) has suggested that many other factors, which may or may not be associated with age, could be causal. Some of these are decreases in physical, mental, or sensory abilities; decline in competitiveness, motivation, curiosity, or interest; and/or illness. As Romaniuk and Romaniuk (1981) phrase it: "Arthritic hands, declining stamina and failing eyesight, for example, may impede an older painter's productivity, but have no effect on the artist's capacity to conceptualize unique relationships in the world" (p. 368).

Very little research of a cross-sectional or longitudinal nature has been done. What there is of all three types will be discussed further in the next section. For now, suffice it to say that it is too early to conclude that older persons are incapable of creative growth. Romaniuk and Romaniuk (1981) sum up the current situation well: "Confusions over prior research findings, especially the failure to distinguish between ability and activity, the status of age as a variable in developmental research, and design problems in untangling the effects of age and cohort influences, have contributed to an unwarrantedly pessimistic view of creativity over the adult life span" (p. 371).

Whatever the case may be as to normal development, the question of when major gains can best be facilitated is even less researched. There are two major points of view on when creativity is likely to develop. The **psychoanalytic school** of thought argues that the first five years of life are critical; if creative attitudes and ability are not inculcated in the child during this period, there is no hope of them later. If a person suddenly appears to become creatively productive at age forty, it is because dormant capacities developed in early childhood are only then being manifested. The second group, the **humanist school** of thought, argues that people who have been low in creative ability can, under the right circumstances, greatly improve it later in life.

Dacey's Peak Periods Theory, I

I believe that the evidence strongly favors the humanist view. In this section, I offer my theory that there are certain peak periods in life during which creative ability can be cultivated most effectively and will examine the evidence in support of this theory. Table 9–1 presents a list of these periods for males and females.

Table 9–1 presents a new theory, and thus it must be considered speculative. Nevertheless, there is some direct evidence from creativ-

Table 9–1

PEAK PERIODS DURING WHICH CREATIVITY MAY
MOST READILY BE CULTIVATED

Males	*Females*
1. 0–5 years old	0–5 years old
2. 11–14 years old	10–13 years old
3. 18–20 years old	18–20 years old
4. 29–31 years old	29–31 years old
5. 40–45 years old	40 (37?)–45 years old
6. 60–65 years old	60–65 years old

ity research to support it, as well as some excellent research from the fields of personality and cognitive development to indicate that these periods are intellectually more volatile than any others. Included in the theory is the concept that large increases in creativity are less likely with each succeeding period. That is, what happens to the person in the early years is far more influential than what happens in the later years. The older people become, the less likely they are to have a sudden burst of high creative production. Let us take a closer look at the dynamics of these six periods.

Period One: Birth to Five Years

Within this period, the first year and a half of life is most crucial. This is mainly because of the development during that time of one of the tiniest components of the brain, the **microneuron**. Though it is miniscule, its role in creative development probably has more significant ramifications than any other physical factor.

The Development of Microneurons. All humans are alike in that the primary pathways of their brains, the **macroneuron** system, are fixed at conception by genetic inheritance. Macroneurons and their many connections appear to be the major vehicles for thought. The average adult human brain is made up of billions of neurons, each of which has an average of one hundred connections with other neurons. In this system alone, the number of possible combinations of neuronal connections seems almost infinite.

But this hardly completes the picture. Juxtaposed between these billions of pathways are tiny switching circuits, made up of the microneurons and their connectors. These additional pathways (see figure 9–1) provide an incredible increase in the number of variations that thought may take.

The crucial variable in this process is the capacity of the micro-neuron to continue to develop not only throughout the prenatal period but for approximately one and a half years after birth (Dacey and Gordon 1971). Furthermore, the way in which these minuscule neurons develop depends greatly on conditions present in the infant's environment.

Effects of the Environment on Microneuron Growth. It seems likely that many factors affect intrauterine and postnatal development of micro-neurons. Unfortunately it has been very difficult to examine these factors in humans. To do so, researchers have to obtain permission to examine samples of brain development in newly deceased infants. They then try to discern whether aspects of the children's environments, such as diet and social interaction, are related to micro-neuronal development. Obviously this is extremely difficult to do because the infants have to have died of causes that did not affect normal brain growth, and the parents have to agree to such an autopsy. On rare occasions such studies have been performed on institutionalized children, but these provide information only on the effects of social (and sometimes dietary) deprivation. Most of our knowledge comes from experiments with development in animal infants, mostly monkeys. Although not permitting certainty, such investigations give us strong reason to speculate on the effects of early experience on human brain growth.

In addition to such obvious environmental forces as diet and social interaction, other more subtle conditions appear also to matter. Noise level is probably important: either too little or too much sound may be detrimental. Well-modulated sounds such as the gentle music heard on some FM radio stations would be likely to have a positive effect. Other factors such as room color and shapes and movements of nursery objects are probably influential too.

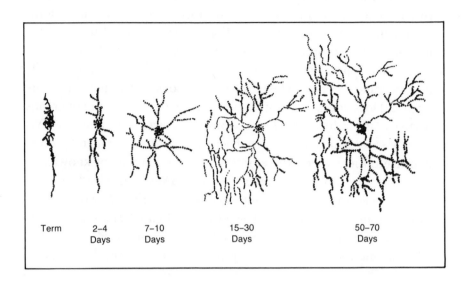

Figure 9–1. STAGES IN THE EARLY DEVELOPMENT
OF MICRONEURONS

The Effects of Deprivation. What happens when a child is deprived of a suitable early environment? It appears that some lower-level socio-economic households may demonstrate an answer. In some such homes, the father is absent, there are numerous other children, the mother must work to support the family, there is the clamor of loud traffic noises and continuous boisterous activity, and the surroundings are dingy and dark colored. Here the hope of good microneural developments is minimal. Certainly such conditions may be found among the middle and upper classes too, but they are likely to be more prevalent in slum areas. Although there are noteworthy exceptions, the children born into such conditions seem rarely to grow to make highly creative contributions. Can we say that early deprivation always causes low creativity? No, but the relationship is obviously strong.

Two aspects of mental functioning are apparently affected by the environment: the ability to take in information, and the ability to process it. The results of studies of institutionalized children indicate sharp contrast in each of these abilities when compared with behaviors of creative children. The contrast is evident in table 9–2.

It would appear that the information intake and processing capabilities are quite different. The problem is to isolate what makes this difference. Does interaction with a rich environment affect the interconnectivity of the brain, as the previously discussed data suggests? We have always assumed that a rich environment will lead to greater information intake and therefore to a greater amount of knowledge about the environment stored in the brain. Does it also lead to more varied modes of thinking or information processing? It would seem that variations in the environment alone would not be enough to alter modes of thinking. In addition, the human learner needs to try out different modes of information processing. He or she learns these

Table 9–2
COMPARISON OF TWO MENTAL ABILITIES IN TWO TYPES OF CHILDREN

Findings for Intake Ability	*Findings for Processing Ability*
Deprived children:	
Fail to attend selectively to their environment	Less able to imagine the consequences of their actions
Fewer cognitive structures	Lowered problem-solving and planning abilities
Lack of sustained attention to tasks	Impulsive, fail to inhibit inappropriate responses
Overly aroused by stimulation	Stereotyped response patterns
Creative children:	
Toleration of ambiguity and inconsistency	Interested in conceptual conflict
Demonstrate many dimensions for judging stimuli	Deal well with inconsistent information
Great category breadth	Search for mediating concepts to explain observations
Great perceptual curiosity	Sensitive to inconsistency in information

Sources: Altman 1967, Beritoff 1965, Konorski 1967, Rosenzweig 1964.

primarily through interpersonal interaction with significant others, who encourage dealing with information in an exploratory manner.

The Need for More Information. Our understanding of the development of creativity will be tremendously facilitated when we know more about microneuronal growth patterns. What is needed is an acceptable technique for determining the degree of multiplication, migration, and interconnectivity of microneurons. One such technique is now being used successfully with higher primates. It employs the measurement of cortical excitability as an index of brain development using the maximal electroshock seizure technique. Another technique currently being employed in Czechoslovakia is the selective destruction of particular cells or areas of the brain by antibodies.

It may well turn out, however, that behavioral measures that are found to be caused by, or at least highly correlated to, growth in the microneuronal system will be the most convenient method of assessing growth patterns of the system. When this is more fully developed, teams of neurophysiologists and behavioral scientists should be able to answer many important questions having to do with the prediction, causation, and facilitation of creativity.

On this last question, J.McV. Hunt's refutation (1969) of the now famous allegation that compensatory education of low-income children cannot work is of interest. Hunt argues that projects like Head Start and, in fact, early childhood education in general, may be failures because the attempt to make an impact on the child's development comes too late. He says that "mankind has not yet developed and deployed a form of early childhood education (from birth to age five) to permit him to achieve his full genotypic potential." He argues that even if the genetic factors within a particular racial group do make for lower intelligence (minorities are of course the typical targets of this charge), there is reason to believe that appropriate environmental stimulation could improve this situation over a relatively short period of time. He cites the increase in height of Western humans of an average of more than one foot within a two-century time span as evidence of the responsiveness of genetic structures to the environment.

Changes in neurological factors (microneurons, mainly) influencing intelligence and creativity might be brought about not only through educational stimuli (for instance, creative playthings), but also through neurosurgery and chemical and electronic stimulation. Of course, neurological factors are likely to be necessary, but most unlikely to be sufficient, to ensure creative productivity.

The Critical Period Hypothesis. A number of theorists, notably those of the psychoanalytic school believe that the first five years of life are not only a peak, but are also critical, in fact absolutely essential, for the development of creativity. They believe this is so, not because of brain physiology, but because of early interactions with parents. To them, people are more or less creative, depending on their childhood experiences and subconscious processes; trying to develop a person's creativity after this time will prove fruitless.

Alfred Adler argued that unless some injury, illness, or other privation occurred during this period and was then compensated for, creativity is almost certain not to follow. For Otto Rank, parents who nurture the early development of their child's will are the only ones likely to see creativity blossom. Sigmund Freud urged that only the child who successfully deals with the crisis of toilet training (one and a half to three years of age) and resolves his Oedipal or her Electra complex (three to five years) has any chance of creative achievement.

There is no scholar in the creativity field who denies the importance of this first few years of life. A growing number, however, agree that the psychoanalytic school has been too restrictive in its thinking and that there are later periods during which major development can occur. On the basis of her research on children in the first six grades, for example, Dudek (1974) conludes that creativity is more an "attitude or a personality trait, not an ability" and that "it changes in quality as a child grows older" (p. 291).

Each of the periods suggested below (as stages in my theory) is one in which the personality is open to change because life events common at that age force us to look at ourselves anew. Hence the research on which I have depended in suggesting these critical periods results more from the study of personality than from direct investigations of change in creative ability, although there is some of that too.

Period Two: Ten to Fourteen Years

Early adolescence is well established as a highly transitional time of life. It is also widely agreed that females enter this phase about one year before males, physiologically as well as psychologically. Girls precede boys in terms of hormonal change, peak period of growth, and other aspects of puberty. This is also true from the standpoint of interest in heterosexual relationships and other traits of developmental maturity. Hence I have suggested that females are likely to become open to cultivation of their creative abilities one year sooner (at ten years old) than are their male counterparts.

On the basis of extensive investigation, Cornell psychologist Richard Ripple and I (Ripple and Dacey 1969) concluded that since creativity is so much a matter of one's self-concept and motivation, and since early adolescence is a period in which self-concept is being defined, creativity may be fostered during this period. We studied the relationships between ten personality characteristics and verbal creativity, using several hundred junior high school students as subjects. We compared our results with the findings of studies done on elementary school children and on adults. We found the ten personality traits and creativity to be considerably less stable during adolescence than they are for younger or older populations; thus, the relationships are also in a state of flux.

For example, Harrington, Block, and Block (1983) compared scores on two divergent thinking tests and two IQ tests of children when they were four or five years with evaluations of their creativity by their sixth-grade teachers six or seven years later. The correlation between a composite score on the divergent thinking tests and the teachers' ratings was .45. Thus for these eleven-year-olds, scores on these measures or creative ability indicate somewhat greater stability in the second half of their childhoods.

Assuming that instability during early adolescence is caused by the teenager's need to reexamine and redefine her or his personality traits, we designed programmed instruction in creative thinking based on this need and significantly raised the scores of the majority of eight-graders in the study.

In his follow-up of Dewing's 1968 study of seventh-graders, Howieson (1981) examined the correlations among their scores on the Torrance Test of Creative Thinking and their "nonacademic creative achievements" ten years later. The relationships for the males were moderate (correlations of .30–.44), but low for the females. The author suggests that there might be a "sleeper" effect, in which some of the males and many of the females who demonstrated creative potential in the seventh grade would be likely to fulfill it later on in life.

It seems clear that the young adolescent is open to growth in creative thinking. Can adults also grow in creative ability? Before we examine the remaining periods separately, let's consider research that has studied creativity across the adult span.

Development of Creativity across The Adult Life Span

A number of studies have attempted to determine at what age creativity peaks in adults. Of course, studying when it reaches its zenith is quite a different thing from investigating when it can best be fostered, but these results are relevant here. We will consider these overall studies of adult creativity before looking more specifically at the three peak adult periods.

Psychohistorical Studies of Creativity Achievement

Herbert Lehman examined biographical accounts of the work of several thousand individuals born since 1774 (the birth date of his first subject). He studied the ages at which these persons made their contributions, and he compared the contributions of deceased persons with those still living (1953). On the basis of this study, he concluded; "On the whole it seems clear that both past and present generation scientists have produced more than their proportionate share of high-quality research not later than at ages 30 to 39, and it is useless to bemoan this fact or to deny it" (p. 251).

Figure 9–2 portrays Lehman's general results. By Median %, Lehman means the average percentage of creative products produced by all of his subjects for each decade of life.

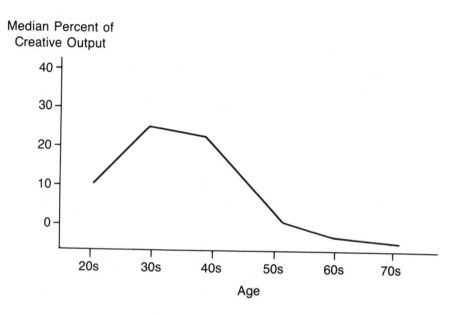

Median Percent of
Creative Output

Source: Adapted from Lehman 1953.

Figure 9–2. RELATION BETWEEN AGE AND CREATIVE
OUTPUT–LEHMAN'S FINDINGS

In a report of his own research on this subject, Wayne Dennis (1966) criticized Lehman's work, stating that it included many individuals who died before they reached old age. Dennis points out that this biased the study statistically, because we cannot know what proportion of creative contributions these deceased people would have made had they lived.

Dennis studied the biographies of 738 creative persons, all of whom lived to the age seventy-nine or beyond, and whose contributions were considered valuable enough to have been reported in biographical histories. He did this because "it is our view that no valid statements can be made concerning age and productivity except from longitudinal data involving no dropouts due to death" (p. 2). He looked at the percentage of works performed by these persons in each of the decades between the ages of twenty and eighty. When creative productivity is evaluated in this way, the results are quite different.

He found that scholars and scientists (with the exception of mathematicians and chemists) usually have little creative output in their twenties. For most of them, the peak period is between their forties and sixties, and most produce almost as much in their seventies as they did in their earlier years. The peak period for artists tended to be their forties, but they were almost as productive in their sixties and seventies as they were in their twenties. Figure 9–3 depicts these relationships.

Dennis offers an interesting hypothesis to explain the difference in creative productivity among the three groups (artists, scholars, and scientists): that the output curve of the arts rises earlier and declines earlier and more severely because productivity in the arts is primarily a matter of individual creativity. Scholars and scientists require a greater period of training and a greater accumulation of data than do others. The use of accumulated data and the possibility of receiving assistance from others causes the scholars and scientists to make more contributions in later years than do those in art, music, and literature.

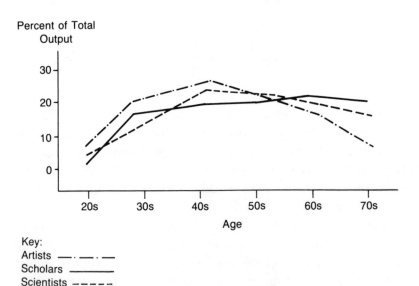

Source: Dennis 1966.

Figure 9–3. RELATION BETWEEN AGE AND CREATIVE
OUTPUT–DENNIS'S FINDINGS

Most of the productive persons in Dennis's study were males. It would be interesting to investigate the patterns of productivity among a comparable all-female group.

More recent studies by Dean Simonton (1975, 1976, 1977a, 1977b, 1984) have attempted to resolve the differences between the Lehman and Dennis studies. In general, Simonton found evidence that quantity declines with age, which favors Lehman, but that quality does not, which favors Dennis. Unfortunately, because of differences in design and criteria (for example, differing data sources, differing criteria for inclusion in the studies), it cannot be said that this issue has been fully resolved.

Cross-sectional Studies of Creative Productivity

The studies discussed in the previous section are of people who were unusually gifted, almost all of whom are now deceased. The first large-scale study to look at the creative productivity of *typical* people at various ages was completed by Alpaugh, Renner, and Birren (1976, also described in Alpaugh and Birren 1977). They administered two batteries of creativity tests (those of Guilford and of Barron and Welsh) to 111 schoolteachers aged twenty to eighty-three. Their findings support the decremental model described earlier. One major criticism of their research is that the tests they used are almost certainly not equally valid for all age groups. The younger subjects are much more likely to have had experience with these types of materials than are the older ones.

An effort to evaluate the effects of aging while avoiding the problem of using age-related materials has been made by Jaquish and Ripple (1980a, 1980b). These researchers gathered data on six age groups across the life span: ten to twelve years (61 people); thirteen to seventeen (71 people); eighteen to twenty-five (70 people); twenty-six to thirty-nine (58 people); forty to sixty (51 people); and sixty-one to eighty-one (39 people). There were a total of 350 subjects in the study.

The definition of creativity in this study was restricted to the concepts of fluency, flexibility, and originality; these are collectively known as divergent thinking abilities. These three traits were measured through the use of an auditory exercise, which was recorded on cassette. Known as the Sounds and Images Test, it elicits responses to the "weird" sounds presented on the tape. Responses are then scored according to the three traits of divergent thinking. The researchers believe that this test is so unusual that no age group is likely to have had more experience with it than any other.

A number of interesting findings have resulted from this study, as may be seen from table 9–3 and figures 9–4, 9–5, and 9–6.

On all three measures of divergent thinking, as figures 9–4, 9–5, and 9–6 make clear, the scores generally increased slightly across the first five age groups. Scores for the forty- to sixty-year-old group increased significantly, and for the sixty-one- to eighty-one-year-old group decreased significantly below the scores for any of the younger age groups. Furthermore, when decline in divergent thinking did occur, it was more pronounced in quantity than in quality. That is, there were greater age differences in fluency (a measure of quantity) than in originality (a measure of quality). Finally, it is not known to what extent the oldest subjects were affected by hearing loss, particularly of high and low tones. Obviously, this could be an alternative explanation of the findings for the oldest group.

Probably the most important finding of the study had to do with the relationship between divergent thinking and self-esteem, which

Table 9–3

MEANS FOR DIVERGENT THINKING AND
SELF-ESTEEM SCORES

Age Group	Fluency	Flexibility	Originality	Self-esteem
	Mean	Mean	Mean	Mean
10–12	20	13	14	30
13–17	29	18	18	33
18–25	31	19	19	34
26–39	30	18	19	37
40–60	36	21	20	38
61–81	22	15	15	32

Source: Jaquish and Ripple 1980.

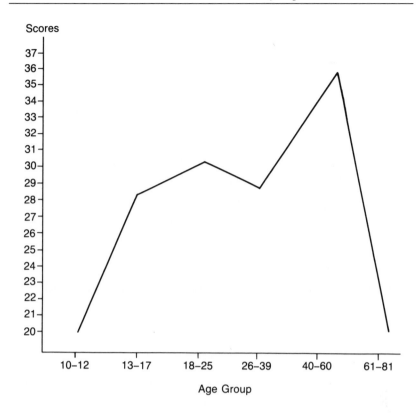

Source: Jaquish and Ripple 1980a and 1980b.

Figure 9–4. SCORES FOR THE FLUENCY SCORES

was measured by the Coopersmith Self-esteem Inventory, as can be seen in figure 9–7.

Figure 9–7 indicates that self-esteem follows a pattern quite similar to that of the other three traits. Of special interest is the relationship between self-esteem and divergent thinking for the oldest group: the correlations were moderately high in every case. This indicates that if older adults manage to maintain a high level of self-esteem, their level of divergent thinking does not decrease significantly. Thus self-esteem may be seen as having mediating effect that alters the picture

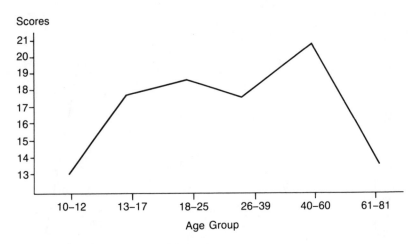

Source: Jaquish and Ripple 1980a and 1980b.

Figure 9-5. SCORES FOR THE FLEXIBILITY MEASURE

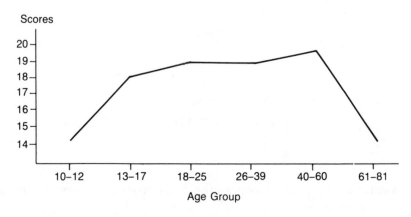

Source: Jaquish and Ripple 1980a and 1980b.

Figure 9-6. SCORES FOR THE ORIGINALITY MEASURE

of decline in creative abilities over the years. Jaquish and Ripple conclude that "there is much more plasticity in adult development than
has been traditionally assumed. Such an interpretation should find a
hospitable audience among those people concerned with educational
intervention. If the creative abilities of older adults were to be realized

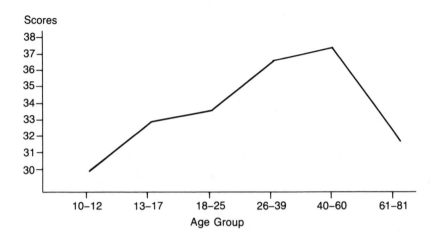

Source: Jaquish and Ripple, 1980a and 1980b.

Figure 9-7. SCORES FOR THE SELF-ESTEEM MEASURE

in productivity, it would be difficult to overestimate the importance of the formation of new attitudes of society, teachers in continuing adult education programs, and in the older adults themselves" (p. 33).

The results of these cross-sectional studies must be accepted cautiously, however, because of one more problem from which each suffer: inequality of the educational backgrounds of the subjects. In the words of Baltes and Schaie (1974): "It seems fair to assume that older people . . . were exposed to shorter periods of education. Furthermore, their education probably relied more heavily on principles of memorization and less heavily on those of problem solving" (p.36). (For more on this topic, see Dacey 1982.)

There is no direct evidence as to what could be the ideal periods in adult life to try to foster creativity. What follows is a description of what these periods are likely to be, based on personality research on adults (these periods were outlined in table 9-1).

Two major personality studies are relied on as supporting the next three stages. One of the studies, by Roger Gould and his colleagues, and the theory of adult personality development derived from it, has been described in Gould's book *Transformations* (1978). The other investigation, with the resulting adult personality theory, by Daniel

Levinson and his associates is explained in Levinson's book *Seasons of a Man's Life* (1978).

Both studies have limitations. Gould's work involved more than one thousand subjects, but over half were in some sort of therapy and may have been quite different from the others. Much of his research relied on responses to a questionnaire and was restricted to those between the ages of sixteen and forty-five. Levinson's work involved much more extensive interview techniques but included only forty subjects, all of them men. It covered their lives from age seventeen to forty-five, although they were between the ages of thirty-five and forty-five at the time of the study; thus much of the data comes from their memories of earlier occurrences.

Despite these important limitations, the theories that have resulted from these investigations offer a clear-cut look at the major tasks of adults and have received considerable acclaim in the literature. Their implications for developmental periods of creativity will now be discussed.

Dacey's Peak Periods Theory, II

Period Three: Eighteen to Twenty

Gould (1978) calls the period from age eighteen to twenty the peak time for "leaving our parent's world." Of it he says:

> Thus the most important goal of this stage is to achieve a sense of independence from one's parents. This new independence ought to be of several types. Youth gain physical independence from their parents by moving out of the home. When they form other love relationships and begin to recognize their own sexuality, they gain emotional independence. Economic independence comes from getting a full-time job and taking care of one's own finances. Finally, it is necessary to gain confidence in one's own ability to think rationally (p. 37).

Levinson (1978) refers to this stage of life as the "early adult transition." He sees it as composed of two major tasks:

One task is to terminate the adolescent life structure and leave the pre-adult world. A young man has to question the nature of the world and his place in it. It is necessary to modify existing relationships with important persons and institutions, and to modify the self that formed in pre-adulthood. Numerous separations, losses and transformations are required. The second task is to make a preliminary step into the adult world: to explore its possibilities, to imagine oneself as a participant in it, to make and test some tentative choices before fully entering it. The first task involves a process of termination, the second a process of initiation (p. 51).

Both of these quotations clearly emphasize the need to examine and change one's self-image. This is obviously an atmosphere in which, if other conditions are present (opportunity and encouragement, for example), a more creative persona may emerge.

Period Four: Twenty-eight to Thirty

Gould found that the primary cause of conflict at this stage of life is parenthood. As adults attempt to encourage values in their children, they become aware of uncertainty in their own values. The divorce rate escalates at this time, as spouses attempt to adjust to one another's developing values and realize that they no longer agree as much as they thought they had.

There is a positive side to the increased conflict of this transitional period. Gould cites Bertrand Russell's description of this stage as "intellectually the highest point of my life." Gould believes that the "age-thirty" crisis often forces us to know ourselves for what we really are. He suggests that "our confidence in the world increases as we accept the limitations of our powers and the complexity of reality . . . in short, we come to see that life is not fair."

Levinson and his team also discovered that most men go through a developmental crisis at this time. They see it as more related to vocational problems, however:

One suggestive metaphor for the developmental crisis is a man alone on a body of water trying to get from Island Past to Island Future. He fears he will not reach Future. He feels that he can move neither forward nor backward, that he is on the verge of drowning. A man may experience himself as swimming alone, as rowing a leaky boat, or as captain of a luxurious but defective ship caught in a storm. There are wide variations on the nature of the vehicle, the sources of threat and nature of Past and Future. The critical thing is that the integrity of the enterprise is in serious doubt: he experiences the imminent danger of chaos, dissolution, the loss of the future (p. 108).

As one writer suggested, "Whatever people do during their twenties, they want to do something else during their thirties." Women who raised a family in their twenties feel the world of work looks exciting, whereas career women begin to yearn for their own family. For men, the family may figure less centrally, but the desire for change is usually no less intense. As with the previous period, this increased search for a new way to be is sometimes the perfect breeding ground for creativity.

Period Five: Forty to Forty-five

Many psychologists have suggested that the period around the age of forty is one of serious change in self-perception. Jung (1933) described this as a time of reversal, from greater individuation to greater integration. Buhler (1935) defined it as a period of creative expansion, in which the person strives to advance the world creatively through physical or mental activities. Neugarten (1968, 1973) suggests that it is an age during which such traits as mastery, competence, self-awareness, and control of the environment are enhanced. Loevinger (1977) names it the "autonomous" stage, during which there is greater conceptual complexity, and physiological and psychological aspects become integrated. And of course Erikson (1950, 1959) marked it as the beginning of "generativity." It has frequently been referred to as the period of **midlife crisis** or of **midcourse correction.**

But is forty the critical age, for both men and women? None of these theorists is willing (or perhaps able) to specify the age of this stage. Further, several researchers (for example, Barnett and Baruch 1978, Giele 1982, Gilligan 1979, 1982, Rossi 1980) have suggested that the Levinson and Erikson positions are biased in favor of the male experience, and that females may actually tend to become generative (and therefore creative) several years earlier than, and in different ways from, men. Ryff (1983), in the only study to date that has attempted to resolve this question, produced conflicting evidence as to gender differences. Thus it may be that this peak period for women should be something like thirty-seven to forty-two years old. Also, there is nothing sacred about the period being five years long. But this must await much more study.

For now, I suggest no difference between men and women for this stage. So let us look further at the two studies that do claim to have evidence in favor of the early forties as a peak period of change. Gould (1978) describes it as a time to deal with and overcome five "major false assumptions" about the nature of life:

1. "The illusions of life can last forever."
2. "Death can't happen to me or my loved ones."
3. "It is impossible to live without a protector [a parent or guardian.]"
4. "There is no life beyond this family."
5. "I am innocent."

Gould and his associates suggest that most of us reject these myths during this period, and so it can be a major time of change: "Mid-life, then, is not a sedentary or bucolic period. In fact, mid-life is every bit as turbulent as adolescence, except we can use all this striving to blend a healthier, happier life. For unlike adolescents, in mid-life we know and accept who we are" (1978, p. 211).

Levinson agrees that this period lasts about five years, although he only speaks of it from the standpoint of men. He claims the period consists of three major tasks:

1. The review, reappraisal, and termination of the early adult period
2. Decisions as to how the period of middle adulthood should be conducted
3. Dealing with the **polarities** that are the source of the deep division in the man's life at this stage.

Resolution of the conflict between these opposing tendencies is a critical task in the lives of all of us. Levinson also argues that resolution of the polarities is especially likely to lead to creativity, and so I will describe them in some detail here.

Levinson draws on the theory of psychoanalyst Carl Jung in his description of the four polarities with which middle-aged people must contend. Jung (1933) suggested that the experience of thousands of generations of humans has gradually produced deep-seated ideas within each of us which sooner or later call for resolution. Levinson found that four become preeminent in the later thirties and early forties.

Young/Old. We begin to age at birth, but even though we recognize we are always growing older, we maintain a strong interest in holding on to our youth. Everyone wants to grow old, but no one wants to age. In Jung's theory, the word *young* represents fertility, growth, energy, potential, birth, and spring. *Old,* on the other hand, encompasses termination, death, completion, ending, fruition, and winter. At about the fortieth birthday there comes a sense of wanting to leave a legacy: most people want to feel that their life has made some important difference to the world; they want to be remembered. Therefore it is typical at this time that the individual becomes more creative and often works harder to make a contribution that will be considered worthwhile by those who will follow.

Destruction/Creation. People going through the midlife crisis realize not only the potential of the world to destroy but also their own capacity to be destructive. They recognize evil within themselves, and that they have sometimes been very hurtful, even to those they love most. They see themselves as both victim and villain "in the continuing tale of man's inhumanity to man."

Masculinity/Femininity. Jung's concept of sex role change is especially relevant here. In his theory, it is argued that all persons have both masculine (**animus**) and feminine (**anima**) natures; we only emphasize the side that matches our gender because of the demands of society. This emphasis usually costs us greatly. Jung believed that a rich adult life can only be achieved by compensating for that part of us that was denied in childhood.

According to Levinson, femininity has a number of negative connotations to men in young adulthood. To many men, it means physical ineptness, incompetence, lack of ambition, and worst of all, emotionality. Now the mature male changes this view and is able to allow himself to indulge the feminine aspects of his personality. He now feels secure enough in his self-concept to be dependent, to have strong feelings, and to want to nurture others. Neugarten (1973), believes that the female now achieves a greater self-assertiveness, as a compensation for years of being dependent and supportive. She refers to the trend in both genders to reverse their earlier tendencies as the "crossover" effect.

Attachment/Separation. By this last polarity, Levinson means that each of us needs to be attached to fellow members of society but also to be separate from them. In childhood, there is a clear attachment to the mother and later to family. During adolescence, there is a switch to a need for separateness from family and attachment to friends. Adolescents not only detach themselves from family identity but temporarily separate from society in general in order to try new identities. Throughout their twenties and thirties, most people return to an attachment to family, but this time to their own new ones and to those they believe can help them with their careers.

Now, in the midlife transition, a new separateness, perhaps a second adolescence of a sort, takes place. The man, especially if he has been successful, begins to look inwardly and to gain greater awareness of his sensual and esthetic feelings. He gains more rapport with himself by being temporarily separate from others. Sometimes he emerges with a stronger relationship with his spouse; sometimes he decides he needs to end that relationship, perhaps to start a new one. At any rate, it is rare indeed when the midlife transition results in no change at all.

Unfortunately, we know much less about how women face the second half of their lives. There are, of course, wide variations on this theme. Nevertheless, it seems safe to conclude, even on the basis of this limited evidence, that midlife is a time of considerable turmoil for both men and women and is therefore a prime time when dormant creative ability may be realized.

Period Six: Sixty to Sixty-five

For most men and for a growing number of women, this is the period in which retirement occurs. Even if a woman has not been in the labor force, she has many adjustments to make because of the effect of the change on her husband. Thus most adults are faced with a major adjustment of self-concept at this time in their lives.

Although some fare badly as a result of this change and begin withdrawing from society, others use it as a chance to pursue creative goals that had previously been impossible for them. Obviously a majority of the "young old" (the new term for those who are sixty to seventy-five) do not suddenly become creative, but a substantial number do. Of the highly productive people Lehman studied (1953, 1962), more than one hundred began their major productivity in the years after sixty.

In addition to highly visible contributions, it seems clear that many of the elderly become creative in less newsworthy ways. Gerontologist Jack Botwinick, who presents an excellent analysis of this topic in his book *We Are Aging* (1981), suggests that many elderly persons exercise a newfound creativity by mentoring younger people. Though largely unheralded, such guidance and encouragement of younger creators unquestionably has invaluable benefits for society.

This is not to say that maintaining or increasing creative performance in one's later years is easy. Clearly there are inherent problems that are not easily overcome. Psychologist B.F. Skinner (1983), who has had a sixty-year-long career of high creative achievement, states that productivity is difficult for the elderly because they tend to lose interest in work, find it hard to start working, and even when they do, work more slowly:

> It is easy to attribute this change to them, but we should not overlook a change in their world. For motivation, read reinforcement. In old age, behavior is not so strongly reinforced. Biological aging weakens reinforcing consequences. Behavior is more and more likely to be followed by aches and pains and quick fatigue. Things tend to become not worth doing in the sense that the aversive consequences exact too high a price. Positive reinforcers become less common and less powerful. Poor vision closes off the world of art, faulty hearing the enjoyment of highly fidelitous music. Foods do not taste as good, and

erogenous tissues grow less sensitive. Social reinforcers are attenuated. Interests and tastes are shared with a smaller number of people (p. 28).

This is not to say that this course of events is inevitable. In fact, Skinner has a number of fascinating suggestions for overcoming these problems (1987). Gerontologist Bernice Neugarten (1968) agrees that the decline in creativity in the later years is most likely due to a social stereotype. She argues that the aging process is one of a "continually changing sense of self and a changing set of adaptations. With the passage of time, life becomes more, not less, complex; it becomes enriched, not impoverished" (p. 98). As the elderly increase in number and in the respect paid them, the stereotype may wither away, and more and more people who are entering old age should view themselves as having a fresh new opportunity to fulfill their potentials.

It is increasingly clear that creativity may blossom at any age. My theory of "the peak periods of creative growth" is not meant to disparage the fact. However, it seems that the evidence points rather solidly to the six periods identified by my theory as those with the best opportunities.

10

The Role of the Family

Chapter Highlights:

Characteristics of the Families of Highly Creative Adolescents
Principal Conclusions

Key Terms and Concepts:

Critical periods
Figural content
Left-handedness/lateral dominance
Semantic content

Social (or behavioral) content
Symbolic content
Trauma

In all of the preceding chapters, the emphasis has been on the traits that make an individual creative. Now we turn to look at how the family influences those characteristics.

Characteristics of the Families of Highly
Creative Adolescents

The family lives of highly creative young people differ from those of ordinary adolescents in a number of important ways, according to the results of a study that my colleagues and I recently completed (Dacey, in press). Fifty-six families of one hundred New England–area adolescents participated in this study. Half of the families were selected because one of the parents was identified as being in the top 5 percent of his or her profession in creativity by members of that profession. The other half were included because one of the teenaged members was identified by knowledgeable staff as being in the top 5 percent of his or her school system as highly creative.

The actual creative achievements of these nominees were then scrutinized and scored by a panel of faculty and graduate students at Boston College specializing in this field before the nominees' families were invited to participate. Of sixty-one families nominated, three were eliminated by this procedure, and two declined to participate.[a] Data for the fifty-six participating families were compared with a comparable set of data gathered from twenty other families selected because no one in them was identified as creative.

The research consisted of fifty minutes of testing administered to the children, followed by two hours of interviewing of the family members on a varity of topics concerning the family's life-style. All interview sessions were conducted so that no family member was aware of the responses of the others. Perceptions of each of the members were later compared (and found to be surprisingly in accord). Almost all sessions were held from 7:00–10:00 P.M. at the homes of the families.

To determine creativity levels of participants in the study, each person was asked to describe and, where possible, provide hard evidence of her or his own and the other family members' creative productions (the latter as a means of cross-validation). Such evidence included

---

[a]Although most observers would agree that the criterion for participation was very high, no one who is nationally famous was included in the sample. The lives of the famous are so different because of their fame as to be ungeneralizable to more ordinary people. Some of the participants in the study have won prizes and awards at the national level, but they are not famous.

publications, awards, and media articles describing their achievements. No test data was used as evidence. For each case, the assembled evidence was rated by the research team (interscorer reliabilities averaged correlations of .83). This method is the same as that defined by Amabile (1983a): "A product or response is creative to the extent that appropriate observers independently agree it is creative. Appropriate observers are those familiar with the domain in which the product was created of the response articulated. Thus, creativity can be regarded as the quality of products or responses judged to be creative by appropriate observers" (p. 31).

Four types of creativity (Guilford 1975) were rated on a 1–9 scale. These four types, and examples of each, are shown in table 10–1. The points on the rating scale are described in table 10–2.

The quality level of the person's products and the level of recognition received for them were jointly considered in making the four evaluations. Needless to say, the two types of criteria are highly correlated, and therefore considering them jointly caused few prob-

Table 10–1
TYPES AND EXAMPLES OF CREATIVITY IN THE STUDY

Type	Example
Figural	Sculpture, architecture, cabinet making
Symbolic	Mathematics, music, ballet
Semantic	Journalism, play writing
Social (behavioral)	Psychology, teaching, school politics

Table 10–2
RATING SCALE CRITERIA

9	Highest level	(National
8		(
7		(Regional
6		(
5		(Local
4		(
3		(No Recognition
2		(
1	Lowest level	(

Table 10–3
EXAMPLES OF THE ACHIEVEMENTS OF HIGHLY RATED YOUTH

Age	Gender	Achievement
13	F	Choreographed and starred in a junior high school assembly ballet program.
12	M	Wrote and produced a half-hour radio play.
19	F	Had lead in university plays two years in a row.
11	F	Organized and led several clubs in school; organized and led summer day care for twelve preschool children.
15	F	Student director of Shakespeare's *Tempest* in junior high; recipient of districtwide acting award.
20	M	Wrote and illustrated three children's books for a major publishing company, all of which are selling well.
18	M	Won scholarship to Harvard University for innovative approach to mathematics in regional science fair.
14	M	Won regional architecture contest for drawings of bulidings.
15	F	Won regional writing contest for short-story writers.
18	M	Hired by advertising company because of imaginative drawings.
14	M	Had music written for saxophone published in regional music magazine.
20	F	Had two poems published in college poetry magazine, and one in a national magazine.

Note: All of the above participants had other achievements, too numerous to mention here.

lems. A total score, composed of the sum of these four scores, was also computed. Table 10–3 describes examples of achievements that received scores of 8 or 9, as well as the age and gender of those subjects who received those ratings.

These are the types of data used in the conclusions made from this study:

1. Correlations among creativity tests and ratings of creative achievements.

2. T-tests of differences of means (a test that shows if mean differences are large enough to be trusted) for high- and low-creative samples.

3. Answers to forty-two interview questions analyzed qualitatively.

4. The parents of twenty-five of the most creative youth were invited to spend an evening in discussion of numerous topics as to what produces creative children. There were five three-hour sessions, with five different families participating in each. These were taped and were also analyzed qualitatively.

Principal Conclusions

Genes versus the Environment. In those families that were selected because one of the parents had clearly demonstrated high creativity, slightly over half of the children were also above average in creativity. In the group of families chosen because a school system had nominated a teenaged family member as being extremely creative, only one third of the parents were above average in creative achievement. Although this finding cannot be considered definitive in the "nature versus nurture" debate, it does offer some credence to the position that environmental factors such as parenting style and home atmosphere play the greater role.

Rules for Behavior. The parents of creative teenagers refrain from imposing rules on them. These parents averaged less than one specific rule, such as number of study hours, bedtimes, or sexual activity, for their children's behavior. The group of twenty families with no highly creative members averaged six rules.

The parents of the creative youth are not permissive, however (Goertzel, Goertzel, and Goertzel 1978, Taylor 1964a and 1964b). Rather, they put forth and model a clear set of values, and encourage their children to decide which behaviors exemplify those values. As one Jewish man put it, "I can't think of any rules we've had for our kids—we just wanted each to become a "Mensch" [a truly admirable person]." Most of these parents remarked that they had surprisingly few problems with discipline.

Paper-and-Pencil Tests Poor Predictors of Adolescents' Levels of Creative Achievement. Six abbreviated versions of creativity tests were administered to the youths in this study. Although some of their correlations with the creativity ratings were significant, all were rather low. It was hoped that one or more of these short tests would prove to be a good predictor of the much more laborious rating method, but, probably because the shortened adaptations were used, this did not occur. Thus it would be inappropriate (and probably unfair) to discuss them further here. (See also Treffinger 1980, 1985, 1986.)

Of course, the achievement ratings may themselves lack validity, but their high correlations with other factors in this study offer encouraging evidence of construct validity. A strong possibility is that creativity is a relatively unstable trait as compared with, for example, shyness, and is most unstable during the adolescent years (Dacey 1986, Ripple and Dacey 1969).

Critical Periods. Many subjects spoke of a "critical moment" in their lives, a time when, for various reasons, their self-image was unusually open to change. At this moment, if the right event occurred, they become inspired to think more imaginatively and to take greater risks in acting on their thoughts. The right event might include encouragement from a teacher or parent, or rare good fortune in some endeavor.

On the basis of the testimony of these subjects, and also on the basis of new findings on personality development by other researchers (Gould 1978, Levinson 1978, Vaillant 1977), it seems likely that six periods in life may be pinpointed as having the greatest opportunities for such critical moments (Dacey 1986, Jaquish and Ripple 1980a and 1980b, Ripple and Dacey 1969). These are: the first five years of life; the early years of adolescence; early adulthood (around age nineteen; from twenty-nine to thirty-one; the early forties; and sixty to sixty-five. Unfortunately, it appears that such opportunities become less likely with each succeeding period.

Humor. Joking, trick playing, and family "fooling around" take an important place in these families (Derks 1985, Torrance 1979, Wicker, 1985). Family members often have comical names for each other and use a vocabulary understood only by them.

Both parents and children in this study were asked to rate thirteen traits, such as "having a high IQ" and "being popular with peers," as they pertain to the child (Getzels and Jackson 1962). "Sense of humor" was ranked much higher than by the comparison families. It was in the top half for most of the responses.

Other Outstanding Traits. Contrary to the stereotype, creative children see themselves as getting along well with others and ranked this trait highly (it also appeared in the top half of the ranking most of the time). They regard themselves as being "different" and say they thought this at an early age (usually before six). Most feel that this has been an asset.

The adolescents chose "best able to look at things in a new way and discover new ideas" as the trait best describing them, and gave lowest ranks to "healthiest" and "has the most energy." Their parents agreed that "having outstanding traits of character such as honesty and trustworthiness" best describes them, followed by "best able to look at things in a new way and discover new ideas." Parents ranked "best-looking" and "healthiest" as lowest.

"Getting highest grades" and "having the highest IQ" were ranked moderately low by most (Stanley, George, and Solano 1977). As has been found in other studies (Getzels and Jackson 1962, MacKinnon 1978, Taylor and Getzels 1975), internal states such as imagination and honesty are much more valued than such readily observable traits as grades and health.

Housing. Most of the families of the creative live in decidedly different kinds of houses from other people. Some are modernistic; quite a few were located on rocky ledges in the woods, for example. Others are ancient; one family lives in a converted nineteenth-century town hall. Another bought a two-room eighteenth-century home, then added ultramodern bedrooms and kitchen to the back of it. Many are unconventionally furnished.

The insides of their homes are usually quite different too. Many were decorated with surprising collections, such as Turkish teapots. In one home, a room was devoted to housing forty-seven unusual birds. (It should be noted that most of the families were middle or upper middle class; it is difficult to find successfully creative persons who are also poor.)

Recognition and Reinforcement at an Early Age. Parents in the study were asked to say at what age they first suspected that their child had unusual abilities and what made them think so. Most noticed signs such as distinctive thought patterns or high problem-solving ability before the child had reached age three. Although few had set out to foster these traits in their child, most reported that they found it exciting and tried to encourage these tendencies.

Furthermore, they usually provided a wide range of opportunities (lessons, equipment, contacts, situations) that cultivated the traits. Without exception, they were delighted to find that their child was exhibiting signs of high creativity. Most of the children said that they felt strong encouragement from their parents.

Life-styles of the Parents. Most of the parents in these families were able to tell of some aspect of their lives that is uncommon. For instance, most of the mothers work at jobs that few women have; they are attorneys, surgeons, or artists, for instance. Virtually all the parents have well-developed interests aside from work, and many of these are unusual. In a substantial number of families, the children share in their parents' interests too.

Trauma. Creative children suffer a larger number of traumatic incidents than do ordinary children. These are occurrences that cause grief, anger, or both, and seriously disrupt the child's life. The parents of the creative youth in this study remember two to nine of these incidents, as opposed to one to three in the comparison group of families. Several theorists believe that dealing with childhood trauma is a major cause of creativity, particularly among writers (Adler, cited in Ansbacher and Ansbacher 1956, Goertzel, Goertzel, and Goertzel 1978, and Kris 1965).

Schools Don't Matter. The children in this study and their parents see their schools as ranging from the highly traditional to the highly innovative, but they all agree on one thing: few of the schools have any effect on creativity. This is reinforced by the finding that the correlation between creativity ratings of the Boston College panel and the innovativeness of the school was quite low. Perhaps there are schools or individual teachers who help students expand their creativity, but there was little evidence of it in this study. (The next chapter treats this problem in much greater detail.)

Harder Workers. Subjects in this study agree with Thomas Edison that creativity is "one part inspiration and 99 parts perspiration." Almost without exception they say they work considerably harder than do their schoolmates and have done so since starting school. This was true in a wide range of work, jobs, homework, and chores, for example.

Left-handedness/Lateral Dominance. Several theorists have suggested that left-handedness should be more common among the highly creative because it is an indication that they are dominated by the right sides of their brains, which in turn causes more interhemispheric communication. The left side is seen by some as the "logical" side, the right as the "intuitive" side. It is now clear that the situation is much more complicated than this (Springer and Deutsch 1981), but this study does offer some support for the theory.

In the general population, 5–10 percent are left-handed. Of those who scored in the lower half of the creativity scale in this study, this percentage is 8, whereas 20 percent of those who scored high in creativity are left-handed.

Sex Differences. Although the fathers had higher scores than the mothers in almost all categories, the gender of the youth in this study made no significant difference in their creativity ratings. This appears to be accounted for by changing perceptions of the female gender role in American society, which in turn may be encouraging female productivity more than in the past.

Both parents agreed that almost twice as many of the highly creative teenagers have a strong sense of identification with their mothers. From the interview data, it seems likely that these adolescents imitate their fathers' successes but rely more on their mothers for encouragement.

Parents' Judgment of Their Children's Creativity. In each family, the parents were asked to evaluate each child's level on the four types of creativity. These ratings were then compared with those given by the Boston College panel. Mothers and fathers were in strong agreement with each other, and with the panel's overall ratings, on all but the social ratings.

Number of Collections. The more highly creative adolescents were more likely to have a larger number of collections, and these collections were unusual for their age, such as campaign pins and models of prehistoric birds.

Because this study is based primarily on self-report and retrospective case study data, no claims for causal relationships between family lifestyle and creativity may be made. However, the number of strong, clear differences found between the high and low creativity families are powerful indications that the family is an important, and quite possibly the major, force in the etiology of creative ability.

11

The Role of the Society

Chapter Highlights:

The Schools and Creative Thinking
The Effects of the Schools
Training Teachers to Cultivate Creativity in Their
Students
Evaluating the School
The Role of Societal Rewards
The Role of the Culture
Nine Features of the Creativogenic Study
The Effects of Society in Modern Times on the
Creativity of Jews

Key Terms and Concepts:

Creativity of the Jewish
people
Creativity-relevant skills
Creativogenic society
Domain-relevant skills
Epicyclical theory

Intrinsic motivation
principle
Task motivation
Three components of
creativity

Important People:

Theresa Amabile   Silvano Arieti

I n the last chapter, the evidence presented clearly indicates that the family is a major influence in creative development. Is this also true of the larger society? In this chapter, three societal elements are examined: the typical school experience, societal rewards, and the overall cultural environment.

The Schools and Creative Thinking

The Effects of the Schools

Schools suppress creativity.

How can this be stated so categorically? The reasoning goes as follows: Most young children are naturally curious and highly imaginative. Then, after they have attended school for a while, something happens. They become more cautious and less innovative. Worst of all, they tend to change from being participators to being spectators. Unfortunately, it is necessary to conclude from the investigations of many researchers (most of whom have been professional educators) that our schools are the major culprit.

What would cause a school and its teachers to squelch students' imagination and originality? Some light may be shed on this problem by a study of first graders done by psychologist E.P. Torrance (1963) and described in chapter 2. When he administered the same test two years later to the same children, when they were about to enter the third grade, the change was striking: boys were superior to girls on all of the toys, even including the nurse's kit. Torrance concluded that elementary school teachers (most of whom are female) teach young girls that they "should not question the *status quo*." As he puts it, "You often hear teachers say, 'I need some strong boys to help me.' Girls are more likely to be praised for being 'lady-like.' "

Another element may be deduced from the research of Adorno, et al. (1950). They devised a test of "authoritarianism." It was known that people who have this personality characteristic become quite angry when those in an "inferior" position fail to behave in a subservient way. Authoritarians want instant obedience from those "below" them. These researchers learned from these studies that authoritarian people also feel that *they* should be subservient to those they perceive as being above them. Thus the "authoritarian" is someone who has an exaggerated sense of social hierarchies, of "pecking orders," if you will. Dominance and subordination are the key factors in life for them.

The test was refined and then administered to hundreds of persons in nearly four hundred American occupations. Would you like to guess what job type came out on top? No, it was not teachers. The number one spot went to state police, followed closely by army officers (soldiers in general were in the bottom half). Teachers were third!

Let us look at what the first two occupations have in common. Among their mutual trademarks:

Both bear arms and are allowed by society to use them to enforce orders.

Both wear uniforms that have abundant signs of rank: collar pins, arm patches, hat bands, "scrambled eggs" on the visors of senior officers.

If their orders are not obeyed, the court system, whether public or military, will deal out punishments.

Those whose station is below them must salute them. This practice developed in medieval Europe, when the serfs were forced to grasp the forelocks of their hair and pull their heads down, as a gesture of respect for the lord of the manor as he rode around inspecting his fields.

Those whose station is below male officers must call them "sir." This also derives from the medieval term for the lord, "sire."

But teachers do not engage in such a rigamarole, do they? No, but the differences are there. Not many teachers are seen publicly disagreeing with their principal, superintendent, or school committee on important issues. On the other hand, in most school systems, they can expect relatively complete obedience in their classrooms, and that infringements will be duly punished by their superiors. When they close that classroom door, their reign is more or less supreme (although it must be admitted there are numerous exceptions). In fact, it was not so long ago that if you complained to your parents that the teacher had punished you, you could expect to be punished again!

So far, it must appear that teachers are the sole culprits in this issue. Clearly, however, the whole educational system is involved. There are many stories of teachers who have attempted to organize innovative school projects, only to have the principal or school committee block them as being "too risky." As an example of an impediment at the national level, it may be noted that at present, approximately 95 percent of the federal special budget is spent on those below average in ability; a mere 5 percent goes to developing better education for the gifted.

Nevertheless, the question of why some schoolteachers are so authoritarian (and thus anticreative) still remains. There are several studies that have indicated that schoolteachers are likely to come from families in which the father is an extremely powerful personality, and with such a model, a bright young woman was naturally attracted to a vocation where she could imitate her father's power.

The research by Adorno, et al. was done some years ago, and no doubt the teaching profession has changed significantly since then. Further, there are a greater number of jobs that offer positions of power for women. But teaching still has a strong attraction for the authoritarian. Clearly, some people go into teaching in order to dominate others, and some people do it in order to help their students flourish. That there may be more of the former seems to be evidenced by the decline we see in creative scores the longer children are in school, and not just for females.

A study carried out by my colleagues and me at Cornell University (Dacey and Ripple, 1967) points to an explanation of how the process eventually suppresses the creativity of both genders. We studied the creative abilities of 1,200 seventh and eighth graders in forty-five school systems located in three states. One of the main instruments

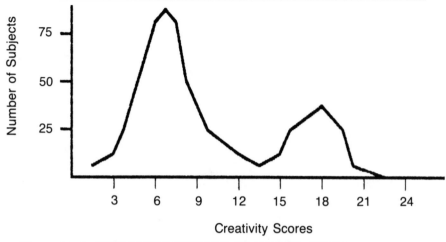

Figure 11–1. THE DISTRIBUTION OF JUNIOR HIGH
SCHOOL CREATIVITY SCORES

was the Story-writing Test described in chapter 2. The results of this test are charted in figure 11–1.

As you can see, the largest group of students scored in the bottom third of the possible range of scores (top score on this test is 22). Students in this large group averaged about 7. A smaller group of students scored in the top third, and averaged around 18. Although the overall mean score was 10.2, very few students actually got that score.

Such a finding really surprised us. It is known that almost all human traits and abilities (for example, IQ, height, and watermelon-seed spitting) are "normally distributed," if enough people are tested. This means that most people are average, with only a few getting the lowest or highest scores. A normal distribution of scores produces what looks like a bell-shaped curve on a graph. Figure 11–2 illustrates how IQ scores are distributed for Americans.

This holds true for any age and for any intelligence test. A chart of the number of notes a person can sing would look much like this. Most traits produce a graph like this one, it is normal and bell-shaped.

So why are the creativity scores shown in figure 11–1 distributed so differently? Well, one obvious explanation would be that this reflects genetic inheritence: most people inherit only a little creative

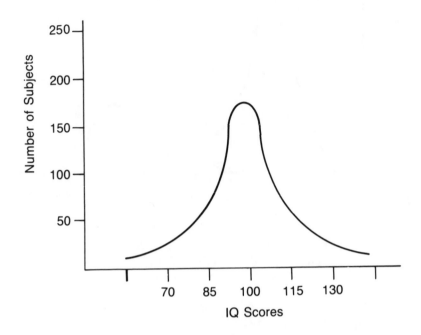

Figure 11-2. TYPICAL DISTRIBUTION OF IQ SCORES

ability, and a few lucky people inherit a lot. If this were so, it would produce a graph such as is seen in figure 11-1. But there are several problems with this hypothesis. For one thing, it does not explain *why* creativity should be different from all the other traits. In addition, as was discussed in the last chapter, there is little other evidence that creativity is so highly influenced by genes.

We came to a different conclusion. We asked ourselves, what if at birth, creativity is naturally distributed just like IQ, but then is affected adversely by some major experience such as attending school? Such an effect could, over time, move everyone's score lower on the graph. It would not affect the *shape* of the distribution, however—it would still be bell-shaped, but with a lower average.

But suppose the suppressing affect of schooling is only powerful enough to affect some of the students—the bottom three-fourths, for example. Suppose those in the top quarter of creative ability are impervious to the effect—they go on being creative no matter how they are treated by the school system. If this were the case, then we would expect a curve just like the one we see in figure 11–1. Figure 11–3 shows two curves—one depicting the present situation, and one showing the normal curve that would exist if not for the negative effect of schooling.

Our Cornell group saw the results as clearly supporting the hypothesis that teachers, especially elementary school teachers, are guilty of suppressing creativity.

Further evidence of this problem comes from research on the results of the Two-String Test, described in chapter 2. We looked at the effects of education on functional fixity as seen in the Two-String Test. About 90 percent of sixth graders studied could solve the problem within the fifteen minutes allowed. Eighty percent of ninth graders could do so, 50 percent of college students were successful, and only about 20 percent of graduate students achieved a solution.

We concluded that education interferes with the required problem-

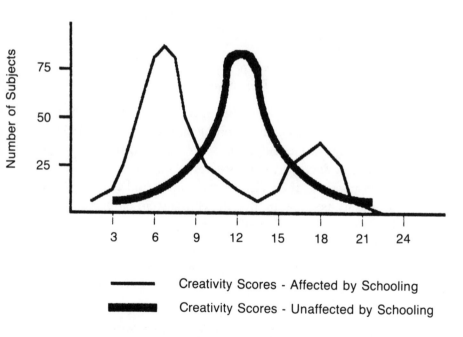

Figure 11–3. A COMPARISON OF CREATIVITY SCORES BEFORE AND AFTER SCHOOLING (THEORETICAL)

solving skill—the ability to redefine the clothespin and the rat trap as weights. The more education a person has, the more rigid her or his perception of function. In addition, education tends to encourage complexity of thought. Thus advanced education is more likely to produce a convoluted problem-solving style. This works against producing simple ideas, which constitute many of the world's greatest solutions.

Finally, my research on creative families, reported on in the previous chapter, reinforces the conclusion that schools generally do not reinforce creative thinking. As was noted, neither the parents for the children regarded their schools as having any real impact on their talents. Thus was true whether the school was viewed as traditional or innovative.

Whatever the dynamics of schools are that cause the problem, no amount of money will correct it, so long as teachers are unable to participate in its correction. Obviously, teachers do not suppress creativity on purpose, but apparently they need to learn to avoid what seems to be a natural impulse.

Training Teachers to Cultivate Creativity in Their Students

Recognizing this tendency, a number of efforts have been made to encourage teachers to overcome this problem. E.P. Torrance (1975) has been a leader in this. He and his associates at the University of Minnesota have conducted twenty studies of ways to help teachers cultivate creativity in their elementary school students. Unhappily, results of the studies indicate that the efforts were unsuccessful. Torrance hypothesizes a number of causes:

> "Personality characteristics [of the teachers] and their perceptions of social expectations" make them unable to change their teaching styles.

> Change is difficult because the average teacher "seems to be preoccupied with the critical and the remedial." It was found that the average teacher frequently interrupts students with evaluative

remarks on their thinking and with attempts to improve their work.

Teachers fail to reinforce interesting, original responses, perhaps because they just do not recognize them as such.

They also fail to protect a student who "is definitely superior to the others in creative thinking abilities, [who] almost always experiences pressures to reduce his productivity and/or originality and is frequently not given credit for the positive contribution he makes to the group's success."

Students need vehicles for creative writing, such as a class newspaper or school magazine, which give them motives for high-quality efforts. These are seldom provided, as they can be quite time consuming for staff.

Two of my colleagues and I reasoned that the teacher's inability to cultivate creativity probably results from deeply learned attitudes and values, and thus it would take substantial time and effort to overcome these unconscious biases (Treffinger, Ripple, and Dacey 1968). An extensive program of lectures, exercises, and discussions was designed which required a full week of day and evening sessions. We measured teacher attitudes before and after the experience, and the questions they were asked are presented below. Perhaps you would like to try answering them as though you were a teacher yourself.

ATTITUDE OF TEACHERS TOWARD CREATIVE STUDENTS

Please indicate the level of your agreement with each statement by placing a number in the blank before it. Choices are: 1 = strong agreement, 2 = agreement, 3 = no opinion, 4 = disagreement, and 5 = strong disagreement.

_____ 1. The creative child is a liability to my classroom because of his disruptive manner.

_____ 2. Creative problem-solving ability is probably a natural strength that some students have and others do not, so that most of our efforts to improve it in our students are in vain.

_____ 3. The creative child is not likely to be well liked by his classmates.

_____ 4. It is possible to improve pupils' ability to think creatively and to solve problems through direct instruction in creativity.

_____ 5. Only a few people in every thousand can truly be considered creative.

_____ 6. Because of the explosion of knowledge in the world, children cannot be taught how to cope with every situation they will ever meet; this indicates the need for teaching creative thinking if we can.

_____ 7. I think I could identify the children in my class who are the most creative.

_____ 8. Most paper-and-pencil tests of creativity do not *really* measure creative abilities of pupils.

_____ 9. The most typical creative person is the "nonconformist" type who may well be in need of a bath.

_____ 10. Even if it is possible to teach children to become more creative, there are serious questions about the necessity or wisdom of doing so.

_____ 11. Creative people are made, not born.

_____ 12. "Creativity" is something that is found among only a few people; most of us lack it almost entirely.

_____ 13. There is a very thin line that divides the very creative act from the pathological.

_____ 14. If we were to try to teach pupils to become more creative, we run the risk of creating a nation of nonconforming individuals who will be unable to maintain normal social relations.

You are seen to be in favor of cultivating creativity if you placed a 1 or a 2 in front of statements 3, 4, 6, 7, and a 4 or a 5 in front of the rest.

At the end of the weeklong series of sessions with the teachers, we found that significant changes in their attitudes had occurred. They had adopted much more positive feelings about creativity and those who have it in abundance. No follow-up of the teachers' classroom performance was possible in this study. However, it does offer some hope that with sustained efforts, schools can become places for enhancing creative talent.

Evaluating the School

It is important to note that negative findings about the impact of educators apply only to schools in general. Certainly there are many schools and many teachers for whom this description is inaccurate. If only you can find them! For another publication (Dacey, forthcoming), I designed a checklist that parents can use to investigate their child's potential classroom situation before allowing the child to enroll in it. It is reproduced here as an indication of the kinds of behaviors and values that mark such teachers.

CHECKLIST FOR SELECTING TEACHERS

Get permission from the school principal to be allowed to sit in one or more classrooms in order to observe the teacher. When you observe one of the behaviors or attitudes on the list below, make a checkmark beside it. If you like, you could make one checkmark for every time you observe the behavior or attitude. The more checkmarks, the more likely that teacher will be to cultivate your child's creativity.

_____ Sets up the discovery process by encouraging students to initiate their own learning and to study independently.

_____ Reinforces and sustains student perplexity.

_____ Rewards and redirects student questions back to the student.

_____ Refrains from being overly critical.

_____ Encourages free exchange of ideas.

_____ Supports students in seeking evidence for their viewpoints.

_____ Looks for quality over quantity in the students' work.

_____ Rewards imaginative efforts.

_____ Uses a wide variety of teaching methods.

_____ Has a warm, friendly relationship with students.

_____ Refrains from being evaluative—encourages students to judge their work themselves.

_____ Has many resources readily available within the classroom.

_____ Encourages questioning and is not shaken by unexpected questions.

_____ Helps students develop self-respect.

_____ Fosters a variety of types of teacher-pupil interactions.

_____ Listens attentively and respectfully to students' statements.

_____ Treats students androgynously and encourages it in them.

_____ Is personally friendly and open with students.

_____ Employs a variety of teaching methods, student groupings, and instructional aids.

_____ Takes time to allay fears and anxieties that often plague creative students.

_____ Provides for student presentations.

_____ Is able to discuss his or her views of the creative process with you knowledgeably.

Also in this publication I listed some suggested criteria to look for in school programs that are likely to help teachers foster creativity. It is reproduced here for the same reason.

CHECKLIST FOR SELECTING A PROGRAM FOR THE CREATIVELY GIFTED

_____ Acceptance in the existing gifted program includes measurement of creative abilities.

_____ A mentor program (specialists in the community volunteer their time to advise and encourage those interested in their field) is available to talented and creative students.

_____ Provides adequately for intra- and interscholastic competitions (for example, science fairs, math games, poetry and debating contenst, "Olympics of the Mind," and so forth.)

_____ Has spaces set aside for long-term projects and research.

_____ Offers students instruction in what creativity is and how they may nurture it.

_____ Has specialist(s) on the staff who holds degrees or other training in teaching the creatively gifted.

_____ These personnel belong to state and/or national organizations for the creatively gifted (perhaps you should join one yourself).

_____ The principal is committed to the program, as seen in his or her economic policy toward it, for example.

_____ There is a generous field trip policy.

_____ Psychology staff (counselor, school psychologists) cooperate well with the program.

_____ Teachers not involved in the program say they believe it is a good one.

_____ Student members of the program tell you that they like it.

I recognize that this section is not likely to make some of my colleagues in the schools happy. I hope that the inclusion of these two checklists indicates my faith that not all are guilty of creativity assassination, and that the readers of this book will be able to use it in their own work so that they can avoid being among the guilty.

The Role of Societal Rewards

Amabile, Hennessey, and Grossman (1986) point to the story of the young Albert Einstein as an example of the effects of motivation on creativity. Amabile has been a leader in researching this topic, and has proposed the **intrinsic motivation principle:** "When people are primarily motivated to do some creative activity by their own interest in and enjoyment of that activity, they may be more creative than they are when primarily motivated by some goal imposed on them by others . . . . Sylvia Plath, for example, appeared to be crippled for long periods of time by a concern with evaluation and competition and the demands that other made on her" (1983a, p. 15).

Amabile is not the first to study effects of incentives. Lepper, Greene, and their associates (Greene and Lepper 1974, Lepper, Greene, and Nisbett 1973, Lepper and Greene 1975, Lepper et al. 1982) have researched what they call the overjustification effect. They found that when too much extrinsic motivation is present (things like pay, praise, or promotion), creativity is dampened. This is also true when a person's natural intrinsic interest in a project is undermined by, for instance, giving unnecessary rewards or motivational instructions on choices (Amabile 1982a, 1982b, Amabile and Gitomer 1984, Amabile, DeJong, and Lepper 1976, Amabile, Hennessey, and Grossman 1986, Berlas, Amabile, and Handel 1979, Garbarino 1975, Greene and Lepper 1974, Lepper and Greene 1975, Lepper Greene, and Nisbett 1973, Kernoodle-Loveland and Olley 1979).

These researchers have learned that rewards can cause a narrow focus on the task, with the goal of getting it done quickly and without risk. People begin to see themselves as being controlled by the payoff and gradually come to lose what intrinsic interest in the task itself they may have had.

As a result of this research, Amabile (1982a, 1982b, 1983a, 1983b) has proposed her own theory of the impact of the social environment on creativity. It has two parts:

1. An objective method of measuring creativity, described in chapter 10.

2. A theory of the **three components of creativity**. Amabile suggests that there are three basic components necessary for any creative performances (see figure 11–4):

The three components are:

1. **Domain-relevant skills** are similar to what we commonly refer to as talent or expertise. A certain degree of technical skill is required before one can perform in any given domain of activity. For example, a good working knowledge of language and of the

1
DOMAIN-RELEVANT SKILLS
INCLUDES:
—Knowledge about the domain
—Technical skills required
—Special domain-relevant "talent"

DEPENDS ON:
—Innate cognitive abilities
—Innate perceptual and
  motor skills
—Formal and informal
  education

2
CREATIVITY—RELEVANT SKILLS
INCLUDES:
—Appropriate cognitive style
—Implicit or explicit
  knowledge of heuristics for
  generating novel ideas

DEPENDS ON:
—Training
—Experience in idea generation
—Personality characteristics

3
TASK MOTIVATION
INCLUDES:
—Attitudes toward the task
—Perceptions of own motivation
  for undertaking the task

DEPENDS ON:
—Initial level of intrinsic
  motivation toward the task
—Presence or absence of
  salient extrinsic constraints
  in the social environment
—Individual ability to
  minimize cognitively extrinsic
  constraints

Source: Amabile 1983b, p. 362. Copyright 1983 by the American Psychological Association. Reprinted by permission of the publisher and author.

Figure 11–4. AMABILE'S COMPONENTIAL THEORY OF CREATIVITY

use of metaphor and imagery might be considered domain-relevant skills for the poet.

2. **Creativity-relevant skills** include all those strategies or dispositions an individual brings to a task that facilitate the creative process. Examples include the ability to break functional fixity (see chapter 2), to suspend judgment, and to take risks.

3. **Task motivation** can be seen as the most important determinant of the difference between what a person *can* do and what he or she *will* do. The former is determined by the level of domain-relevant and creativity relevant skill; the latter is determined by these two in conjunction with an intrinsically motivated state.

The first two components have been considered in different ways by many creativity researchers. Amabile's original contribution comes with the prominent role she gives to task motivation.

According to this framework, task motivation is responsible for determining whether the creative process will begin at all and whether it will continue. The domain-relevant and creativity-relevant skills make their contribution after the process has begun and is being sustained by the motivated individual. This complex relationship is carefully detailed by Amabile in figure 11–5, which you may want to study carefully. The role of the three creativity components is made clear in this diagram.

The implications of the research of Amabile and her colleagues for cultivating creativity are many, and the work has only just begun. Obviously, the major idea is to promote intrinsic motivation, especially among gifted children. Amabile, Hennessey, and Grossman (1986) offer three basic ideas:

1. One way would be to structure the child's work environment so that competition, external rewards, external evaluation, and other constraints are de-emphasized. Children could be taught to rely more on self-evaluation and self-reward systems. Rewards and evaluations could certainly be used, but in a way that did not lead to children's focusing on these external inducements (p. 30).

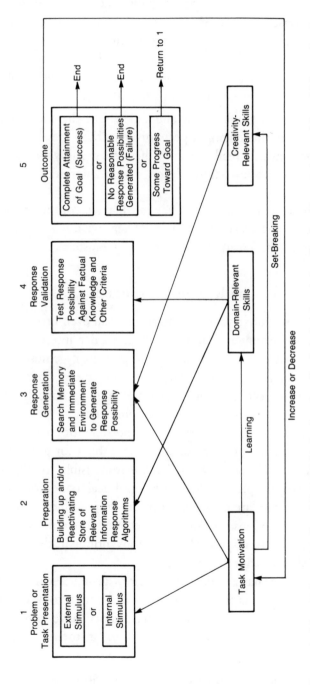

Source: Ambile 1983b, p. 357. Copyright 1983 by the American Psychological Association. Reprinted by permission of the publisher and author.

Figure 11–5. AMABILE'S THEORETICAL FRAMEWORK OF CREATIVITY

2. Teach children ways to cognitively distance themselves from the extrinsic constraints placed on them, without ignoring those constraints completely. The point is to teach children to cognitively keep reward, competition, evaluation, and other constraints in their place, so that these factors do not overwhelm children's intrinsic enjoyment of their work (p. 30–31).

3. Ask children to think about and talk about the most fun, interesting, and challenging aspects of what they are doing. Help them find ways to really explore their most enjoyable activities and to make the less enjoyable ones most interesting (p. 31).

Amabile and Hennessey feel it is vital that we continue studying how motivation and creativity interact. "Then, we might run less risk of losing any of the creativity of our young Einsteins" (p. 31).

The Role of the Culture

In this section, we move to a consideration of an even broader aspect of the social environment: culture.[a] Of particular interest is something that has been noted since antiquity, that great geniuses do not appear at regular intervals in history. During some periods, clusters of brilliant persons, often interacting with each other, have flourished; other periods have been devoid of such eminence.

Why? Does the time in history make it possible for creative potential to achieve fulfillment? For example, was a thirst for philosophical drama during the Golden Age of Greece responsible for the abundance of illustrious playwrights? Were political conditions in the United States of the late eighteenth century responsible for inspiring the writers of the Constitution? Were economic conditions in the Western Hemisphere responsible for the inventions in the late nineteenth and early twentieth centuries?

Or is it the case that genius is the result of genetics, which cannot be predicted, except that the irregularity of extremes is to be expected? If so, then the great epochs of creative history have come about because geniuses happened to have been born in them.

---

[a]Most of the ideas in this section have been summarized from those presented in chapters 13 and 14 of Silvano Arieti's excellent book *Creativity: The Magic Synthesis.*

One of the first to study the question scientifically was the anthropologist G. Kroeber (cited in Arieti, 1976). He noted that not only have clusters of geniuses appeared irregularly, but when they do, it is almost always in one particular field of endeavor. Solitary contributions such as those of Copernicus and Kepler have been rare. Kroeber also suggested that cultural improvement tends to start in one small area and then sweeps through the culture. Thus he concluded that cultural conditions are the crucial factor. He argued that "Genetics leaves only an infinitesimal possibility for the racial stock occupying England to have given birth to no geniuses at all between 1450 and 1550 and whole series of geniuses in literature, music, science, philosophy, and politics between 1550 and 1650" (p. 10).

However, arguing that the state of the times is the crucial variable begs the question, what is there *about* the times that causes genius to surface? Another anthropologist, P. Gray (cited in Arieti, 1976), offers a theory.

Calling it an **epicyclical theory,** Gray suggests there are three types of periods that are repeated throughout history: social, economic, and political. In each type of cycle, things go from good to bad to good again. The cycles are relatively independent of each other, but when more than one peaks at the same time—they become "florescent and developed," in Gray's terminology—the odds that creative potential will be realized are greatly increased. When the peaks of all three coincide, genius becomes certain. Of course, Gray's theory is much more complicated than this, but these are its essentials. In a marvelously cocksure statement, Kroeber summarizes this point of view; "If we are interested primarily in culture and how it works, we can *disregard personalities except as inevitable mechanisms* or measures of cultural expression [italics added]" (1966, p. 10).

The great psychologist William James (1880) took issue with the cultural position, believing the *interaction* of highly creative individuals to be causative. Whenever they get together, the community starts "vibrating": "Blow must follow blow so fast that no cooling can occur in the intervals. Then the mass of the nation grows incandescent, and may continue to glow by pure inertia long after the originators of its internal movement have passed away. We often hear surprise that in these high tides of human affairs . . . individual geniuses should seem so exceptionally abundant."

Well-known psychologist Silvano Arieti also rejects emphasis on cultural factors. He asks, "Can we see Shakespeare only as an inevitable mechanism of Elizabethan culture? Had he not been born, could another Englishman of his time have expressed the culture of his period as well, or achieved such heights?" (p. 299). He holds that people become "geniuses" because of the juxtaposition of three factors:

1. The culture is right. The airplane would not have been invented if the gasoline engine had not been invented—it propelled the Wrights' plane, as well as fueling the public's interest in travel.

2. The genes are right. The person's intelligence, which is powerfully influenced by genes, must be high. Creativity, which may or may not be genetic, must also be high.

3. The interactions must be right. Arieti offers the example of Freud, Jung, and Adler (see chapter 3). If Jung and Adler had not had Freud to compete over—and against—it is questionable whether either would hold such a high position in psychology today. Freud too worked hard to refute his own mentors.

This is not to say that all creative achievement is born of competition, although much surely has been. Ultimately, there is always something mysterious about high creativity. Arieti summarizes it well: "Actually, *the significant synthesis is the creative process itself.* It is so significant and unpredictable as to appear magic. Even when a culture is propitious, the significant synthesis occurs in a very small percentage of its people" (p. 302).

Still, cultures may be positive or negative toward genius. Arieti labels the culture that facilitates creativity a **creativogenic society.** Such a society should of course be based on fair and just laws. He points to Franklin D. Roosevelt's concept of a society that fosters the "four freedoms": freedom from fear and want, freedom of speech and worship. A society that does not offer such freedoms would stifle creativity. But the availability of these four freedoms would not in themselves guarantee the emergence of genius either.

Nine Features of The Creativogenic Society

What would? Arieti proposes nine features that he believes are essential to the creativogenic society:

1. *The availability of culture (and certain physical) means.* Mozart would not have been successful had he been born in Africa, nor would Michelangelo have been in Alaska.

2. *Openness to cultural stimuli.* Not only must the means be available to the creative person, but the population (or at least some significant part of it) must also desire the results. The "Dark Ages" were not very hospitable time in which to be a genius.

3. *Stress on becoming, not just being.* "A culture that puts emphasis *only* on immediate gratification, sensuousness, comfort, and immediate pleasure does not promote creativity" (p. 314).

4. *Free access to cultural media for all citizens, without discrimination.* In the past, essential information has been made available only to a privileged class—the clergy, the wealthy, the religious or ethnic majority, and, most often, members of the male sex. This, Arieti says, is the major explanation for the underrepresentation of women on the historical lists of great achievements. A number of authors have suggested that the woman's role as bearer of children sublimates—that is, assuages the need—to be creative. Arieti says this is a false explanation, in that the female gender role is one cast on women by society, one that has left little choice in the matter.

5. *Freedom, or even moderate discrimination, after severe oppression or absolute exclusion.* This incentive is not recommended by Arieti, of course, but from it he predicts that increased contributions will be made by women and minorities in the near future.

6. *Exposure to different and even contrasting cultural stimuli.* Although cultures are strongly reinforced not to change (people usually believe that time has proved their value), the incorporation of new stimuli from other cultures make creativity more likely. American democracy has obviously benefited here.

7. *Tolerance for and interest in diverging views.* This concept is the same as that described at length in chapter 2 of this book.

8. *The opportunity for interaction between significant persons.* As we

found in the study of families of the creative, described in chapter 10, crucial influences on the lives of the young can come from many quarters, but only if they live in a society that permits and encourages interaction with others who have different views. Clearly the Warsaw ghetto of World War II, for instance, made contact between Christians and Jews virtually impossible, cutting off the chance for exchange of imaginative ideas.

9. *The promotion of incentives and awards.* When Arieti wrote this, Amabile had not yet produced her findings on the negative effects of reinforcements; today he might not include it. However, he does seem to have been aware of the problem, for he says, "The greatest award to creativity is creativity itself" (p. 324).

How can we discover whether these nine factors are really creativogenic? Arieti suggests we look at a group of individuals who have been creative far beyond what would have been expected of a group their size: the Jews.

The Effects of Society in Modern Times on the Creativity of Jews

The long history of persecution of the Jews is well documented, and Arieti states that not until Napoleon Bonaparte rose to power at the beginning of the nineteenth century did they find a champion of their human rights. However, with certain well-known exceptions, the wave of liberation that began in Europe in 1848 has continued to the present.

Have these more positive conditions resulted in the creativity of Jewish people? As Arieti documents extensively, the answer is a resounding yes. These are two examples from the many he gives:

"Of the four people who have revolutionized the socio-cultural world since [1848], two (Freud and Einstein) have been Jews, and one (Marx) was the son of Jewish parents converted to Christianity" (p. 326). The fourth was Darwin.

In the period 1901–70, the number of Jewish winners of the Nobel Prize has been twenty-eight times greater than that of the rest of the world. Second place goes to French non-Jews, at six times greater.

Arieti finds that most of the time, the nine features he suggests have been present in Jewish life, and when they were not, Jewish creative production has suffered severely. Of special importance have been five characteristics of modern Jews:

1. A well-established love of education, the pursuit of which liberation made possible. "When the love of education is well established, it is relatively easy to make the transition from exclusive study of religious books to studies including other disciplines as well" (p. 334).

2. Jews have had little prejudice against women who have wished to pursue careers; consequently the list of female Jewish innovators is a long one.

3. Centuries of oppression have caused a universal desire in them to excel, in part as a means to safety.

4. "Sensitized as they were to society's unfairness, they were always in favor of social innovations and reforms" (p. 335).

5. Their interactions with persons of different backgrounds has been facilitated by their migrations to avoid persecution and to achieve better lives. As a result many have international relationships.

Thus in the case of Jewish creativity, Arieti's theory seems to stand up well. He urges that if we would cultivate eight of his creativogenic features (number five—freedom after severe persecution—is excluded for obvious reasons), "we may find that these features can benefit Jews and non-Jews alike, and as a matter of fact the whole of mankind."

As we can see from chapters 10 and 11, social factors play complex roles, positive and negative, in the development of creativity. In the next chapter. I will attempt to summarize all of the factors considered in this book.

12

Helping Children Become Creative Adults: A Summary

Chapter Highlights:

Physical Aspects of Creativity
Personality Factors in Creativity
Mental Factors in Creativity
Family Factors
In Conclusion

T he principle goal of this book has been to describe what creative persons are like and why they think the way they do. We have investigated their personalities, brains, abilities, attitudes, thinking styles, families, and developmental patterns. Inherent in each of these considerations are implications for raising children to be creative. In this chapter, the most significant of these implications are described. This will also serve as a summary of the book itself, divided into four parts: physical, personality, mental, and family aspects of creativity.

Physical Aspects of Creativity

Genetic Inheritance. There is some evidence that creative parents are more likely to have creative children. However, this may not be caused by the inheritance of creative ability itself.

What is inherited is intelligence, and creativity is based on that, according to the threshhold hypothesis. This hypothesis states that creative ability is highly related to IQ at the lower and middle levels. That is, those with moderate IQ levels are usually more creative than those with low IQ. However, having a high IQ does not ensure greater creativity than having a moderate IQ. The cut-off point appears to be around 120. If your IQ is higher than 120, whether or not you will be highly creative depends much more on factors such as personality, motivation, and opportunity than on intelligence.

The Growth of Microneurons. Children inherit their macroneural system at the moment of conception. Macroneurons form the main electrical pathways of the brain. However, microneurons, the small electrical pathways that run between macroneuronal lines, continue to grow for about one and half years after birth. This growth can be stimulated in infants by providing a moderately stimulating environment. This includes well-modulated sounds (such as classical music and soft, but not punk, rock music), pleasant pastel colors, and little toy birds hanging over the baby's crib.

Overemphasis on Words. Verbal ability lies mainly in the left hemisphere of the brain. There is evidence that when words are emphasized in a child's education, the left hemisphere of the brain comes to dominate thinking. Creative people, however, appear to have a more even balance in the interactions between their hemispheres, which improves communication between the two halves. This in turn may make the production of unusual ideas more likely. A variety of visual, auditory, tactile, and olfactory experiences are needed to compensate for what is largely a verbal world. The book *Drawing on the Right Side of the Brain* (Edwards, 1979) offers excellent advice on this.

Lefthandedness. There was a time when left-handed children were forced to be right-handed; left-handedness was considered "sinister." This practice may well have suppressed creativity. Left-handers are disproportionately represented among the creative. For example, nearly half the students in one architectural school are left-handed, as are 65 percent of the students in a major art school.

Personality Factors in Creativity

Tolerance of Ambiguity. It is a natural reaction of parents to protect their children from threatening or fearful situations. Being too protective, though, is not in their best interest. They should be introduced to unusual situations in increasingly challenging steps, and helped to deal with the fears these experiences produce. In World War II, for example, there was a study of the ability of soldiers to deal with beach invasions. To the surprise of the researchers, it was found that those who had had difficult childhoods often did much better than those whose childhoods had been placidly safe. Surviving a hail of bullets is not the same as being creative, but the two skills may have something in common.

Stimulus Freedom. Parents have a tendency to introduce rules into the lives of their children; thus those children naturally learns to search for rules when they encounter a new situation. However, this tendency is often counterproductive. Creative persons have two distinct tendencies when it comes to rules: when a situation is restrictive, they are likely to break the rules to the extent that they need to in order to achieve their goals; and probably more important, when a situation is ambiguous, they do not feel the need to make up rules to guide their behavior, as most of us do.

The parents in the CRC study typically refrain from imposing rules on their children. Instead, they allow the child to decide for herself how the family's values should be carried out in behavior. In this, the old proverb applies: people get better at doing the things they are encouraged to practice. And practicing deciding how one should behave ultimately leads to creative decisions.

Functional Freedom. Probably the most direct way to help a child to be functionally free is to provide practice in it. For example, play a game with him in which he is to think of all the ways a paper clip may be used. Ask him to think of lots of uses for a stone. Point out to him when he is being functionally fixed in his problem-solving efforts.

Flexibility. This calls for paying attention to the whole of a problem, rather than fixating on some part of it. Relevant to this skill is Carl Jung's distinction between people who are perceptors versus people who are judges. Judges are likely to get stuck on some part of a problem because they are so worried about getting the right (or at least an acceptable) answer to the problem. Perceptors are more likely to wait until they have all the relevant information before they come to a decision about the problem. Of course, having a completely open mind is not functional; eventually some conclusion must be reached. However, those who are willing to look at the broader implications before jumping to a conclusion are more likely to be successful.

Risk Taking. Obviously, willingness to take risks is a necessary part of the creative personality, but parents who cultivate risk taking must take big risks themselves. I am reminded of a time when my three- and four-year-old daughters cooperated in creating a birthday card for their grandfather (the four-year-old composed it, her sister colored it). Then they asked me if they could mail it. The mailbox was three blocks away, which involved crossing two side streets. Finally I agreed but followed them to their goal, dodging from tree to tree in an effort to keep them from knowing I did not completely trust their ability. I know I must have looked foolish, but I remind you of Otto Rank's dictum in raising creative children: they should be allowed to do whatever they want to do, as long as it does not violate the rights of others or compromise their own safety.

Preference for Disorder. As Barron and Welsh have pointed out, it is not disorder itself that creative persons prefer, but the opportunity to impose their own order on complex situations. Nevertheless, they often seem to prefer "messes." Therefore, it may be necessary to allow them to live in sloppy surroundings.

Delay of Gratification. It is not easy to inculcate this value in a child, although creative children tend to accept it more readily. Reading stories about putting off rewards until greater ones can be attained is helpful. Activities that give practice in delaying gratification, such as participating in a savings account, also help.

A Positive Attitude toward Hard Work. Reading stories that glorify hard work, like the Horatio Alger stories of old, will work here too. Another technique is to be sure that children learn to work for their spending money. In fact, they should learn that all rewards are contingent upon their own effort.

Androgyny. The best way to teach androgynous sex roles to children is to model them yourself. Androgyny is a complicated concept, and explanations of it will not do. The child has to see and be willing to imitate those who follow its precepts. The second-best technique is to encourage friendships with other children and adults who are themselves androgynous.

Good Feelings about Being Different. Most parents really do not want their children to be independent; they are not in favor of the child's having a will of his own. As Otto Rank has pointed out, if you let children have their own way, then you are responsible for what happens. *It is much easier to say no.* Then, at least, if things go wrong, it is not your fault. But creative people *are* different, and they need to feel that their parents back them in being so.

Mental Factors in Creativity

Problem-solving Skills. The appendix to this book has a rather large section listing ways to foster problem-solving skills.

Remote Associations and Divergent Thinking. Chapter 6 offered a number of suggestions, such as brainstorming and synectics, for building these skills. Isaksen and Treffinger (1985) suggest these "ideastarters.":

If I had my way . . .
If I could do anything, I would . . .
If I were king (queen) . . .
If I had a magic wand I would . . .
I wish . . .
I hope . . .
I'd really like . . .
It would sure be helpful if . . .
Why don't we . . .
Let's consider . . .
I would if we could . . .
It would make my day if . . .

A Clear, Relaxed Mind. A clear, relaxed mind is essential to original thinking. Yoga (especially the "sponge position" described in chapter 6) is an excellent way to achieve this condition.

Perceptual Set. Young children tend to have few blinders when it comes to perceiving the world, but as they grow older they develop expectations about what they are going to perceive. This "sets up" misperceptions. Many techniques are suggested in the resources listed in the appendix which can alleviate this problem. The "Know Your Orange" game is an example:

"KNOW YOUR ORANGE"

Instructions: In groups of five to eight, children are each presented with an orange and told to "get to know it." They study their orange for size, bumps, and dents, and any other noticeable traits. Then the participants' names are written on the oranges with a felt-tipped pen, and the oranges are placed in a large bag. Reaching in one at a time without being allowed to look, each child tries to find his or her orange. Amazingly, most of the time they can. Each child's orange is returned to the bag after her or his turn.

Next, the children take turns telling how they recognized their orange. Then they are asked to suggest other objects that could be used, and what they would look for in those objects. Finally, they are asked to suggest ways they can become more sensitive to differences in the world around them (for example, use senses other than the visual, have contests to see who noticed the most facets of an object or the most interesting facets).

Before playing this game, children think all oranges are basically alike. it makes them realize there are many subtle differences to be noticed. This is a lesson that most creative adults seem to have learned.

Ego-control and Resiliency. Ego-control is the ability to express or contain impulses, feelings, and desires. Ego-resiliency is the ability to know when to do so. A child comes to possess these abilities only to the extent that you are able to explain them to her and back up your explanations with examples. The best examples, of course, will come from her own behavior. You will need to "seize the moment of opportunity" by being ready to point out when she has appropriately expressed or contained her impulses, feelings, and desires.

Memorizing Techniques. Here again, games are useful aids. "Kim's Game" is an example:

"KIM'S GAME"

Instructions: Arrange objects on a flat area in groups of three or four. For example, place a grape, a plum, an apple, and a nut near each other. Any other types of small objects will do—such as sewing things, a bolt, a screw and a nail, a spoon, a knife, and a fork.

Cover the objects before bringing the child or children in to observe them. Explain to them that this game was described by Rudyard Kipling in his book *Kim*, which is about training young children to spy on the enemy during the revolution in India. When the group is settled, uncover the area for ten to thirty seconds (the amount of time depends on the age of the children—try it yourself first), then recover it. Ask the observers to write down each object they remember having seen. If everyone remembers them all, add some more objects and/or shorten the observation time.

Now retry the experiment with the same number of objects, but use different ones, and ones not associated with each other. Almost certainly the children's success rate will fall. Ask them to explain, and when they point out the help that association was to their ability to observe (children this age will usually notice it), ask them to suggest ways they can use this technique in their regular lives.

If this activity is done in a group, no doubt some children will do better than others. Encourage the group to discuss why this was so. Ask the more successful children to share any techniques they used, other than association, to do well with this task. Have them suggest other ways of improving memory, and you do so too.

Use of Opposite Thinking Patterns. In the first chapter, Jackson and Messick's model called for being able to think both analytically and intuitively, and both reflectively and spontaneously. And in chapter 6, Guilford's model called for thinking convergently and divergently. Most of us seem to become much better at one or the other of these pairs; few maintain a balance between the two, but that is what must be done in creative production. Probably the best help for a child would be to point out which type of thinking he is using in a particular situation, and suggest to him that he try its opposite.

Extra Encouragement During the Two Critical Periods of Potential Growth. In the first five years of life and during the first two years of adolescence, children have the best opportunities to blossom as creative thinkers. This is not to say that other years are unimportant, but that children will benefit from extra help during these critical years.

Family Factors

An Unusual House. To be honest, I do not know whether living in an unusual house (ultramodern or ancient, unexpected location, unconventional furniture, and so forth) promotes creativity, or vice versa. However, there is considerable evidence that the environment in general affects thought patterns, so it probably does in this case too.

Limited Rules, Reinforced Values. Remember that the parents in the CRC study who are most successful have the fewest rules for their children's behavior and the mildest forms of punishment for infractions (usually they just express disappointment). Everyone gets better at what they practice, so a child should be given as much practice as possible in determining his own rules for behavior.

Family Discussions about Creativity. Too often we find that parents erroneously assume that their children understand and accept their values. Family discussion of these values, especially those in which parent praises a child's creative achievements, can have powerful effects.

Turning Traumatic Incidents into Object Lessons. To say that "every cloud has a silver lining" may be trite, but research suggests that people who are able to find some benefit in injury, illness, and even tragedy are also most likely to become creative.

Avoiding Judgments. Many of the parents in the CRC study strongly urged avoiding being the judge of a child's products. If a child's efforts are regularly appraised, she will come to rely on it. She will fail to develop her own ability to be both self-critical and self-approving, two traits that are essential in the creative process.

Family Collections. Family collections are valuable in a number of ways. They offer an avenue for the intergenerational sharing of ideas. They afford a chance for recognition by parents and siblings, even to younger members of the family. Most important, they cultivate a child's categorizing ability. Psychologist Jerome Bruner (Bruner, Goodnow, and Austin, 1956) calls this capacity the basis of all thinking. He fosters categorization in young children by playing the game pictured in figure 12–1. The materials for include:

Three string loops, laid out as in the figure

Nine shapes—three each of squares, ovals, and triangles, each set including one white, one black, and one striped shape

The child is told that all triangles should be put in one loop, and all black shapes should be put in the other. Any shapes that fit both

Bruner's Categories Game

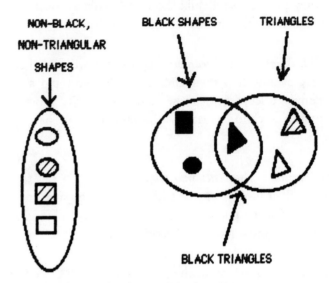

Source: Adapted from Bruner, Goodnow and Austin, 1956.

Figure 12–1. BRUNER'S CATEGORIES GAME

categories should be put in the center. Any shapes that do not fit either category should be left out.

Obviously, this game can be made more or less complicated by adding or deleting categories. Children seem to love playing the game, and there is good evidence that practice with it definitely does cultivate the same kind of thinking that collecting fosters (that is, categorical thinking, a foundation of creative thinking) and is especially good training for the young child.

In Conclusion

This is a long list, and many of the recommendations are difficult to follow, whether one is seeking to apply them to one's children or to oneself. No one ever said that high creative achievement would be easy. Clearly, it is a case of being disappointed often in the pursuit of only very occasional moments of passionate delight. But just as clearly, such moments are worth many disappointments. It is my sincere hope that readers of this book may have many such passionate experiences, and that this book will have made them more likely to occur.

Appendix

Cultivating Creativity
An Annotated Bibliography

Appendix

Cultivating Creativity: An Annotated Bibliography

Highlights:

Works That Cover the Life Span
General Problem Solving
Early Childhood
Childhood
Youth
Adulthood

=============

T echniques designed to foster creativity will be described in this appendix. There has been a vast array of suggestions, largely because so many people (teachers, psychologists, educational researchers, business entrepreneurs, and others) have thought of ways to make people more creative.

Unfortunately, this situation has sometimes resulted in these authors' putting the cart before the horse. That is, much of this work has been done without a clear definition of creative thinking, and without an understanding of how creativity develops. This has occurred because the desire to enhance creativity in our society has often been greater than the desire to study it. There are literally thousands of publications on this topic, many more than on the areas discussed earlier in the book.

Sorting the wheat from the large pile of chaff has not been an easy job. Although I have described those I believe to be the best, no doubt other authors would not agree with all my selections. There is only room in this book for brief examples of the various approaches. I have organized them into six categories: a general category for books and articles that cover the life span, a list of resources on general problem solving skills, and four age group sections (early childhood, childhood, youth, and adulthood). However, I believe that these annotated references should provide the reader with an effective start in learning more about this fascinating aspect of creativity research.

Works that Cover the Life Span

Anderson, H.H. *Creativity and its cultivation.* New York: Harper, 1959. Although dated, many of the articles collected in this book offer suggestions that are still extremely useful.

Barron, F. *Creative person and creative process.* New York: Holt, Rinehart and Winston, 1969. This is one of the best of the early textbooks, especially from the psychoanalytic viewpoint. Barron advocates what he calls "altered states of consciousness" as means to more creative thinking. These include intensification of aesthetic sensibilities, unusual patterns, promotion of intuition, devotion to "higher purposes," and mystical experiences.

Biondi, A.M. (Ed.) *The creative process.* New York, D.O.K. Publishers, 1972. See also *Have an affair with your mind.* Buffalo, N.Y.: Creative Education Foundation, 1974. Editor of the *Journal of Creative Behavior,* Biondi is a well-known theorist in the field.

Bloomberg, M. (Ed.) *Creativity: Theory and research.* New Haven, Conn.: College and University Press, 1973. This book covers the major theoretical approaches to creativity, which include the psychoanalytic, holistic, environmental, associative, factorial, cognitive-developmental, and humanistic theories. A book of readings, it incorporates some of the finest articles ever written in this field.

Gowan, J.C. "Some new thoughts on the development of creativity." *Journal of creative behavior,* 1977, *11*(2), 77–90. Noting that for creativity, "variability in individuals far exceeds the limits of variability characteristic of other traits and abilities," Gowan asks what besides ability could account for this. His answer is "psychological openness." His article explores the ramifications of attempting to evoke this trait. See also Gowan, J.C., "The facilitation of creativity through meditational procedures." *Journal of creative behavior,* 1978, *12,* 156–160.

Lobuts, J.F., Jr., and Pennewill, C.L. "Do we dare to restructure the classroom environment?" *Journal of creative behavior*, 1984, *18*(4), 237–246. Examines the problems inherent in attempting to change the teaching/learning situation.

Moffat, J.A., and Shephard, W.J. "Facilitation: A selected bibliography." *Journal of creative behavior*, 1983, *17*(1), 65–70. An extensive list of books and articles, divided into four areas: the person, the process, the product, and the environmental press.

Parnes, S.J. *Creative behavior guidebook*. New York: Scribner's, 1967. A classic.

Shallcross, D.J. *Teaching creative behavior: How to evoke creativity in children of all ages*. Englewood Cliffs, N.J. Prentice-Hall, 1981.

Torrance, E.P. *Guiding creative talent*. Englewood Cliffs, N.J.: Prentice-Hall, 1962. Another "oldie-but-goody."

Wittmer, J., and Myrick, R. *Facilitative teaching*. Pacific Palisades, Calif.: Goodyear, 1974. A general text on the subject.

General Problem Solving

What follows is a list of resources selected from among the great number that have been published in recent years. It is not annotated because the basic topic of each is the same.

Adams, J. *Conceptual blockbusting*. (3rd ed.) Reading, Mass.: Addison-Wesley, 1986.

Chance, P. *Learning to think*. New York: Teachers College Press, 1985.

Daniels, P.B. *Strategies to facilitate problem-solving*. Provo, Utah: Brigham Young University, 1964.

Davis, G.A. *Psychology of problem-solving: Theory and practice*. New York: Basic Books, 1973.

Davis, G.A. "In pursuit of frumious creativity." *Journal of creative behavior*, 1975, *9*, 75–79.

Feldhusen, J.F., and Treffinger, D.J. *Creative thinking and problem solving in gifted education* (3rd ed.). Dubuque, Iowa: Kendall-Hunt, 1985.

Firestein, R., and Treffinger, D.J. "Creative problem solving: guidelines and resources for effective facilitation." *Gifted/creative/talented*, 1983 (January-February), 2–10.

Firestein, R., and Treffinger, D.J. "Ownership and converging: Essential ingredients of creative problem solving." *Journal of creative behavior*, 1983, *17*(1), 32–38.

Frederiksen, N. *Implications of theory for instruction in problem solving*. Princeton, N.J.: Educational Testing Service, 1983.

Gall, M., and Mendelsohn, G.A. "Effects of facilitating techniques and subject-experimenter interaction on creative problem solving." *Journal of personality and social psychology*, 1967, *5*(2), 211–216.

Haley, G.L. "Creative response styles: The effects of socioeconomic status and problem-solving training." *Journal of creative behavior*, 1984, *18*(1), 25–40.

Isaksen, S.G. "Toward a model for the facilitation of creative problem solving." *Journal of creative behavior*, 1983, *17*(1), 18–31.

Isaksen, S.G., and Parnes, S.J. "Curriculum planning for creative thinking and problem solving." *Journal of creative behavior*, 1985, *19*(1), 1–29.

Kramer, D.E., and Bavern, C.D. "The effects of behavioral strategies on creativity training." *Journal of creative behavior*, 1984, *18*(1), 23–24.

Maier, N.R.F. "Reasoning in humans: The solution of a problem and its appearance in consciousness." *Journal of comparative psychology*, 1931, *12*, 181–194.

Maier, N.R.F. *Problem solving and creativity in individuals and groups.* Belmont, Calif.: Brooks/Cole, 1970.

Mendelsohn, G.A., and Gall, M.D. "Personality variables and the effectiveness of techniques to facilitate creative problem solving." *Journal of personality and social psychology*, 1970, *16*(2), 346–351.

Newell, A., Shaw, J.C., and Simon, H.A. "Elements of a theory of human problem solving." *Psychological review*, 1958, *65*, 151–166.

Newell, A., Shaw, J.C., and Simon, H.A. "The process of creative thinking." In Gruber, H.E., Terrell, G., and Wertheimer, M., *Contemporary approaches to creative thinking.* New York: Atherton, 1962.

Noller, R.B. *Scratching the surface of creative problem solving: A bird's eye view of CPS.* Buffalo, N.Y.: D.O.K. Publishers, 1977.

Prince, G.M. *The practice of creativity: A manual for dynamic group problem-solving.* New York: Harper and Row, 1970.

Renzulli, J.S. "Guiding the gifted in the pursuit of real problems: The transformed role of the teacher." *Journal of creative behavior*, 1983, *17*(10), 49–59.

Treffinger, D.J. "George's group: A creative problem-solving facilitation case study." *Journal of creative behavior*, 1983, *17*(1), 39–48.

Early Childhood (Birth to Five Years Old)

General

Lehane, S. *The creative child: How to encourage the natural creativity of your preschooler.* Englewood Cliffs, N.J.: Prentice-Hall, 1979. This is an excellent source of activities that are soundly based on developmental psychology. Covers "the dreamer stage" (two years old), "the poet stage" (three to five), the inventor stage (four to six), and creative environments.

Remote Association/Divergent Thinking

Cornelia, G.M., and Yawkey, T.D. "Imaginativeness in preschoolers and single parent families." *Journal of creative behavior*, 1985, *19*(1), 56–66. Explores ramifications for eliciting divergent ideas in children who live with one parent.

Flack, J.D. *Once upon a time.* East Aurora, N.Y.: United Disseminators of Knowledge, 1986. Uses fairy tales to provide a springboard for creative thinking and problem solving.

Pelligrini, A.D. "The effects of exploration training on young children's associative fluency." *The creative child and adult quarterly*, 1982, *VII*(4), 226–233. Looks at exploration as a means of cultivating improvement of creative abilities.

Shaw, J.M., and Cliatt, M.J.P. "A model for training teachers to encourage divergent thinking in young children." *Journal of creative behavior*, 1986, *20*(2), 81–88. Suggests a method that helps children become inventors rather than just responders.

Yawkey, T.D. "Creative dialogue through sociodramatic play and its uses." *Journal of creative behavior*, 1986, *20*(1), 52–60. Author claims that sociodramatic play situations offer an ideal medium for stimulating imagination. See also Yawkey, T.D., "Effects of social relationships, curricula, and sex differences on reading and imaginativeness in young children." *Alberta journal of educational research*, 1980, *26*(3), 159–168; Yawkey, T.D. "Sociodramatic effects and sex differences on selected cognitive academic and play-related abilities in five-year-olds." *Contemporary educational psychology*, 1983.

Object Play

Hollman, J. "Games to promote creativity." *English journal*, January 1981, *70*, 83–85.

Piaget, J. *Play, dreams and imitation in childhood.* New York: Norton, 1965. A most seminal work in this area.

Trostle, S.L., and Yawkey, T.D. "Creative thinking and the education of young children: The fourth basic skill." *Journal of early childhood*, 1982, *14*(2), 67–71. The ability to play well with objects in their world is beginning to be seen as the "fourth aspect" of the essentials in early childhood learning.

Trostle, S.L., and Yawkey, T.D. "Facilitating creative thought through object play in young children." *Journal of creative behavior*, 1983, *17*(3), 181–189. Builds on their first article. "Objects facilitate cognitive and social growth and become the sensorial building blocks of all adaptive development and creativity" (p. 182).

Yawkey, T.D., and Hrncir, E.S. "Pretend play tools for oral language growth in preschool." *Journal of creative behavior*, 1982, *16*(4), 265–271. Further use of play to foster creativity in early childhood.

Role Played by Grandparents

Robertson, J. "Grandmotherhood: A study of role conceptions." *Journal of marriage and the family*, 1977, *39*(1), 165–174. Looks at four aspects of the grandparenting role.

Strom, R., and Strom, S. "Creative curriculum for grandparents." *Journal of creative behavior*, 1984, *18*(2), 133–141. Suggests numerous activities through which grandparents are especially able to cultivate creativity.

Childhood (Five to Twelve Years Old)

General

Barron, F. *Creative person and creative process.* New York: Holt, Rinehart and Winston, 1969. Psychoanalyst Barron offers many insights into the relationships between childhood experiences and creative development. Of special interest is his chapter on the relevance of *The Education of Henry Adams.*

Belliston, L., and Belliston, M. *How to raise a more creative child.* Allen, Tex.: Argus Communications, 1982. This is the original how-to-do-it type of book, and many of the eighty suggestions for "things parents can do" are quite good. These suggestions are preceded by explanations of various aspects of creative thinking, some of them reinforced by scientific study, and some highly speculative.

Darrow, H.F. *Independent activities for creative learning.* New York: Teachers College Press, 1986.

Gehlbach, R.D. "Creativity and instruction: The problem of task design." *Journal of creative behavior*, 1987, *21*(1), 34–47. Offers a paradigm by which "educational efforts to foster creativity can become much more systematic than has been generally true in the past (p. 47).

Haylock, D.W. "Mathematical creativity in schoolchildren." *Journal of creative behavior*, 1987, *21*(1), 48–59. Describes typical high-attaining creative math students, and hypothesizes how they got that way.

Mack, R.M. "Are methods of enhancing creativity being taught in teacher education programs as perceived by teacher educators and student teachers?" *Journal of creative behavior*, 1987, *21*(1), 22–33. Describes a survey of 62 teacher educators and 388 student teachers, to whom enhancement techniques are seldom taught. Offers several remedies.

Navarre, J. "Incubation as fostering the creative process." *The gifted child quarterly*, 1979, *23*(4), 792–800.

Otto, H.A. "The potential of people." *Elementary school guidance and counseling*, 1979, *14*(2), 92–96. Offers action-oriented concepts useful to guidance counselors in the elementary schools.

Shallcross, D. *Teaching creative behavior.* Buffalo, N.Y.: Bearly Limited, 1985. A concise, well-written resource book for teachers who are concerned with fostering creativity and developing self-confidence and sensitivity among students.

Simple gifts: The education of the gifted, and creative. A book of readings. Madison: University of Wisconsin, 1978. Contains twenty articles from twelve telecasts on education for promoting creativity.

Torrance, E.P., and Torrance, J.P. *Is creativity teachable?* Bloomington, Ill.: Phi Delta Kappa Educational Foundation, 1973. Based on their long experience in designing educational experiences, the authors explain their convictions about the best ways to cultivate creativity.

Treffinger, D., Hohn, R., and Feldhusen, J. *Reach each you teach.* East Aurora, N.Y.: United Disseminators of Knowledge, 1983. Practical guidelines and resources for designing curriculum and individualized units. Uses a planning matrix to relate specific content to thinking processes.

Wallach, M.A., and Kogan, N. *Creativity and intelligence in children's thinking.* New Brunswick, N.J.: TRANS-action, 1967. This is one of the most seminal studies of creativity in the childhood years ever produced. The methods used, as well as their analysis, opened many doors for creativity researchers.

Training for the Integration of Brain Hemisphere Functions

Barr-Johnson, V. "Challenging the right side of the brain." *The creative child and adult quarterly,* 1982, *VII*(4), 218–225. Describes techniques used to stimulate "right-brained" thought and their effect on performance.

Edwards, B. *Drawing on the right side of the brain.* Los Angeles: J.P. Tarcher, 1979. Uses many imaginative techniques to foster "right-brained" approach to art.

Sensory Awareness

Van Matre, S. Acclimatizing. Martinsville, Ind.: American Camping Association, 1975. See also *Acclimatization,* 1972, by the same author and publishers.

Adult Modeling

Glover, J.A. *Becoming a more creative person.* Englewood Cliffs, N.J.: Prentice-Hall, 1980. Has a chapter devoted to family interactions with many good suggestions.

Rejskind, F.G. "Autonomy and creativity in children." *Journal of creative behavior,* 1982, *15*,(1), 58–67. Explores the role of parents in developing the child's independence from them.

Torrance, E.P. *Creativity.* Washington, D.C.: National Education Association, 1963. One of the earliest publications to inform teachers how they can organize their classrooms to foster creativity in their students. This booklet may be obtained inexpensively by writing the NEA. Most of the ideas may be readily adapted by parents too.

Training Programs

These are programs specifically designed to enhance the creative abilities of elementary aged students.

Covington, M.V., Crutchfield, R., Davies, L., and Olten, R.M. *The productive thinking program: A course in learning to think.* Columbus, Ohio: Merill, 1974.

The Creative Problem Solving Program. Described in Noller, R.B., Parnes, S.J., and

Biondi, A.M., *Creative actionbook*. New York: Scribner's, 1976, and Parnes, S.J., Noller, R.B., and Biondi, A.M. *Guide to creative action*. New York: Scribner's, 1977. (Also used with older individuals.)

Davis, G.A., and Houtman, S.E. *Thinking creatively: A guide to training imagination*. Madison: University of Wisconsin, 1968.

Feldhusen, J.F., Treffinger, D.J., and Bahlke, S.J., "Developing creative thinking: The Purdue creativity training program." *Journal of creative behavior*, 1970, *4*, 85–90. Also described in Feldhusen, J.F., Speedie, S.M., and Treffinger, D.J. "The Purdue creative thinking program: Research and evaluation." *National society for performance an instruction journal*, 1971, *10*, 5–9.

Khatena, J. "Identification and stimulation of creative imagination imagery." *Journal of creative behavior*, 1978, *12*, 30–38.

Myers, R.E., and Torrance, E.P. The *Imagi/craft* and *Ideabooks* Series, Boston: Ginn, 1964-1965.

Renzulli, J. *The enrichment triad method*. Wethersfield, Conn.: Creative Learning Press, 1976.

Renzulli, J., and Callahan, C. *New directions in Creativity: Mark I, II, and III*. New York: Harper and Row, 1973.

Each of the above-listed programs is reviewed in Feldhusen, J.F., and Clinkenbeard, P.R. "Creativity instructional materials: A review of research." *Journal of creative behavior*, 1986, *20*(3), 153–182. This work is the best and most up-to-date review available at present. If only one work can be read on this topic, this is the one. Includes an extensive bibliography. In their reviews of the above-listed programs, the authors stress that each has strengths and weaknesses and that evaluating the effectiveness of each is a complex task.

Another good, but older, review can be found in Mansfield, R.S., Busse, T.V., and Krepelka, E.J., "The effectiveness of creativity training, *Review of educational research*, 1978, *48*, 517–536. See also Rose, L.H., and Hsin-Tai, L., "A meta-analysis of long-term creativity training programs." *Journal of creative behavior*, 1984, *18*(1), 11–22.

Creative Problem Solving

An extensive program designed to help teachers and others cultivate creativity in students is Isaksen, S.G., and Treffinger, D.J., *Creative problem solving: The basic course*. Honeoye, N.Y.: Center for Creative Learning, 1985. It is listed separately here because, since this particular approach has become quite popular, there are now numerous programs and books that use and extend it. Among the best of them are the following:

Draze, D. *Options: A guide to creative decision-making*. San Luis Obispo, Calif.: Dandy Lion, 1982. An extensive collection of practical activities to help balance creative thinking and critical decision-making skills in problem solving. Many reproducibles.

Draze, D. *Primarily problem solving.* San Luis Obispo, Calif.: Dandy Lion, 1986. Motivating, easy-to-use guide that provides creative problem solving practice activities for children.

Duling, G. *Creative problem solving for an eency-weency spider.* East Aurora, N.Y.: United Disseminators of Knowledge, 1985a. Helps children in the primary grades learn the basic steps of creative problem solving using a familiar children's song and related activities.

Duling, G. *Creative problem solving for the 4th little pig.* East Aurora, N.Y.: United Disseminators of Knowledge, 1985b. Children will relate easily to this extension of the familiar story, "The Three Little Pigs."

Standish, B. *Creativity for kids* (series). East Aurora, N.Y.: United Disseminators of Knowledge, 1985.

. . . *Through word play.* A unique approach to bring creative thinking into your reading and language arts program.

. . . *Through word analysis.* Raise creative thinking by teaching word analysis skills.

. . . *Through vocabulary development.* Uses creative thinking to strengthen and improve vocabulary development.

. . . *Through writing.* New and different activities to help students apply creative thinking in writing.

Eberle, B. *Help! In solving problems creatively at home and school.* Carthage, Ill.: Good Apple, 1984. Parents and teachers can use this brief booklet to learn, enjoy, and apply the basics of creative problem solving.

Eberle, B. *Scamper.* East Aurora, N.Y.: United Disseminators of Knowledge, 1977. A book of imagination games to teach students to use the SCAMPER checklist to generate new ideas.

Eberle, B. *Scamper on.* East Aurora, N.Y.: United Disseminators of Knowledge, 1984. A follow-up to the original SCAMPER book, this collection includes new and more sophisticated games.

Eberle, B., and Stanish, B. *CPS for kids.* East Aurora, N.Y.: United Disseminators of Knowledge, 1985. An excellent resource for teaching students the stages of the creative problem-solving process.

Noller, Ruth B. *Scratching the surface of creative problem solving.* East Aurora, N.Y.: United Disseminators of Knowledge, 1977. A "bird's eye view" of the CPS process.

Noller, R.B., Heintz, D., and Blaeuer, D. *Creative problem solving in mathematics.* East Aurora, N.Y.: United Disseminators of Knowledge, 1978. This book asks you to assume an attitude of imagination and resourcefulness and to sweep away some "cobwebs" that might blur your mathematical vision.

Ricci, J. and Treffinger, D.J. *Adventures in creative thinking.* East Aurora, N.Y.: United Disseminators of Knowledge, 1982. Activities to promote creative thinking and problem solving at home or in school. Helps to link home and school as a partnership for developing students' thinking skills.

Stanish, B., and Eberle, B. *Be a problem solver.* East Aurora, N.Y.: United Disseminators of Knowledge, 1984. Provides posters to use as starting points for practicing CPS with students.

Youth (Twelve to Eighteen Years Old)

General

Baroody, A., Brumley, S., Hocevar, D., and Ripple, R.E. "Influencing teachers' attitudes about creativity." *Child study journal*, 7, 1–7, 1976.

Gowan, J.C., and Olson, M. "The society which maximizes creativity." *The national/state leadership training institute on the gifted and the talented*, 1980, *1*, 113–125. Focuses on cultural and societal influences on the development of "youthful genius."

Henegar, L.E. "Nurturing the creative promise in gifted disadvantaged youth." *Journal of creative behavior*, 1984, *18*(2), 109–115. The author believes that mainstream education has discriminated against disadvantaged youth, and offers many suggestions on how this problem might be rectified.

Human quest. San Luis Obispo, Calif.: Dandy Lion, 1986. Fourteen areas of human development and expression are explored, including invention, communication, transformation, and others, with challenging exercises and projects.

Parnes, S. *Making the point about creativity*. Buffalo, N.Y.: Bearly Limited, 1981. A practical, personal guide to help you discover the excitement, enjoyment, and effectiveness of creative problem solving.

Standish, B. *Mindglow*. Carthage, Ill.: Good Apple, 1986. Activities to stimulate and celebrate creativity! Each activity has a full-page, thought-provoking photograph, a philosophical statement, and activities with suggestions for follow-up or extension.

Treffinger, D.J., Ripple, R.E., and Dacey, J.S. "Teachers' attitudes about creativity." *Journal of creative behavior*, 1968, *2*(4), 242–248. Examines an approach to improving teachers' valuing of creative behavior, so that they become more likely to foster it in their students.

Williams, A.J., and Poole, M.E. "The school experience of talented adolescents." *The creative child and adult quarterly*, 1981, *4*, 103–108. Compares approaches to cultivating creativity to those for cultivating ability and personality.

Problem Finding

Getzels, J.W., and Csikszentmihalyi, M. "From problem solving to problem finding." In Taylor, I.A., and Getzels, J.W., Eds., *Perspective in creativity*. Chicago: Aldine, 1975. In their ground-breaking longitudinal study of artists from the years in art school to their careers several years later, these researchers found that the ability to *find* problems is as vital to their success as problem *solving*. The article offers a number of means to build problem-finding skills.

Use of Microcomputers

Tisone, J.M., and Wismar, B.L. "Microcomputers: How can they be used to enhance creative development?" *Journal of creative behavior*, 1985, *19*(2), 97–103. This article encourages teachers to build their own computer courseware for their classes. "These programs will also facilitate, encourage, and motivate students to take a more active role in their own creative development" (p. 103).

Writing Imaginatively

Glover, J.A. *Becoming a more creative person*. Englewood Cliffs, N.J.: Prentice-Hall, 1980. Contains a chapter that gives a wide variety of ideas on encouraging creative writing.

Imagination unlimited. Cleveland: Cleveland Public Schools, 1969. A guide for the recombination of ideas into something new. It emphasizes avoiding obstacles such as the fear of being different and inadequate motivation.

Terrell, D.L. "The TCB in clinical-forensic psychological evaluation: A case study of exceptionality." *Journal of non-white concerns*, 1982, *10*, 64–72. Argues that the writing test known as Themes Concerning Blacks (TCB), normally used as a projective instrument, often elicits highly creative responses from blacks. The author claims that responses reflect insightful feelings and self-knowledge of the creative black.

Training for the Integration of Brain Hemisphere Functions

Edwards, B. *Drawing on the right side of the brain*. Los Angeles: J.P. Tarcher, 1979. Uses numerous imaginative techniques to foster a right-brained approach to art. An example is inverted drawing. This approach attempts to "force the cognitive shift from the dominant left-hemisphere mode to the subdominant right-hemisphere mode" (p. 53). A series of specific instructions are given for attempting to copy a picture that is presented to the drawer upside down. Because an interpretation of the picture is allegedly suppressed by its inversion, the right side of the brain takes over and a much better copy is made.

Remote Association/Divergent Thinking

Belcher, T.L. "Modeling original divergent responses: An initial investigation." *Journal of educational psychology*, 1975, *17*, 351–358. Investigates the effects of modeling originality and fluency of ideas on the behaviors of observers.

Evans, R.G., and Forbach, G.B. "Facilitation of performance on a divergent measure of creativity: A closer look at instructions to "be creative." *Applied psychological measurement*, 1983, *7*, 181–187. Examines the role of instructions on the production of divergent ideas.

Mednick, S.A. "The associative basis of the creative process." *Psychological review,* 1962, *69,* 220–227, 232. Starting with a clear-cut theory, Mednick set out to test it with well-designed research. An example of this system is *practicing for a test.* One of the best ways, it appears, to improve abilities is to practice taking tests of creativity. In fact, dreaming up your own version of some of these tests, and particularly the Remote Associates Test, may be one of the best methods. (See chapters 5 and 7 for more on this test.) Anything that encourages people to "dig deeper" for more, and for more remote, ideas is a step in the right direction.

Facilitating Imagery

Sheehan, P.W., McConkey, K.M., and Law, H.G. "Imagery facilitation and performance on the creative imagination scale." *Journal of mental imagery,* 1978, *2,* 265–274. Argues that numerous unusual situations, such as anesthesia, hallucination, and age regression can be effective in eliciting imaginative images. Considers other approaches for facilitating vivid imagery.

Adulthood

General

Albrecht, K. *Brain building: Easy games to develop your problem-solving skills.* Englewood Cliffs, N.J.: Prentice-Hall, 1984. See also Albrecht, K., *Brain power: Learn to improve your thinking skills.* Englewood Cliffs, N.J.: Prentice-Hall, 1980. Deals not only with positive aspects of successful thinking but also with the fears of success that impede many people.

Clinton, B.J., and Torrance, E.P. "S.E.A.M.: A training program for developing problem identifcation skills." *Journal of creative behavior,* 1986, *20,*(2) 77–80. Focuses on helping those in supervisory positions deal with the meanings of problem identification.

Davis, G.A. *Creativity is forever.* Dubuque, Iowa: Kendall-Hunt, 1986. A valuable overview of many general concepts.

Hanks, K., and Parry, J. *Wake up your creative genius.* Los Altos, Calif.: Kauffman, 1981. Designed to maximize the number of bright ideas that hit their target.

Jones, M. *Getting high on creativity.* New York: R. Rosen Press, 1982. A lighter approach.

MacKinnon, D.T. *In search of human effectiveness.* Buffalo, N.Y.: Creative Education Foundation, 1978. MacKinnon is well known in the field for his research on the personality characteristics of the highly creative. In this insightful book, he discusses his ideas on "transliminal experience," the conflict between theoretical and aesthetic values, "personal soundness," and liberation and breadth of experience. ·

Patterson, B.H. "Creativity and androgogy: A boon for adult learners." *Journal of creative behavior*, 1986, *20*(2), 99–109. Helpful in dealing with concerns of the elderly.

Torrance, E.P. *The search for satori and creativity.* Buffalo, N.Y.: Creative Education Foundation, 1979. The most prolific writer on the topic, and in some ways the absolute best. This book represents Torrance's furthest venture in his quest for new approaches to creativity. It was written while he was a fellow of the Japan Society for the Promotion of Science, and a visiting professor at Osaka City University. He explains the concept of *satori:* "To attain expertness in any worthwhile skill, Japanese commonly expect that it will require many years of intensive training and practice. They regard short cuts as harmful. In 'expertness,' the highest point attainable is 'satori,' a sudden flash of enlightenment" (p. ix). This book is replete with ideas for cultivation, covering such new topics as "highlighting the essence," combination and synthesis, extending the boundaries, and rich and colorful visualization.

von Oech, R. *A kick in the seat of the pants.* New York: Harper and Row, 1986. See also von Oech, R., *A whack on the side of the head.* New York: Warner Books, 1983. Among the most enjoyable and easy to read of the general how-to books.

Whimby, A., and Lockhead, J. *Problem solving and comprehension.* Hillsdale, N.J.: Erlbaum, 1986.

Hypnosis

Bowers, P.G. "Effect of hypnosis and suggestions of reduced defensiveness on creativity test performance." *Journal of personality*, 1967, *35*, 311–322. This study demonstrated that "hypnosis and instructions were 'defense-reducing' techniques," which in turn increased scores on creativity tests.

Meditation

Cowger, E.L., Jr. and Torrance, E.P. "Further examination of the quality of changes in creative functioning resulting from meditation (Zazen) training." *The creative child and adult quarterly*, 1982, *VII*, (4), 211–217. Describes the effects of meditation on performance on a number of measures of creativity.

Gowan, J.C. "The facilitation of creativity through meditational procedures." *Journal of creative behavior*, 1978, *12*, 156–160. Argues the case that transcendental mediation is effective in decreasing anxiety, controlling stress, promoting psychological openness, and thus in fostering creativity.

Cultivating the Incubation Process

Olton, R.M., and Johnson, D.M. "Mechanisms of incubation in creative problem solving. *American journal of psychology*, 1976, *89*, 617–630. Describes such techniques as set breaking, elimination of fatigue, stress reduction, unconscious mental work, and facilitating the effects of incidental and selective forgetting.

Vance, M. *Creative thinking*. Chicago: Nightingale-Conant, 1982. Director of "idea and people development" at the Walt Disney company, Vance offers many techniques for fostering the deeper aspects of creativity. He bases his approach on his life cycle theory: unconscious incompetence; conscious incompetence; conscious competence; and unconscious competence.

Self-management

Glover, J.A. *Becoming a more creative person*. Englewood Cliffs, N.J.: Prentice-Hall/Spectrum, 1980. This book advocates "self-management" through the personal application of B.F. Skinner's behavior modification techniques. For example, the chart might show the number of times per day you tried to use an imaginative word in your conversation rather than an ordinary one. If you reach a previously set goal, such as the use of ten imaginative words a day for five straight days, you can allow yourself to have "a special treat—things you wouldn't ordinarily have—as reinforcing consequences for the performance of your goal behavior, be they edible goodies, special activities, or whatever" (p. 84).

Producing Remote Associations

Gall, M., and Mendelsohn, G.A. "Effects of facilitating techniques and subject-experimenter interaction on creative problem solving." *Journal of personality and social psychology*, 1967, 5, 211–216. The results of this study raise doubts about the efficacy of incubation in covergent solutions and point to the importance of social psychological variables, at least for females.

Gordon, W.J.J. "On being explicit about the creative process." *Journal of creative behavior*, 1972, 6, 295–300. See also *Synectics: The development of creative capacity*. Cambridge, Mass.: Synectics Education Press, 1970, and *The metaphorical way of learning and knowing: Applying Synectics to sensitivity and learning situations*. Cambridge, Mass.: Porpoise Books, 1973. The founder of a technique known as synectics, Gordon has made many contributions to education and management science. He is a proponent of "making the strange familiar," and "making the familiar strange." The method is the opposite of those described above, in that he emphasizes the *dissociation* between things. The role of metaphor (see chapter 5) is vital in his approach. He also deemphasizes roles of inspiration and being a "genius," believing that everyone can greatly improve his or her creative abilities (see chapter 6).

Koestler, A. *The act of creation*. New York: Macmillan, 1964. Koestler argues that creations come about through the association of two frames of references that are normally seen as incompatible. The leap from one frame of reference to another often causes us to feel a sudden tension, which be relieved only by crying or laughing (or occasionally both). For example, this is his explanation for the way humor works. Jokes about the clergy and sexuality abound, because we normally see the two as incongruous. Koestler advocates approaching problems with the intention of producing such unusual associations.

Osborn, A.F. *Applied imagination.* (3rd ed.). New York: Scribner's, 1963. The "grand old man" of creative problem-solving techniques, Osborne pioneered group production of imaginative associations through the use of brainstorming. Two basic principles of brainstorming are: don't edit your own ideas—even if they are silly, express them; and never criticize anyone else's ideas—silly thoughts often generate creative associations (see chapter 6).

Rothenberg, A. "Homospatial thinking in creativity." *Archives of general psychiatry,* 1976, *33,* 17–26. An extension of the ideas presented in the Osborn article.

Rothenberg, A. "The process of Janusial thinking in creativity." *Archives of general psychiatry,* 1971, *24,* 195–205. Janus was the Roman god with two faces. Rothenberg believes that much of creative thought involves " 'oppositional thinking'— the capacity to conceive and utilize two or more opposite or contradictory ideas, concepts, or images *simultaneously.*" It is possible through practice, he believes, to produce high-quality associations through this cognitive ability.

Sarnoff, S.A. "The associative basis of the creative process." *Psychological review,* 1962, *69,* 220–227. This seminal work is discussed in detail in chapter 5.

Skinner, B.F. "A lecture on 'having' a poem." *Cumulative record: A selection of papers* (3rd ed.). Englewood Cliffs, N.J.: Prentice-Hall, 1972; and "A behavioral model of creation." In Rothenberg, A., and Hausman, C.R. (Eds.), *The creativity question.* Durham, N.C.: Duke University Press, 1976. No bibliography on association would be complete without the ideas of this well-known psychologist.

Training for the Integration of Brain Hemisphere Functions

de Bono, E. *Lateral thinking: Creativity step by step.* New York: Harper and Row, 1970. See also de Bono, E., *New think.* New York: Avon, 1971, and *The CORT thinking skills program,* New York: Pergamon Press, 1984. Emphasizes methods called the "structural association technique of reversal" and the "random association technique."

Herman, N. "The creative brain." *Training and development journal,* October, 1981, 11.16. Herman explains his six stages of problem solving and the side of the brain that probably dominates each. He offers solid suggestions for facilitating the process.

Creative Leadership/Management

Burgelman, R.A., and Sayles, L.R. *Inside corporate innovation: Strategy, structure, and managerial skills.* New York: Free Press, 1986.

Fiene, J.F. "Elements of leadership which impede creativity." *Creative child and adult quarterly,* 1979, *4,* 37.

Hanson, H.L. *Managing creative assets.* Edina, Minn.: Chiefton, 1985.

Johne, F.A. *Industrial product innovation.* New York: Nichols, 1985.

Keil, J.M. *The creative mystique: How to manage it, nurture it, and make it pay.* New York: Wiley, 1985.

Kuhn, R.L. (Ed.). *Frontiers in creative and innovative management.* Cambridge, Mass.: Ballinger, 1986.

Parnes, S.J. *A new generation of leadership.* Los Angeles: National/State Leadership Training Institute of the Gifted and Talented, 1977. Emphasizes creativity in leadership roles.

Raudsepp, E. "Establishing a creative climate." *Training and development journal,* April, 1987, 49–53. Offers "two dozen ways to turn on your organization's light bulbs."

Ray, M. *Creativity in business.* Garden City, N.Y.: Doubleday, 1986.

Rickards, T. *Stimulating innovation: A systems approach.* New York: St. Martin's Press, 1985.

Mentoring

Noller, R.B. *Mentoring: An annotated bibliography.* Buffalo, N.Y.: Bearly Limited, 1983; and Frey, B.A., and Noller, R.B., "Mentoring: A legacy of success." *Journal of creative behavior, 1983, 17,*(1), 60–64. Noller is an acknowledged leader in the effort to promote mentoring in a variety of settings, for children as well as for adults.

Rivchun, S.B. "Be a mentor and leave a lasting legacy." *Association management,* August 1980, *32,*(8), 71–74. Discusses motivations for mentoring.

Glossary

Numbers in parentheses indicate the chapter in which the word or phrase will be found.

ACQUIESCING PERSONALITY (3): One of Rank's three personality types. A person who automatically (and usually subconsciously) makes sure that his or her choices coincide with those of authority figures in order to avoid their disapproval. See *authoritarianism*.

ANALYTIC THINKING (1): One of the mental processes described by Jackson and Messick in their theory of creativity. Refers to the ability to solve problems logically.

ANDROGYNY (2): Refers to those persons who are found to have higher than average male *and* female elements in the personalities. They are more likely to behave in a way appropriate to the situation, regardless of their gender. One of eight essential personality characteristics of the creative person.

ANIMA (9): The feminine nature of all persons, including males, according to Jung.

ANIMUS (9): The masculine nature of all persons, including females, according to Jung.

APPROPRIATENESS (1): The second characteristic of a creative product in Jackson and Messick's theory. Refers to the correctness or goodness of the product, within a particular context.

APRAXIA (4): The inability to perform physical functions that require hand-eye coordination, such as combing one's hair.

ARMCHAIR SPECULATION (5): The antiquated approach to research that involved making guesses on the basis of one's own personal experience, as opposed to empirical research.

ASKING QUESTIONS TEST (2): Torrance's test of verbal creativity.

ASSOCIATIONISM (5): The theory that ideas, especially creative ideas, come not from carefully laid-out mental plans but from a series of trial-and-error efforts to solve a problem

ASYMMETRY (2): Lack of balance. An aspect of preference for disorder, which is one of eight essential personality characteristics of the creative person.

AUTHORITARIANISM (6): Having a strong sense of one's place in society's power structure; knowing "who's above you and who's below you" in terms of control.

BEM SEX ROLE INVENTORY (7): A measure of androgyny.

BICAMERAL MIND (4): The ancient idea that the mind is split into two "chambers": one part into which the gods or the "muse" placed ideas, and one part from which these ideas were put into words.

BIPOLAR (8): Items on a scale are called unipolar because they are rated from one extreme to the other—that is, they have two poles.

BRAINSTORMING (6): Osborn's technique for group problem solving.

CASE STUDY APPROACH (5): An intense study of the mental functioning (and often of other facets) of the creative person. As opposed to the empirical methods of research that gather less data about a group of people.

CEREBRAL LOCALIZATION (4): The concept that the various forms of thought, sensation, and action are located in specific centers of the brain.

COGNITION (6): One of Guilford's five mental operations. Calls for discovery, rediscovery, or recognition.

COGNITIVE MOBILITY (5): The ability to switch from lower, more unconscious mental processes to higher, more conscious processes, and back again, depending on the demands of a problem.

COGNITIVE PHENOTYPE (4): One of five aspects of Findlay and Lumsden's theory of creativity. Refers to the individual's genetically and environmentally determined manner of thinking.

COGNITIVE STYLE (5): Refers to the manner of an individual's thinking. Examples of it are field dependence versus independence and cognitive mobility.

COLLECTIVE UNCONSCIOUS (3): Vague memories of the experiences of the whole human race, stored in everyone's unconscious mind.

COMPENSATORY THEORY (3): Adler's idea that the creative act is primarily an attempt to compensate for some perceived inferiority.

COMPLEX (8): Besemer and O'Quin's term for one of the criteria of their elaboration and synthesis category.

COMPLEXITY (2): Having many facets. An aspect of preference for disorder, which is one of eight essential personality characteristics of the creative person.

CONDENSATION (1): The fourth criterion for the creative product, according to Jackson and Messick's theory of creativity, involves the unification of complex information, expressed in a highly condensed form.

CONSTRAINTS (1): The way in which transformation is judged, in Jackson and Messick's theory of creativity. Refers to rules within which an effort must be confined.

CONTEXT (1): The appropriateness of a product is judged in terms of its context—that is, the setting in which the product is found.

CONVERGENT THINKING (6): One of Guilford's five mental operations. Calls for thinking that results in the right answer to a question that can only have one correct answer.

CREATIVE PERSONALITY (3): One of Rank's three personality types. A person capable of "being a minority of one" and therefore of producing creative innovations.

CREATIVE PRODUCT ANALYSIS MATRIX (8): Besemer and Treffinger's name for their model of the three categories that make up a creative product.

CREATIVITY OF THE JEWISH PEOPLE (11): Arieti asserts that the amazingly high level of Jewish creativity in the twentieth century results from ways in which this group fosters his concept of the "creativogenic society."

CREATIVITY QUESTIONNAIRE (7): A test of attitudes toward one's own creative ability.

CREATIVITY-RELEVANT SKILLS (11): One of Amabile's three components of creativity. Refers to a person's strategies or dispositions that facilitate the creative process.

CREATIVOGENIC SOCIETY (11): Arieti's concept of a society that naturally cultivates creativity. He lists nine features of such a society.

CRITERION PROBLEM (7): A test that attempts to measure valid dimensions of a problem may do so inadequately.

CRITICAL PERIOD HYPOTHESIS (9): There are peak periods in life when various human traits are best able to develop. In fact, for some traits such as speaking, if nurturance is unavailable, the trait does not develop at all.

CROSS-SECTIONAL APPROACH (9): Studying the creative productivity of groups of people of different ages.

DACEY'S THEORY (9): Suggests that there are six periods of life, roughly the same for males and females, during which creativity may most readily be cultivated.

DECREMENTAL MODEL (9): Holds that creative change is curvilinear—that is, ability increases through childhood, youth, and early adulthood, then levels out in middle adulthood, and decreases with advancing old age.

DEFENSE MECHANISMS (3): Unconscious mental mechanisms that control behavior by preventing awareness of unpleasant or unacceptable images of the self (see discussion in chapter 3 in the section on Freud).

DELAY OF GRATIFICATION (2): The willingness to work long and hard at a project because the final reward will be great. One of eight essential personality characteristics of the creative person.

DIMENSIONALITY PROBLEM (7): The problem that a test that is supposed to measure some trait may only measure some (or none) of the factors that actually make up that trait.

DIRECT ANALOGY (6): A method within the synectics approach to problem solving.

DIRECT OBSERVATION OF CREATIVE PERFORMANCE (7): A technique that attempts to measure a person's creative ability by watching how that person reacts in a problem situation.

DIVERGENT THINKING (6): One of Guilford's five mental operations. Calls for thinking in different directions, searching for a variety of answers to questions that can have several answers.

DOMAIN-RELEVANT SKILLS (11): One of Amabile's three components of creativity. Refers to a person's talent or expertise.

DUNCKER'S TUMOR PROBLEM (6): Duncker posed the problem of destroying a stomach tumor without hurting the surrounding tissue. Two crossed X ray beams achieve it.

EGO-CONTROL (5): The extent to which a person can express or contain impulses, feelings, and desires.

EGO-RESILIENCY (5): The ability of a person to modify his or her level of ego-control to meet the demands of the situation.

ELABORATION AND SYNTHESIS (8): One of Besemer and Treffinger's three categories that make up a creative product. Refers to the degree to which the product "combines unlike elements into a refined, developed, coherent whole."

ELEGANT (8): Besemer and O'Quin's term for one of the criteria of their elaboration and synthesis category.

ENDOCEPT (3): A primitive organization in the mind of past experiences, perception, memory traces, and images of things and movements.

EPICYCLICAL THEORY (11): Refers to Gray's theory that there are three types of periods that are repeated throughout history: social, economic, and political.

EUREKA PHENOMENON (4): From the Greek story about Archimedes who, when he solved a vexing problem, ran through the streets naked crying, "Eureka!" meaning "I have found it!"

EVALUATION (6): One of Guilford's five mental operations. Calls for reaching decisions about the accuracy, goodness, or suitability of information.

EXPERIENTIAL LISTINGS (7): A technique that attempts to measure a person's creative ability by asking that person to list past achievements.

FANTASY ANALOGY (6): A method within the synectics approach to problem solving.

FIELD DEPENDENCE/INDEPENDENCE (6): *Independence* refers to the ability to look at a whole picture or problem, break it into its parts, and then attend to the more relevant parts while blocking out the less relevant. *Dependence* is the inability to do this.

FIGURAL CONTENT (10): One of four types of the contents of the mind, according to Guilford. Creative examples include sculpture, architecture, and cabinet making.

FLEXIBILITY (2): The capacity to see the whole situation, without becoming fixated on only one significant part of it. One of eight essential personality characteristics of the creative person.

FLEXIBLE (1): One of the personality traits described by Jackson and Messick in their creativity theory. Refers to someone who is less rigid, less neurotic, and less anxious than most.

FREE ASSOCIATION (5): Freud's concept that ideas in the unconscious mind can be discovered when a person responds to a word by saying whatever other word comes to mind. Based on the notion that ideas in the conscious mind are linked to those in the unconscious mind by threads of similarity. Used as a method to foster creative thoughts.

FULLY FUNCTIONING PERSON (3): Rogers's term for a person in excellent psychological health, from whom creativity naturally emerges.

FUNCTIONAL FIXITY (2): The belief that objects have only one, well-established purpose. One of eight essential personality characteristics of the creative person.

FUNCTIONAL FREEDOM (2): The ability to imagine many uses for an object that is usually seen as having only one purpose; to avoid functional fixity. One of eight essential personality characteristics of the creative person.

GENOTYPE (4): One of five aspects of Findlay and Lumsden's theory of creativity. Refers to the individual's genetic constitution.

GERMINAL (8): Besemer and O'Quin's term for one of the criteria of their novelty category.

GESTALT (5): A German word, used in Wertheimer's theory of creativity, which means "pattern or form."

GOOD STUDENT SYNDROME (7): Some students try so hard to get good grades that they lose their adventurous imagination.

HEMISPHERICALITY (4): The apparent specialization of each of the hemispheres of the brain.

HIERARCHY OF NEEDS (3): Maslow's ascending list of the needs possessed by every human being.

HUMANIST SCHOOL OF CREATIVE DEVELOPMENT (9): Argues that under the right circumstances, creative ability can surge at any point in the life span.

IDEA-GENERATION TEST (7): Duncker's test of functional freedom.

IDEAL (6): Bransford and Stein's overall approach to problem solving.

ILLUMINATION (5): The third of Wallas's four stages in the creative process. The idea, solution, or new relationship emerges and all the facts fall into place.

INCUBATION (5): The second of Wallas's four stages in the creative process. The problem is ignored consciously, so that the unconscious mind may work on it.

INGENUITY TEST (4): A multiple choice test of ingenuity, but correct ideas that may tap the extent of coordination between the two hemispheres of the brain.

INNOVATION HIERARCHY OF FINDLAY AND LUMSDEN (4): Describes the interactions among the five aspects of Findlay and Lumsden's theory of creativity.

INTERNAL RELIABILITY (2): A measure of test reliability, which involves the extent to which test takers get about the same score on one part of the measure as they do on another.

INTERSCORER RELIABILITY (2): A measure of test reliability, which involves the extent to which test takers get about the same score no matter who is scoring the test.

INTRINSIC MOTIVATION PRINCIPLE (11): "When people are primarily motivated by their own interest in and enjoyment of" some activity, they are most likely to be creative.

INTUITION (1): One of the mental processes described by Jackson and Messick in their theory of creativity. Refers to the ability to solve problems through unconscious processes.

INVENTIVLEVEL (8): A definition of creative effort used by the U.S. Patent Office.

LATERAL DOMINANCE (4,10): The tendency of all persons to be dominated by one or the other hemisphere of their brains. There is a "crossover" effect, so that right-handed people are dominated by the left hemi-sphere, and vice versa.

LINKING THESIS (4): Findlay and Lumsden's theory that "creative activity is an evolved strategy in which rules of cognitive development act through a joint inheritance of genetic and cultural information."

LOGICAL (8): Besemer and O'Quin's term for one of the criteria of their resolution category.

LONGITUDINAL APPROACH (9): Studying the achievements of a group of people from the time they are all of one age to the time they are another. Several measurements of their achievements (or other traits) may be taken across the time span.

MACRONEURON (9): The basic building block of the brain. Macroneuronal circuits are the major pathways of thought, which are fixed at the moment of conception through genetic inheritance.

MEDIATION (5): One of Mednick's three methods through which remote associations may be achieved. Two ideas with no association between them may nevertheless be brought into mental juxtaposition through their association with a third element.

MEMORY (6): One of Guilford's five mental operations. Calls for retention of what is cognized.

METAPHOR (5,11): Used as a way to stimulate creative thinking.

MICRONEURON (9): The center of the tiny switching circuits that connect macroneural pathways. Apparently can be affected by the environment throughout the first year and a half of life.

MIDCOURSE CORRECTION (9): A period of life during which the individual tries to resolve old issues and makes changes commensurate with a new plan for the rest of his or her life. Synonymous with *midlife crisis*.

MIDLIFE CRISIS (9): A period of life during which the individual tries to resolve old issues and makes changes commensurate with a new plan for the rest of his or her life. Synonymous with *midcourse correction*.

MINIMAL BRAIN DAMAGE (4): The slight brain damage that occurs during birth, usually in passage through the birth canal.

MULTIPLE DOUBLE TECHNIQUE (6): Used as part of Torrance's method for problem solving.

NEUROTIC PERSONALITY (3): One of Rank's three personality types. A person who is forever uncertain about what will happen, because of inconsistent parenting. Often develops phobias.

NORMS (1): A measure of what is usually the case in a particular situation.

NOVELTY (8): One of Besemer and Treffinger's three categories that make up a creative product. Refers to the extent of the product's newness.

OPEN-MINDEDNESS (1): One of four mental traits described by Jackson and Messick in their creativity theory. Refers to the ability to receive new information without prejudice.

ORGANIC (8): Besemer and O'Quin's term for one of the criteria of their elaboration and synthesis category.

ORIGINAL (1): One of four personality characteristics described by Jackson and Messick in their creativity theory. Refers to being highly imaginative.

ORIGINAL (8): Besemer and O'Quin's term for one of the criteria of their novelty category.

PEAK EXPERIENCE (3): Maslow's concept of a momentary flash of insight that brings with it a great joy and gratitude for being alive.

PERCEPTUAL BLOCKS (6): Adam's term for problems that filter out creative thoughts.

PERSONAL ANALOGY (6): A method within the synectics approach to problem solving.

PHRENOLOGY (4): The theory (now in disrepute) that personality traits may be determined by examining the bumps on an individual's skull.

PLENUM (5): A space that is totally filled with objects.

POLARITIES (9): The source of deep division in men's (and perhaps women's) lives that must be dealt with in midlife. There are four: young/old, destruction/creation, masculinity/femininity, and attachment/separation.

PRECOCITY (7): Being able to do things that can usually only be done by someone who is older.

PREFERENCE FOR DISORDER (2): The trait of creative persons who like disorder, because they find it interesting to bring their own personal order to the situation. Includes complexity and asymmetry. One of eight essential personality characteristics of the creative person.

PREPARATION (5): The first of Wallas's four stages in the creative process. The problem is detected, and data relevant to it are identified.

PRODIGIOUSNESS (7): Being able to achieve things that are so rare as to inspire wonder. Refers to truly unusual achievements, as opposed to those that are unusual because of the person's age.

PSYCHIC CENSOR (6): Freud's term for the unconscious mental action that blocks unacceptable thoughts from awareness.

PSYCHOHISTORICAL APPROACH (9): Studying the biographies of highly creative persons to see when they were most and least productive.

PURDUE TEST (7): A test of figural creativity used in industry.

PSYCHOANALYTIC SCHOOL OF CREATIVE DEVELOPMENT (9): Argues that the first five years of life are critical; if creative attitudes and ability are not inculcated in the child during this period, there is no hope of them later.

RECURRENCE (5): Galton's concept that most thinking is merely a reiteration of earlier thoughts.

REFLECTION (1): One of the cognitive traits in Jackson and Messick's theory of creativity. Denotes a slow, cautious approach to problem solving.

REGRESSION (3): A defense mechanism. Reverting to behaviors that were previously successful when current behavior is unsuccessful.

REMOTE ASSOCIATES TEST (7): Mednick's test derived from his remote associates theory, which he claims is a general test of creativity.

RESOLUTION (8): One of Besemer and Treffinger's three categories that make up a creative product. Refers to the degree to which the product fulfills the needs of the problem situation.

RISK TAKING (2): The ability to take a moderate, reasonable risk to attain some creative purpose. One of eight essential personality characteristics of the creative person.

SAVORING (1): The fourth reflexive response of judges to a creative product, according to Jackson and Messick's theory of creativity. Refers to the desire to experience the product repeatedly.

SELF-TRANSCENDENCE (3): Fromm's term for the person in excellent psychological health, who is able to rise "beyond the passivity of existence into the realm of purposefulness and freedom."

SEMANTIC CONTENT (10): One of four types of the contents of the mind, according to Guilford. Creative examples include journalism and playwriting.

SENSITIVE (1): One of the personality traits Jackson and Messick describe in their theory of creativity. Refers to the ability to be aware of the existence of a problem before others are.

SERENDIPITY (5): One of Mednick's three methods through which remote associations may be achieved. Luck is involved, but so is adequate preparation.

SEX ROLE IDENTIFICATION (2): Differences between the two genders that result from societal dictates, rather than from permanent genetic differences.

SEX ROLE IDENTITY TEST (2): A test used to measure one's identity with the sex role of his or her gender.

SIMILARITY (5): One of Mednick's three methods through which remote associations may be achieved. There is some relationship between the two otherwise remote elements.

SOCIAL (OR BEHAVIORAL) CONTENT (10): One of four types of the contents of the mind, according to Guilford. Creative examples include psychology, teaching, and politics.

SOCIODRAMA (6): Torrance's method for problem solving.

SPONTANEITY (1): One of the cognitive traits in Jackson and Messick's theory of creativity. Denotes a carefree, risk-taking approach to problem solving.

STIMULATION (1): The third reflexive response of judges to a creative product, according the Jackson and Messick's theory of creativity. A feeling of being aroused by experiencing the product.

STIMULUS FREEDOM (2): The freedom to bend the rules in a situation that calls for it (in order to be creative), and to avoid assuming that rules exist where none are explicitly stated. One of eight essential personality characteristics of the creative person.

STORY-WRITING TEST (7): Test of verbal creativity.

STRUCTURE OF INTELLECT MODEL (6): Guilford's complex statistical theory that defines 120 aspects of intellectual functioning. See also *cognition, memory, convergent* and *divergent thinking, evaluation,* and *figural, symbolic, semantic,* and *social content.*

SUBLIMATION (3): A defense mechanism. When unable to fulfill one's sex drives, making up for it by being creative in some artistic way.

SUMMARY POWER (1): The way by which condensation is judged, according to Jackson and Messick's theory of creativity.

SUPRA-RATIONAL CREATIVITY (7): The highest type of creativity, which involves unusual levels of insight, intuition, and even revelation.

SURPRISE (1): The first of four reflexive reactions people typically have when they view a creative product.

SURPRISING (8): Besemer and O'Quin's term for one of the criteria of their novelty category.

SYMBOLIC ANALOGY (6): A method within the synectics approach to problem solving.

SYMBOLIC CONTENT (10): One of four types of the contents of the mind, according to Guilford. Creative examples include mathematics, music, and ballet.

SYNECTICS (6): Gordon's approach to problem solving.

TASK MOTIVATION (11): One of Amabile's three components of creativity. Refers to a person's intrinsically motivated state; the difference between what a person can and will do.

TEST-RETEST RELIABILITY (2): A measure of test reliability, which involves the extent to which test takers get consistent scores over several administrations of the test.

THREE COMPONENTS OF CREATIVITY (11): Amabile's componential theory of creativity, which includes domain-relevant skills, creativity-relevant skills, and task motivation.

TOLERANCE OF AMBIGUITY (2): Refers to the capacity for facing the unknown with a relatively high degree of confidence and lack of fear.

TOLERANCE OF INCONGRUITY (1): One of the mental traits described by Jackson and Messick in their creativity theory. Refers to the capacity for dealing confidently with strange and unexpected occurrences. Used interchangeably with *tolerance of ambiguity*.

TRANSFORMATION (1): The third product criterion in Jackson's and Messick's theory of creativity. Involves the capacity for reformulating a situation or field.

TWO-STRING TEST (2): Maier's test of functional freedom.

UNDERSTANDABLE (8): Besemer and O'Quin's term for one of the criteria of their elaboration and synthesis category.

UNIPOLAR (8): Items on a scale are called unipolar because they are rated from low to high—that is, they have one pole.

UNUSUALNESS (1): The first characteristic of a creative product in Jackson and Messick's theory. Refers to the rarity of a product, compared with norms.

USE OF METAPHOR (5): Calling attention to seemingly unsimilar things.

USEFUL (8): Besemer and O'Quin's term for one of the criteria of their resolution category.

VALIDITY (2): The extent to which a test really measures what it is supposed to measure.

VALUABLE (8): Besemer and O'Quin's term for one of the criteria of their resolution category.

VERIFICATION (5): The fourth of Wallas's four stages in the creative process. The idea is tested "against the cold reality of fact—does it work."

WATER JAR TEST (6): Luchin's test of functional freedom.

WELL-CRAFTED (8): Besemer and O'Quin's term for one of the criteria of their elaboration and synthesis category.

WORST-CASE ANALYSIS (6): Bransford and Stein's technique for problem solving.

YOGIC SPONGE POSITION (6): A technique for relaxing the psychic censor so that desirable unconscious thoughts may become conscious.

References

Adams, J. *Conceptual blockbusting* (3rd ed.). Reading, Mass.: Addison-Wesley, 1986.

Adler, A. Disintegration and restoration of optic recognition in visual agnosia. *Archives of neurology and psychiatry*, 1944, *51*, 243–259.

————. *A study of organ inferiority and its physical compensation*. New York: Nervous and Mental Diseases Publishing, 1917.

Adorno, T.W., Frenkel-Brunswick, E., Levinson, D.J., and Sanford, R.N. *The authoritarian personality*. New York: Harper, 1950.

Albrecht, K. *Brain building: Easy games to develop your problem-solving skills*. Englewood Cliffs, N.J.: Prentice-Hall, 1984.

————. *Brain power: Learn to improve your thinking skills*. Englewood Cliffs, N.J.: Prentice-Hall, 1980.

Alpaugh, P.K., and Birren, J.E. Variable affecting creative contributions across the adult life span. *Human development*, 1977, *20*, 240–248.

Alpaugh, P.K., Renner, V.J., and Birren, J.E. Age and creativity: Implications for education and teachers. *Educational gerontology*, 1976, *I*, 17–40.

Altman, J. Postnatal growth and differentiation of the mammalian brain with implications for a morphological theory of memory. In G.C. Quarton (Ed.), *The neurosciences: A study program*. New York: Rockefeller University Press, 1967, 723–743.

Amabile, T.M. *The social psychology of creativity*. New York: Springer-Verlag, 1983a.

————. Social psychology of creativity: A componential conceptualization. *Journal of personality and social psychology*, 1983b, *45*, 357–377.

————. Children's artistic creativity: Detrimental effects of competition in a field setting. *Personality and social psychology bulletin*, 1982a, *8*, 573–578.

————. Social psychology of creativity: A consensual assessment technique. *Journal of social psychology*, 1982b, *43*, 997–1013.

————. Effects of external evaluation on artistic creativity. *Journal of personality and social psychology*, 1979, *27*, 221–233.

Amabile, T.M., DeJong, W., and Lepper, M.R. Effects of externally-imposed deadlines on subsequent intrinsic motivation. *Journal of personality and social psychology*, 1976, *34*, 92–98.

Amabile, T.M., and Gitomer, J. Children's artistic creativity: Effects of choice in task materials. *Personality and social psychology bulletin*, 1984, *10*, 209–215.

Amabile, T.M., Hennessey, B.A., and Grossman, B.S. Social influences on creativity: The effects of contracted-for reward. *Journal of personality and social psychology*, 1986, *50*, 14.

Anderson, H.H. (Ed.). *Creativity and its cultivation*. New York: Harper, 1959.

Ansbacher, H.L., and Ansbacher, R.R. (Eds.). *The individual psychology of Alfred Adler*. New York: Basic Books, 1956.

Arieti, S. *Creativity: The magic synthesis*. New York: Basic Books, 1976.

————. "Creativity and its cultivation: Relation to psychopathology and mental health." In Arieti, S. (Ed.), *American handbook of psychiatry*. New York: Basic Books, 1966, *3*, 722–774.

————. The rise of creativity: From primary to tertiary process. *Contemporary psychoanalysis*, 1964, *1*, 51–68.

Arlin, P.K. Cognitive development in adulthood: a fifth stage? *Developmental psychology*, 1975, *11*, 602–606.

Atkinson, J.W. *An introduction to motivation*. New York: American Book, 1964.

Bakan, P. Hypnotizability, laterality of eye movement and functional brain asymmetry. *Perceptual and motor skills*, 1969, *28*, 927–932.

Baltes, P.B., Reese, H.W., and Lipsett, L.P. Life-span developmental psychology. *Annual review of psychology*, 1980, *31*, 65–110.

Baltes, P.B., Reese, H.W., and Nesselroade, J.R. *Life-span developmental psychology: Introduction to research methods*. Monterey, Calif.: Brooks/Cole, 1977.

Baltes, P.B., and Schaie, K.W. On the plasticity of intelligence in adulthood and old age: Where Horn and Donaldson fail. *American psychologist*, 1976, *31*, 720–725.

————. Aging and IQ: The myth of the twilight years. *Psychology today*, 1974, *3*, 35–40.

————. (Eds.). *Lifespan developmental psychology*. New York: Academic Press, 1973.

Barnett, R.C., and Baruch, G.K. Women in the middle years: A critique of research and theory. *Psychology of women quarterly*, 1978, *3*, 187–197.

Baroody, A., Brumley, S., Hocevar, D., and Ripple, R.E. Influencing teachers' attitudes about creativity. *Child study journal*, 1976, *7*, 1–7.

Barr-Johnson, V. Challenging the right side of the brain. *The creative child and adult quarterly*, 1982, *VII*, (4), 218–225.

Barron, F. The solitariness of self and its mitigation through creative imagination. In Taylor, I.A., and Getzels, J.W. (Eds.), *Perspectives in creativity*. Chicago: Aldine, 1975.

————. *Creative person and creative process*. New York: Holt, Rinehart and Winston, 1969.

————. *Creativity and personal freedom*. Princeton, N.J.: Van Nostrand, 1968.

————. The disposition toward originality. In Taylor, C.W. and Barron, F. (Eds.), *Scientific creativity: Its recognition and development*, New York: Wiley, 1963a, 139–152.

————. The needs for order and for disorder as motives in creative activity. In Taylor, C.W., and Barron, F. (Eds.), *Scientific creativity. Its recognition and development.* New York: Wiley, 1963b, 153–160.

————. *Creativity and psychological health.* Princeton, N.J.: Van Nostrand, 1963c.

Barron, F., Gaines, R., Lee, D. and Marlow, C. Problems and pitfalls in the use of rating schemes to describe visual art. *Perceptual and motor skills,* 1973, *37* (2), 523–530.

Barron, F., and Welsh, G.S. Artistic perception as a factor in personality style: Its measurement by a figure preference test. *Journal of psychology,* 1952, *33,* 199–203.

Belcher, T.L. Modeling original divergent responses: An initial investigation. *Journal of educational psychology,* 1975, *17,* 351–358.

Belliston, L., and Belliston, M. *How to raise a more creative child.* Allen, Tex.: Argus Communications, 1982.

Bem, S. Androgyny versus the tight little lives of fluffy women and chesty men. *Psychology today,* 1975, *9* (4), 58–62.

Bergson, H. *The creative mind.* New York: Philosophical Library, 1946.

Beritoff, J.S. (Beritashvili), *Neural mechanisms of higher vertebrate behavior.* Boston: Little, Brown 1965.

Berlas, S., Amabile, T.M., and Handel, M. Effects of evaluation on children's artistic creativity. Paper presented at the meeting of the *American Psychological Association,* New York, 1979.

Besemer, S.P., and O'Quin, K. Creative product analysis: Testing a model by developing a judging instrument. In Isaksen, S.G. (Ed.), *Frontiers of creativity research: Beyond the basics.* Buffalo, N.Y.: Bearly Limited, 1987, 367–389.

————. Analyzing creative products: Refinement and test of a judging instrument. *Journal of creative behavior,* 1986, *20* (2), 115–126.

Besemer, S.P., and Treffinger, D.J. Analysis of creative products: Review and synthesis. *Journal of creative behavior,* 1981, *15,* 158–178.

Bieri, J., Bradburn, W.M., and Galinsky, M.D. Sex differences in perceptual behavior. *Journal of personality,* 1958, *26,* 1–12.

Biondi, A.M. (Ed.). *The creative process.* New York: D.O.K. Publishers, 1972.

Birren, J.E., and Morrison, D.F. Analysis of the WAIS subtests in relation to age and education. *Journal of gerontology,* 1961, *16,* 363–369.

Block, J.J., and Block, J. The role of ego-control and ego-resiliency in the organization of behavior. In W.A. Collins (Ed.), *Minnesota symposia on child psychology* (Vol. 13). Hillsdale, N.J.: Erlbaum, 1980.

Block, J., and Block, J.H. An investigation of the relationship between intolerance of ambiguity and egocentrism. *Journal of personality,* 1951, *19,* 303–311.

Bloomberg, M. (Ed.). *Creativity: Theory and research.* New Haven, Conn.: College and University Press, 1973.

————. Creativity as related to field independence and mobility. *Journal of genetic psychology,* 1971, *118,* 3–12.

Botwinick, J. *We are aging.* New York: Springer, 1981.

Bowers, P.G. Effect of hypnosis and suggestions of reduced defensiveness on creativity test performance. *Journal of personality,* 1967, *35,* 311–322.

Brabeck, M. Longitudinal studies of intellectual development during adulthood. *Journal of research and development in education,* 1984, *17* (3), 12–25.

Brandwein, P.F. *The gifted student as future scientist.* New York: Harcourt, Brace, 1955.

Bransford, J.D., and Stein, B.S. *The ideal problem solver.* New York: Freeman, 1984.

Briskman, L. Creative product and creative process in science and art. *Inquiry,* 1980, *23,* 83–106.

Brittain, A.W. Creativity and hemispheric functioning. *Empirical study of the arts,* 1985, *3* (1), 105–107.

Bromley, D.B. Some experimental tests of the effect of age on creative intellectual output. *Journal of gerontology,* 1956, *11,* 74–82.

Brown, R., and McNeill, D. The "tip of the tongue" phenomenon. *Journal of verbal learning and verbal behavior,* 1966, *5,* 325–337.

Bruner, J.S., Goodnow, J.J., and Austin, G.A. *A study of thinking.* New York: Wiley, 1956.

Buhler, C. The curve of life as studied in biographies. *Journal of applied psychology,* 1935, *19,* 405–409.

Bull, W.D. The validity of behavioral rating scale items for the assessment of individual creativity. *Journal of applied psychology,* 1960, *44,* 407–412.

Butler, R.N. The creative life and aging. In Pfeiffer, J. (Ed.), *Successful aging.* Durham, N.C.: Duke University Press, 1974.

Butler, R.N. The destiny of creativity in later life: Studies of creative people and the creative process. In Levin, S., and Kahana, R.J. (Eds.), *Psychodynamic studies on aging.* New York: International Universities, 1967.

Campbell, D.T., and Stanley, J.C. *Experimental and quasi-experimental designs for research on teaching.* In Gage Handbook for Research on Teaching. Chicago: Rand McNally, 1963.

Cannington, B.F., and Torrance, E.P. *Sounds and images.* Lexington, Mass.: Ginn, 1965.

Carmichael, L. (Ed.). *Manual of child psychology.* New York: Wiley, 1954.

Cicirelli, J. Form of the relationship between creativity, IQ, and academic achievement. *Journal of educational psychology,* 1965, *56,* 303–308.

Cline, V., Richards, J.M., and Abe, C. Validity for a battery of creativity tests in a high school sample. *Educational and psychological measurement,* 1962, *22,* 781–784.

Coopersmith, S. *The antecedents of self-esteem.* San Francisco: Freeman, 1967.

Covington, M.V., Crutchfield, R., Davies, L., and Olten, R.M. *The productive thinking program: A course in learning to think.* Columbus, Ohio: Merrill, 1974.

Cowger, E.L., Jr., and Torrance, E.P. Further examination of the quality of changes in creative functioning resulting from meditation (Zahen) training. *The creative child and adult quarterly*, 1982, *VII*, (4), 211–217.

Crawford, R.P. *The techniques of creative thinking.* New York: Hawthorn, 1954.

Crovitz, H.F. *Galton's walk.* New York: Harper and Row, 1970.

Cunningron, B.F., and Torrance, E.P. *Sounds and Images.* Lexington, Mass.: Ginn, 1965.

Dacey, J.S. Discriminating characteristics of the families of highly creative adolescents. *The journal of creative behavior,* in press.

———. *Adolescents today* (3rd ed.). Glenview, Ill.: Scott, Foresman, 1986.

———. *Adult development.* Glenview, Ill.: Scott, Foresman, 1982.

———. *Where the world is.* Glenview, Ill.: Goodyear, 1981.

———. *New ways to learn.* Stamford, Conn.: Greylock, 1976.

Dacey, J.S., and Gordon, M. *Implications of post-natal cortical development for creativity research.* Paper presented at the American Education Research Association Convention, New York, February 1971.

Dacey, J.S., and Leona, M. Recent attitude changes among adolescents as observed by adults who work with them. *Adolescence,* in press.

Dacey, J., Madaus, G., and Crellin, D. *Can creativity be facilitated? The critical period hypothesis.* Paper presented at Ninth Annual Convention of the Educational Research Association of New York State, Kiamesha Lake, November 1968.

Dacey, J.S., and Ripple, R.E. The facilitation of problem solving and verbal creativity by exposure to programmed instruction. *Psychology in the schools,* 1967, *4* (3), 240–245.

Dacey, J.S., and Williams, F. Some proposals for the improvement of adolescent life. *Adolescence,* in press.

Daniels, P.B. *Strategies to facilitate problem-solving.* Provo, Utah: Brigham Young University, 1964.

Davis, G.A. In pursuit of frumious creativity. *Journal of creative behavior,* 1975, *9* 75–78.

Davis, G.A. *Psychology of problem-solving: Theory and practice.* New York: Basic Books, 1973.

Davis, G.A., and Scott, J.A. *Training creative thinking.* New York: Holt, Rinehart and Winston, 1971.

Davis, G.A., and Houtman, S.E. *Thinking creatively: A Guide to training imagination.* Madison: University of Wisconsin, 1968.

deBono, E. *The CORT thinking skills program.* New York: Pergamon Press, 1984.

———. *Lateral thinking: Creativity step by step.* New York: Harper and Row, 1970.

———. *New think.* New York: Avon, 1971.

Del Gaudio, A.C. Psychological differentiation and mobility as related to creativity. *Perceptual and motor skills,* 1976, *43*, 831–841.

Dennis, W. Creative productivity between 20 and 80 years. *Journal of gerontology*, 1966, *21*, 1–8.

———. Age and achievement. *Journal of gerontology*, 1956, *II*, 331–333.

Derks, P.L. Abstract: Creativity in Shakespeare's humor. *Journal of creative behavior*, 1985, *19* (3), 218.

Deutsch, F. Mind, body, and art. *Daedalus*, 1960, *51*, 58–89.

Doerr, S.L. Conjugate eye movement, cerebral dominance, and the figural creativity factors of fluency, flexibility, originality and elaboration. *Studies in art education*, 1980, *21*, 5–11.

Dorethy, R., and Reeves, D. Mental functioning, perceptual differentiation, personality, and achievement among art and non-art majors. *Studies in art education*, 1979, *20* (2), 52–63.

Dreistadt, R. The psychology of creativity: How Einstein discovered the theory relativity. *Psychology*, 1974, *II*, 15–25.

Drews, Elizabeth M. *The creative intellectual style in gifted adolescent*. East Lansing: Michigan State University, 1965.

Duckworth, E. *Structure, continuity and other people's minds*. In K. Jervis (Ed.), Reunion, reaffirmation and resurgence. Proceedings of the Miquon Conference on progressive education, 1983, 40–60.

Dudek, Stephanie A. Creativity in young children: Attitude or ability? *Journal of creative behavior*, 1974, *8*, 23–37.

Duncker, K. On problem solving. Trans. by Lees, L.S. *Psychological monographs*, 1945, *58*, Whole no. 270.

Eccles, J. *The brain and unity of conscious experience: The 19th Arthur Stanley Eddington memorial lecture*. Cambridge, England: Cambridge University Press, 1965.

———. The physiology of imagination. *Scientific American*, 1958, *199*, 135–146.

Edwards, B. *Drawing on the right side of the brain*. Los Angeles: J.P. Tarcher, 1979.

Ekvall, G., and Parnes, S.J. *Creative problem solving methods in product development: A second experiment*. Stockholm: Swedish Council for Management and Work Life Issues, 1984.

Erikson, E.H. *Childhood and society* (2nd Ed.). New York: Norton, 1963.

Erikson, E. Identity and the life cycle. *Psychological issues*, 1959, *1*, 148–164.

Evans, R.G., and Forbach, G.B. Facilitation of performance on a divergent measure of creativity: A closer look at instructions to "be creative." *Applied psychological measurement*, 1983, *7*, 181–187.

Falcone, D.J., and Loder, K. A modified lateral eye-movement measure, the right hemisphere and creativity. *Perceptual and motor skills*, 1984, *58* (3), 823–830.

Feldhusen, J.F., and Clinkenbeard, P.R. Creativity instructional materials: A review of research. *Journal of creative behavior*, 1986, *20* (3), 153–182.

Feldhusen, J.F., Speedie, S.M., and Treffinger, D.J. The Purdue creative thinking program. Research and evaluation. *National society for performance and instruction journal*, 1971, *10*, 5–9.

Feldhusen, J.F., Treffinger, D.J., and Bahike, S.J. Developing creative thinking: The Purdue creativity training program. *Journal of creative behavior*, 1970, *4*, 85–90.

Feldman, D.H. *Beyond universals in cognitive development*. Norwood, N.J.: Ablex, 1980.

Feldman, J.F. *Teaching creative thinking and problem solving*. Dubuque, Iowa: Kendal Hunt, 1977.

Fiene, J.F. Elements of leadership which impede creativity. *Creative child and adult quarterly*, 1979, *4*, 37.

Findlay, C.S., and Lumsden, C.J. The creative mind: Toward an evolutionary theory of discovery and innovation. *Journal of social and biological structures*, 1988, *11*, 3–55.

Firestein, R., and Treffinger, D.J. Creative problem solving: guidelines and resources for effective facilitation. *Gifted/creative/talented*, 1983a (January-February), 2–10.

———. Ownership and converging: Essential ingredients of creative problem solving. *Journal of creative behavior*, 1983b, *17* (1), 32–38.

Flanagan, J.C. Definition and measurement of ingenuity. In C.W. Taylor (Ed.), *The second (1957) University of Utah research conference on the identification of creative scientific talent*, pp. 109–118. Salt Lake City: University of Utah Press, 1958.

Flescher, I. Anxiety and achievement of intellectually gifted and creatively gifted children. *Journal of psychology*, 1963, *56*, 251–268.

Franco, L., and Sperry, R.W. Hemisphere lateralization for cognitive processing of geometry. *Neuropsychologia*, 1977, *15*, 107–114.

Frankl, Victor. Self-transendence as a human phenomenon. *Journal of humanistic psychology*, 1966, Fall, 104+.

Frazer, J.G. *The golden bough*. New York: Macmillan, 1922.

Fredericksen, N. *Implications of theory for instruction in problem solving*. Princeton, N.J.: Educational Testing Service, 1983.

Freud, S. Introductory lectures on psycho-analysis, part III. General theory of the neurosis. In *The standard edition of the complete psychological works, vol. XVI*. London: Hogarth Press, 1963.

———. *The interpretation of dreams*. New York: Basic Books, 1960.

———. Creative writers and day-dreaming. In *The standard edition of the complete psychological works, vol IX*. London: Hogarth Press, 1959.

———. Leonardo da Vinci. *The standard edition of the complete psychological works, vol. XI*. London: Hogarth Press, 1957.

———. *The future of an illusion*. New York: Liveright, 1949.

———. *Leonardo da Vinci*. London: Routledge and Kegan Paul, 1948.

———. The relation of the poet to day-dreaming. In *Collected papers, vol. II*. London: Hogarth, 1924.

Frey, B.A., and Noller, R.B. Mentoring: A legacy of success. *Journal of creative behavior*, 1983, *17*, (1), 60–64.

Fromm, E. The creative attitude. In Anderson, H.H. (Ed.), *Creativity and its cultivation*.
New York: Harper, 1959.
————. *Escape from freedom*. New York: Farrar and Rinehart, 1941.
Galin, D. Implications for psychiatry of left and right cerebral specialization. *Archives of general psychiatry, 31,* 1974, 572–583.
Gall, M., and Mendelsohn, G.A. Effects of facilitating techniques and subject-experimenter interaction on creative problem solving. *Journal of personality & social psychology,* 1967, *5* (2), 211–216.
Galton, F. Psychometric experiments. *Brain,* 1879, *2,* 148–162.
————. *Hereditary genius.*New York: Appleton, 1870.
Gamble, K.R., and Kellner, H. Creative functioning and cognitive regression. *Journal of personality and social psychology,* 1968, *9,* 266–271.
Garbarino, J. The impact of anticipated reward upon cross-age tutoring. *Journal of personality and social psychology,* 1975, *32,* 421–428.
Gardner, H. *Art, mind, and brain.* New York: Basic Books, 1982.
————. What we know (and don't know) about the two halves of the brain. *Harvard magazine,* 1978, *80,* 24–27.
————. *The arts and human development.* New York: Wiley, 1973.
Getzels, J.W. *Creativity: Prospects and issues.* In Taylor, I.A., and Getzels, J.W. (Eds.), *Perspectives in creativity.* Chicago: Aldine, 1975.
————. *Creativity and intelligence.* New York: Wiley, 1962.
Getzels, J.W., and Csikszentmihalyi, M. From problem solving to problem finding. In Taylor, I.A., and Getzels, J.W. (Eds.), *Perspectives in creativity.* Chicago: Aldine, 1975.
Getzels, J.W., and Jackson, P.W. *Creativity and intelligence: Explorations with gifted students.* New York: Wiley, 1962.
Getzels, J.W., and Madaus, G.F. Creativity. In R.L. Ebel (Ed.), *Encyclopedia of educational research,* pp. 267–275. New York: Macmillan, 1969.
Ghiselin, B. (Ed.). *The creative process.* (Paperback ed.). New York: Mentor, 1955.
————. *The creative process.* Berkeley: University of California Press, 1952.
Giele, J.Z. (Ed.). *Women in the middle years: Current knowledge and directions for research and policy.* New York: Wiley, 1982.
Gilligan, C. *In a different voice: Psychological theory and women's development.* Cambridge, Mass.: Harvard University Press, 1982.
————. Woman's place in man's life cycle. *Harvard educational review,* 1979, *49,* 431–446.
Ginsberg, H., and Opper, S. *Piaget's theory of intellectual development.* Englewood Cliffs, N.J.: Prentice-Hall, 1969.
Glover, J.A. *Becoming a more creative person.* Englewood Cliffs, N.J.: Prentice-Hall/Spectrum, 1980.
Goertzel, M.G., Goertzel, V., and Goertzel, T.G. *300 eminent personalities.* San Francisco: Jossey-Bass, 1978.

Goertzel, V., and Goertzel, M. *Cradles of eminence.* Boston: Little, Brown, 1962.

Golden, C.J. The measurement of creativity by the Stroop Color and Word Test. *Journal of personality assessment,* 1975, *39,* 502–506.

Goldstein, J.H., and McGhee, P.E. (Eds.). *The psychology of humor.* New York: Academic Press, 1972.

Gordon, W.J.J. On being explicit about the creative process. *Journal of creative behavior,* 1972, *6,* 295–300.

———. *The metaphorical way of learning and knowing.* Cambridge, Mass.: Porpoise Books, 1971.

———. *Synectics: The development of creative capacity.* New York: Harper and Row, 1961.

Gould, R. *Transformations.* New York: Simon and Schuster, 1978.

Gowan, J.C. The facilitation of creativity through meditational procedures. *Journal of creative behavior,* 1978, *12,* 156–160.

———. Some new thoughts on the development of creativity. *Journal of creative behavior,* 1977, *11* (2), 77–90.

———. *Development of the creative individual.* San Diego, Calif.: Robert R. Kapp, 1972.

Gowan, J.C., and Olson, M. The society which maximizes creativity. *The national/ state leadership training institute on the gifted and the talented,* 1980, *1,* 113–125.

Greenacre, P. The childhood of the artist. *Psychoanalytic study of the child,* 12, 47–72. New York: International Universities, 1957, *12,* 47–72.

Greene, D., and Lepper, M.R. Effects of extrinsic rewards on children's subsequent intrinsic interest. *Child development,* 1974, *45,* 1141–1145.

Gruber, H.E. *Darwin on man: a psychological study of scientific creativity.* Chicago: University of Chicago Press, 1981.

Gruber, H.E., Terrell, G., and Wertheimer, M. (Eds.). *Contemporary approaches to creative thinking.* New York: Atheron Press, 1964.

Guilford, J.P. "Creativity: A quarter century of progress. In Taylor, I.A., and Getzels, J.W. (Eds.), *Perspectives in creativity.* Chicago: Aldine, 1975.

———. *The nature of human intelligence.* New York: McGraw-Hill, 1967.

———. Factors that aid and hinder creativity. *Teachers' college record,* 1962, *63,* 391.

———. Traits of creativity. In Anderson, H.H. (Ed.), *Creativity and its cultivation,* pp. 142–161. New York: Harper and Row, 1959a.

———. Three faces of intellect. *American psychologist,* 14, 469–479, 1959b.

———. A revised structure of intellect. *Report of psychology,* Los Angeles: University of Southern California, 1957a, *19,* 1–63.

———. Creative ability in the arts. *Psychological review,* 1957b, *64,* 110–118.

———. Creativity. *American psychologist,* 1950, *5,* 444–454.

Hadamard, J. *The psychology of invention in the mathematical field.* Princeton, N.J.: Princeton University Press, 1945.

Haitte, J.A. Conditions for administering creativity tests. *Psychological bulletin,*

1977, *84*, 1249–1260.

Hallman, R. Techniques of creative teaching. *Journal of creative behavior*, 1967, *1* (3), 325–330.

Hammer, E.F. *Creativity, talent and personality.* Malabar, fla.: Krieger, 1984.

———. *Creativity.* New York: Random House, 1961.

Harrington, David M., Block, Jack, and Block, Jeanne H. Predicting creativity in preadolescence from divergent thinking in early childhood. *Journal of personality and social psychology*, 1983, *45* (3), 609–623.

Harter, S. Effectance motivation reconsidered: Toward a developmental model. *Human development*, 1978, *21*, 34–64.

Hayes, J.R. *The complete problem solver.* Philadelphia: The Franklin Institute, 1981.

Hecaen, H., and Albert, M. *Human neuropsychology.* New York: Wiley, 1978.

Helson, R., and Crutchfield, R.S. Mathematicians: The creative researcher and the average Ph.D. *Journal of consulting and clinal psychology*, 1970, *34*, 250–257.

Henegar, L.E. Nurturing the creative promise in gifted disadvantaged youth. *Journal of creative behavior*, 1984, *18* (2), 109–115.

Hermann, N. The creative brain. *Training and development journal*, October 1981, 11–16.

Hersch, C. The cognitive functioning of the creative person: A developmental analysis. *Journal of projective techniques*, 1962, *26*, 193–200.

Higgins, T.E., and Chaires, W.M. Accessibility of interrelational constructs: Implications for stimulus encoding and creativity. *Journal of experimental social psychology*, *16*, 348–361, 1979.

Hirsch, N.D.M. *Genius and creative intelligence.* Cambridge, Mass.: Sci-Art Publishers, 1931.

Hollman, J. Games to promote creativity. *English journal*, January 1981, *70*, 83–85.

Horn, J.L., and Donaldson, G. Faith is not enough. *American psychologist*, 1977, *32*, 369–373.

———. On the myth of intellectual decline in adulthood. *American psychologist*, 1976, *31*, 701–719.

Howieson, Noel. A longitudinal study of creativity—1965–1975. *Journal of creative behavior*, 1981, *15*, 21–35.

Hudgins, B.B. Effects of group experience on individual problem solving. *Journal of educational psychology*, 1960, *51*, 37–42.

Hunt, J.McV. Has contemporary education failed? Has it been attempted? *Harvard educational review*, 1969, *39* (2), 278–300.

Hutchinson, E.D. *How to think creatively.* New York: Abingdon-Cokesbury, 1949.

Isaacs, N. Children's why questions. In S. Isaacs, *Intellectual growth in young children.* London: Routledge and Kegan Paul, 1930.

Isaksen, S.G. (Ed.). *Frontiers of creativity research: Beyond the basics.* Buffalo, N.Y.: Bearly Limited, 1987, 367–389.

———. Toward a model for the facilitation of creative problem solving. *Journal of creative behavior*, 1983, *17* (1), 18–31.

Isaksen, S.G., and Parnes, S.J. Curriculum planning for creative thinking and problem solving. *Journal of creative behavior*, 1985, *19* (1), 1–29.

Isaksen, S.G., and Treffinger, D.J. *Creative problem solving: The basic course.* Buffalo,
N.Y.: Bearly Limited, 1985.

Jackson, P.W., and Messick, S. The person, the product, and the response: Conceptual problems in the assessment of creativity. *Journal of personality*, 1965, *33*
(3), 309–329.

Jaynes, J. *The origin of consciousness and the breakdown of the bicameral mind.* Boston:
Houghton-Mifflin, 1976.

James, W. *The principles of psychology.* New York: Holt, 1890.

―――. Great men, great thoughts and the environment. *Atlantic monthly*, 1880,
46, 441–459.

Jaquish, G.A., Block, J., and Block, J.H. *The comprehension and production of metaphor in early adolescence: A longitudinal study of cognitive childhood antecedents.*
Unpublished manuscript, 1984.

Jaquish, G.A., and Ripple, R.E. Divergent thinking and self-esteem in preadoles-
cents and adolescents. *Journal of youth and adolescence*, 1980a, *9* (2), 143–152.

Jaquish, G., and Ripple, R.E. Cognitive creative abilities across the adult life span.
Human development, 1980b, *34*, 25–33.

Jones, M. *Getting high on creativity.* New York: R. Rosen Press, 1982.

Jones, E. *The life and work of Sigmund Freud.* New York: Basic Books, 1953.

Jourard, S.M. The "awareness of potentialities" syndrome. *Journal of humanistic
psychology*, 1966, Fall, 139–140.

Jung, C.G. *The spirit in men, art and literature.* New York: Bollingen Foundations,
1966.

―――. *The structure and dynamics of the psyche.* Princeton: Princeton University
Press, 1960.

―――. *Two essays on analytical psychology.* New York: Meridan, 1956.

―――. *Modern man in search of a soul.* New York: Harcourt, Brace, and World,
1933.

Katz, A.N. The relationship between creativity and cerebral hemisphericity.
Empirical studies of the arts, 1986, *4* (2), 97–108.

―――. Creativity and individual differences in asymmetric cerebral hemispheric
functioning. *Empirical studies of the arts*, 1983, *1* (1), 3–16.

Kaufman, B. *Up the down staircase.* New York: Avon, 1966.

Kernoodle-Loveland, K., and Olley, J.G. The effect of external reward on interest
and quality of talk performance in children of high and low intrinsic motivation. *Child development*, 1979, *50*, 1207–1210.

Khatena, J. Identification and stimulation of creative imagination imagery. *Journal
of creative behavior*, 1978, *12*, 30–38.

Khatena, J., and Torrance, E.P. *Thinking creatively with sounds and words.* Lexington,
Mass.: Ginn, 1973.

Kinsbourne, M. Eye and head turning indicates of cerebral lateralization. *Science*,
1972, *176*, 539–541.

Kocel, K., Galin, D., Ornstein, R., and Merrin, E.L. Lateral eye movement and cognitive mode. *Psychonomic science*, 1972, *27* (4), 223–224.

Koestler, A. *The act of creation*. New York: Macmillan, 1964.

Koestner, R., Ryan, R., Bernieri, F., and Holt, K. Setting limits on children's behavior: The differential effects of controlling vs. informational styles on intrinsic motivation and creativity. *Journal of personality*, 1984, *52*, 233–248.

Kogan, N. Stylistic variation in childhood and adolescence: Creativity, metaphor, cognitive styles. In P.H. Mussen (Ed.), *Handbook of child psychology* (Vol. 3). New York: Wiley, 1983.

———. Creativity and cognitive style: A life-span perspective. In Baltes, P.B., and Schaie, K.W. (Eds.), *Lifespan developmental psychology*. New York: Academic Press, 1973.

Kohler, W. *Gestalt psychology*. New York: H. Liveright, 1929.

———. *The mentality of apes*. Trans. by E. Winter. New York: Harcourt, Brace, 1925.

Konorski, J. *Integrative activity of the brain*. Chicago: University of Chicago Press, 1967.

Kramer, E.E., and Bavern, C.D. The effects of behavioral strategies on creativity training. *Journal of creative behavior*, 1984, *18* (1), 23–24.

Kris, E. On inspiration: Preliminary notes on emotional conditions in creative states. In Ruitenbeek, H.M. (Ed.), *The creative imagination*. Chicago: Quadrangle Books, 1965, 145–160.

———. Psychoanalysis and the study of creative imagination. In Ruitenbeek, H.M. (Ed.), *The creative imagination*. Chicago: Quadrangle Books, 1965 23–46.

———. *Psychoanalytic explorations in art*. New York: International Universities, 1952.

Kubie, L.S. *Neurotic distortion of the creative process*. Lawrence: University of Kansas Press, 1958, also New York: The Noonday Press, 1961.

Lange-Eichbaum, W. *The problem of Genius*. Trans. by E. and C. Paul. New York: Macmillan, 1944.

Lasswell, H. The social setting of creativity. In Anderson, H. (Ed.), *Creativity and its cultivation*. New York: Harpers, 1959, 203–221.

Lawson, A.E. Formal operations and field independence in a heterogenous sample. *Perceptual and motor skills*, 1976, *42*, 981–982.

Lehane, S. *The creative child: How to encourage the natural creativity of your preschooler*. Englewood Cliffs, N.J.: Prentice-Hall, 1979.

Lehman, H.C. The psychologist's most creative years. *Psychology*, 1966, *21*, 363–369.

———. The creative production rates of present versus past generations of scientists. *Journal of gerontology*, 1962, *17*, 409–417.

———. *Age and achievement*. Princeton, N.J.: Princeton University Press, 1953.

Lepper, M.R., Sagotsky, G., Dafoe, J.L., and Greene, D. Consequences of superfluous social constraints: Effects on young children's social inferences and subsequent intrinsic interest. *Journal of personality and social psychology, 42* 51–65. 1982.

Lepper, M.R., and Greene, D. Turning play into work: Effects of adult surveillance and extrinsic rewards on children's intrinsic motivation." *Journal of personality and social psychology, 31*, 479–486, 1975.

Lepper, M.R., Greene, D., and Nisbett, R. Undermining children's intrinsic interest with extrinsic rewards: A test of the "overjustification hypothesis." *Journal of personality and social psychology, 28*, 129–137, 1983.

Lesner, W.J., and Hillman, D. A developmental schema of creativity. *Journal of creative behavior*, 1983, *17* (2) 86–94.

Levine, S.H. Play experience is the foundation for rational creativity. *Journal of creative behavior*, 1984, *18*, 90–108.

Levinson, D. *Seasons of a man's life*. New York: Knopf, 1978.

Levy, J. Possible basis for the evolution of lateral specialization of the human brain. *Nature*, 1976, *224*, 614–615.

Levy, J., and Nagylaki, T. A model for the genetics of handedness. *Genetics, 72*, 1972, 117–128.

Levy, J., and Reid, M.L. Variations in writing posture and cerebral organization. *Science*, 1976, *194*, 337.

Levy, J., Trevarthen, C., and Sperry, R.W. Perception of bilateral chimeric figures following hemispheric disconnection. *Brain, 95*, 1972, 61–78.

Levy-Agresti, J. and Sperry, R.W. Differential perceptual capacities in major and minor hemispheres. *Proceedings of the national academy of science, U.S.A.* 1968, *61*, 1151.

Lewis, C. Critical thinking: Providing enrichment for the gifted. *Adapting selected units of study*, 1979, 1, 23–37.

———. Independent study: Problem-solving. Providing enrichment for the gifted: Adapting selected units of study, 1979, *1*, 5–17.

Lobuts, J.F., Jr., and Pennewill, C.L. Do we dare restructure the classroom environment? *Journal of creative behavior*, 1984, *18* (4), 237–246.

Loevinger, J. *Ego development*. San Francisco: Jossey-Bass, 1977.

Lombrosco, C. *The man of genius*. London: Walter Scott, 1889.

Lowenfeld, V. *The nature of creative activity*. London: Routledge and Kegan Paul, 1959.

Lubeck, S., and Biddle, T. Creativity and cognition: A Piagetian framework. *Journal of creative behavior*, 1988, *22* (1), 31–41.

Luchins, A.S. Mechanization in problem solving: The effect of einstellung, *Psychological monographs*, 1952, *54*, (6) (whole no. 248).

Lundsteen, S.W. *Measurement for creative problem solving in kindergarten children*. Paper presented at the National Council on Measurement in Education, April 9, 1980.

Luria, A.R. *The working brain: An introduction to neuropsychology*. New York: Basic Books, 1973.

MacKinnon, D.W. *In search of human effectiveness: identifying and developing creativity*. Buffalo, N.Y. Creative Education Foundation, 1978.

―――. IPAR's contribution to the conceptualization and study of creativity In Taylor, I.A., and Getzels, J.W. (Eds.), *Perspectives in creativity*, Chicago: Aldine, 1975, 60–69.

―――. The nature and nurture of creative talent, *The American psychologist*, 1962, *17*, 484–495.

McLeish, J. *The Ullyssean adult: Creativity in the middle and later years*. New York: McGraw-Hill, 1976.

MacPherson, J.H. A proposal for establishing ultimate criteria for measuring creative output. In Taylor, C.W., and Barron, F., *Scientific creativity*. New York: Wiley, 1963.

Maddi, S.R. Motivational aspects of creativity. *Journal of personality*, 1965, *33*, 330–347.

Maier, N.R.F. *Problem solving and creativity in individuals and groups*. Belmont, Calif.: Brooks/Cole, 1970.

―――. Reasoning in humans: The solution of a problem and its appearance in consciousness. *Journal of comparative psychology*, 1931, *12*, 181–194.

Maltzman, I. On the training of originality. *Psychological review*, 1960, *67*, 229–242.

Mansfield, R.S., Busse, T.V., and Krepelka, E.J. The effectiveness of creativity training, *Review of educational research*, 1978, *48*, 517–536.

Martindale, C., Hines, D., Mitchell, L., and Covell, E. EEG alpha asymmetry and creativity. *Personality and individual differences*, 1984, *5* (1), 77–86.

Maslow, A.H. A holistic approach to creativity. In Taylor, C.W., *Climate for creativity*. New York: Pergamon Press, 1972, 287–293.

―――. *The psychology of science*. Harper and Row, 1966.

―――. *Toward a psychology of being*. New York: Van Nostrand, 1962.

―――. Peak experiences as acute identity experiences. *American journal of psychoanalysis*, 1961, *21*, 254–260.

―――. Creativity in self-actualizing people. In Anderson, H.H. (Ed.), *Creativity in its cultivation*. New York: Harper and Brothers, 1959a.

―――. Cognition of being in the peak experiences. *Journal of genetic psychology*, 1959b, *94*, 43–66.

―――. *Motivation and personality*. New York: Harper, 1954.

May, R. *The courage to create*. New York: Norton, 1975.

―――. Creativity and encounter. In Ruitenbeek, H.M. (Ed.). *The creative imagination*. Chicago: Quadrangle Books, 1965, 283–292.

―――. The nature of creativity, in Anderson, H.H. (Ed.), *Creativity and its cultivation*. New York: Harper, 1959.

Mednick, S.A., and Mednick, M. An associative interpretation of the creative process. In Taylor, C.W. (Ed.), *Widening horizons in creativity*. New York: 1964.

Mednick S.A. Research creativity in psychology graduate students. *Journal of consulting psychology*, 1963, *27* (3), 265–266.

————. The associative basis of the creative process. *Psychological review*, 1962, *69*, 220–232.

Mendelsohn, G.A., and Gall, M.D. Personality variables and the effectiveness of techniques to facilitate creative problem solving. *Journal of personality & social psychology*, 1970, *16* (2), 346–351.

Michael, W.B. *Teaching for creative endeavor.* Bloomington: Indiana University Press, 1968.

Milner, M. *On not being able to paint.* New York: International Universities Press, 1957.

Moffat, J.A., and Shephard, W.J. Facilitation: A selected bibliography. *Journal of creative behavior*, 1983, *17*, 65–70.

Moreno, J.L. *Psychodrama.* New York: Beacon House, 1946.

Murray, H.A. Vicissitudes of creativity, in Anderson, H.H. (Ed.), *Creativity and its cultivation.* New York: Harper, 1959

Myers, R.E., and Sperry, R.W. Interhemispheric communication through the corpus callosum. Mnemonic carry-over between the hemispheres. *Archives of neurology and psychiatry*, 1958, *80*, 298–303.

Myers, R.E., and Torrance, E.P. *The image/craft and ideabooks series:* Boston: Ginn, 1964–1965.

Navarre, J. Incubation as fostering the creative process. *The gifted child quarterly*, 1979, *23*, (4), 792–800.

Neimark, E.E. Individual differences and the role of cognitive style in cognitive development. *Genetic psychological monographs*, 1975, *91*, 171–225.

Neugarten, B.L. Time, age, and the life cycle. *American journal of psychiatry*, 1979, *136*, 887–894.

————. Personality change in late life: A developmental perspective. In Eisdorfer, C., and Lawton, M.P. (Eds.), *The psychology of adult development and aging.* Washington, D.C.: American Psychological Association, 1973, 311–335.

————. The awareness of middle age. In Neugarten, B.L. (Ed.), *Middle age and aging.* Chicago: University of Chicago Press, 1968, 93–98.

Newell, A., Shaw, J.C., and Simon, H.A. The process of creative thinking. In Gruber, H.E., Terrell, G., and Wertheimer, M., *Contemporary appraoches to creative thinking.* New York: Atherton, 1962.

————. Elements of a theory of human problem solving. *Psychological review*, 1958, *65*, 151–166.

Noller, R.B. *Mentoring: An annotated bibliography.* Buffalo, N.Y.: Bearly Limited, 1983.

————. *Scratching the surface of creativity problem solving: A bird's eye view of CPS.* Buffalo, N.Y.: D.O.K., 1977.

Noller, R.B., Parnes, S.J., and Biondi, A.M. *Creative actionbook.* New York: Scribner's, 1976.

Noppe, L.D. The relationship of formal thought and cognitive styles to creativity. *Journal of creative behavior*, 1985, *19*, 88–96.

Obler, L., and Fein, D. *The exceptional brain.* London: Ky.: Guilford Press, 1987.

Olton, R.M., and Johnson, D.M. Mechanisms of incubation in creative problem solving. *American journal of psychology,* 1976, *89,* 617–630.

Ornstein, R. The split and whole brain. *Human Nature,* 1978, *1,* 76–83.

———. *The psychology of consciousness* (2nd ed.). New York: Harcourt Brace Jovanovich, 1977.

Osborn, A.F. *Applied imagination.* New York: Scribner's, 1963.

Otto, H.A. The potential of people. *Elementary school guidance and counseling.* 1979, *14* (2), 92–96.

Parnes, S.J. *A new generation of leadership.* Los Angeles: National/State Leadership Training Institute of the Gifted and Talented, 1977.

———. *Creative behavior guidebook.* New York: Scribner's, 1967.

Parnes, S.J., and Harding, H.F. (Eds.). *Source book for creative thinking.* New York: Scribner's, 1962.

Parnes, S.J., Noller, R.B., and Biondi, A.M. *Guide to creative action.* New York: Scribner's, 1977.

Pasternak, B. The artist and the public. *New York Times book review,* Nov. 1, 1959, 5.

Patrick, C. Creative thought in artists. *Journal of psychology,* 1937, *4,* 35–73.

———. Creative though in poets. *Archives of psychology,* 1935, *26,* 1–74.

Pearlman, C. Teachers as informational sources in identifying and rating student creativity. *Education,* 1983a, *103,* 215–222.

———. A theoretical model of creativity. *Education,* 1983b, *103,* 294–305.

Pearson, K. *The life, letters and labours of Francis Galton.* Cambridge, England: Cambridge University Press, 1914.

Pelligrini, A.D. The effects of exploration training on young children's associative fluency. *The creative child and adult quarterly,* 1982, *VII* (4), 226–233.

Penfield, W., and Roberts, L. *Speech and brain mechanisms.* Princeton: Princeton University Press, 1959.

Piaget, J. The cognitive unconscious. In Inhelder, B., and Chipman, H. (Eds.), *Piaget and his school.* Berlin: Springer-Verlag, 1976.

———. *To understand is to invent.* New York: Viking Press, 1973.

———. *Psychology of intelligence.* Totowa, N.J.: Littlefield, Adams, 1966.

———. *Play, dreams and imitation in childhood.* New York: Norton, 1962.

———. *The construction of reality in the child.* New York: Ballantine, 1954.

———. *The origins of intelligence in children.* New York: International Universities, 1952.

Pickering, G. *Creative malady.* New York: Oxford University Press, 1974.

Poincaré, H. Mathematical creation. In Poincare, H., *The foundation of science.* Lancaster: Science Press, 1946.

Prince, G.M. *The practice of creativity: A manual for dynamic group problem-solving.* New York: Harper and Row, 1970.

Quarton, G.C. The enhancement of learning by drugs and the transfer of learning by macromolecules. In Quarton, G. (Ed.), *The neurosciences: A study program.* New York: Rockefeller University Press, 1967, 747.

Rank, O. Life and creation. In Ruitenbeek, H.M. (Ed.), *The creative imagination.* Chicago: Quadrangle Books, 1965, 67–96.

––––––. *Will therapy and truth and reality.* Trans. by J. Taft. New York: Knopf, 1945.

Rejskind, F.G. Autonomy and creativity in children. *Journal of creative behavior,* 1982, *15* (1), 58–67.

Renzulli, J.S. Guiding the gifted in the pursuit of real problems: The transformed role of the teacher. *Journal of creative behavior,* 1983, *17* (10), 49–59.

Renzulli, J. *The enrichment triad method.* Wethersfield, Conn.: Creative Learning Press, 1976a.

––––––. *New directions in creativity: Mark A and B; Mark I, II and III.* New York: Harper and Row, 1976b.

Ripple, R.E., and Dacey, J.S. Relationships of some adolescent characteristics and verbal creativity. *Psychology in the schools,* 1969, *6* (3), 321–324.

Rivchun, S.B. Be a mentor and leave a lasting legacy. *Association management,* August 1980, *32* (8), 71–74.

Robertson, J. Grandmotherhood: A study of role conceptions. *Journal of marriage and the family,* 1977, *30* (1), 165–174.

Roe, A. Painters and painting. In Taylor, I.A., and Getzels, J.W. (Eds.), *Perspectives in creativity.* Chicago: Aldine, 1975.

––––––. *The making of a scientist.* New York: Dodd, Mead, 1966.

––––––. A psychological study of eminent psychologists and anthropologists, and a comparison with biological and physical scientists. *Psychological monographs,* 1953, *67* (2).

––––––. A psychological study of eminent biologists. *Psychological monographs,* 1951, *65* (14).

––––––. The personality of artists. *Educational and psychological measurement,* 1946, *6,* 401–408.

Rogers, C.R. *On becoming a person: A therapist's view of psychotherapy.* Boston: Houghton Mifflin, 1961.

––––––. Toward a theory of creativity. In Anderson, H.H. (Ed.), *Creativity and its cultivation.* New York: Harper, 1959.

Rogers, E.M. *Diffusion of innovations.* (3rd ed.) New York: The Free Press, 1983.

Rokeach, M. *The open and closed mind.* New York: Knopf 1960.

Romaniuk, J.G. Training creativity in the elderly: An examination of the attitudes, self-perception and abilities. Unpublished Ph.D. dissertation, University of Wisconsin, 1978.

Romaniuk, J.G., and Romaniuk, M. Creativity across the life span: A measurement perspective. *Human development,* 1981, *24,* 366–381.

Rose, L.H., and Hsin-Tai, L. A meta-analysis of long-term creativity training programs. *Journal of creative behavior,* 1984, *18* (1), 11–22.

Rosenzweig, M. Effects of heredity and environment on brain chemistry, anatomy and learning ability in the rat. In Edwards, A.J., and Cawley, J.F. (Coordinators), *University of Kansas symposium: Physiological determinates of behavior.* Lawrence: University of Kansas School of Education Publications, June 1964, *14.*

Rosner, S., and Abt, L.E. (Eds.), *The creative experience.* New York: Grossman, 1970.

Rossi, A.S. Life-span theories and women's lives. *Signs: Journal of women in culture and society,* 1980, *6,* 4–32.

Roth, N. Free association and creativity. *Journal of the American academy of psychoanalysis, 1976, 4.*

Rothenberg, A., and Hausman, C.R. *The creativity question.* Durham, N.C.: Duke University Press, 1976.

Rothenberg, A. The process of Janusian thinking in creativity. *Archives of general psychiatry,* 1971, *24,* 195–205.

Ruitenbeek, H.M. (Ed.), *The creative imagination.* Chicago: Quadrangle Books, 1965.

Ryff, C.O. Subjective experience of the life span transition. In Rossi, A.S. (Ed.), *Gender and the life course.* New York: Aldine, 1983, 97–113.

Sarnoff, D.P., and Cole, H.P. Creative and personal growth. *Journal of creative behavior,* 1983, *17* (2), 95–102.

Sarnoff, S.A. The associative basis of the creative process. *Psychological review,* 1962, *69,* 220–227.

Saul, R.E., and Sperry, R.W. Absence of commissurotomy symptoms with agenesis of the corpus callosum. *Neurology,* 1968, *18,* 307.

Schaie, K.W. Quasi-experimental research designs. In Birren, J.E., and Schaie, K.W. *Handbook of the psychology of aging.* New York: Van Nostrand and Reinhold, 1977.

———. Translations in gerontology—from lab to life: intellectual functioning. *American psychologist,* 1974, *29:* 802–807.

Schwartz, G., and Bishop, P.W., (Eds.), *Moments of discovery* (2 vols.) New York: Basic Books, 1958.

Shallcross, D.J. *Teaching creative behavior: How to evoke creativity in children of all ages.* Englewood Cliffs, N.J.: Prentice-Hall, 1981.

Sheehan, P.W., McConkey, K.M., and Law, H.G. Imagery facilitation and performance on the creative imagination scale. *Journal of meantal imagery,* 1978, *2,* 265–274.

Simon, H. Motivational and emotional controls and cognition. *Psychological review,* 1967, *74,* 29–39.

Simonton, D.K. *Genius, creativity and leadership.* Cambridge, Mass.: Harvard University Press, 1984.

———. Creativity age and stress. *Journal of personality and social psychology,* 1977a, *35,* 791–804.

————. Eminence, creativity and geographical marginality. *Journal of personality and social psychology,* 1977b, *35,* 805–816.

————. Biographical determinants of achieved eminence. *Journal of personality and social psychology,* 1976, *33,* 218–276.

————. Age and literary creativity. *Journal of cross-cultural creativity,* 1975, *6,* 259–277.

Simple gifts: The education of the gifted, and creative. A book of readings. Madison: University of Wisconsin, 1978.

Singer, J.L. Imagination and writing ability in young children. *Journal of personality,* 1961, *29,* 396–413.

Skinner, B.F. *Upon further reflection.* Englewood Cliffs, N.J.: Prentice-Hall, 1987.

————. Origins of a behaviorist. *Psychology today,* September 1983. *17* (2), 22–33.

————. A lecture on "having" a poem. *Cumulative record: A selection of papers* (3rd ed.). Englewood Cliffs, N.J.: Prentice-Hall, 1972.

————. *Beyond freedom and dignity.* New York: Knopf, 1971.

————. *The technology of teaching.* Englewood Cliffs, N.J.: Prentice-Hall, 1968.

————. *Verbal behavior.* Appleton-Century-Crofts, 1957.

————. *Science and human behavior.* New York: Macmillan, 1953.

————. *Walden Two.* Englewood Cliffs, N.J.: Prentice-Hall, 1948.

Smith, F. *The creative impulse.* New York: Knopf, 1984.

Smith, P. (Ed.). *Creativity.* New York: Hastings House, 1959.

Speedie, S.M., Treffinger, D.J., and Houtz, J.C. Classification and evaluation of problem-solving tasks. *Contemporary educational psychology,* 1976, *1,* 52–75.

Sperry, R.W. Lateral specialization in the surgically separated hemispheres. In Schmitt, F.O., and Worden, F.G. (Eds.), *The neurosciences third study program.* Cambridge, Mass.: MIT Press, 1974.

————. Brain bisection and consciousness. In Eccles, J. (Ed.), *Brain and conscious experience.* New York: Springer-Verlag, 1966.

Spotts, J.V., and Mackler, B.U. Relationships of field-dependent and field-independent cognitive styles to creative test performance. *Perceptual and motor skills,* 1967, *24,* 239–268.

Springer, S.P., and Deutsch, G. *Left brain, right brain.* San Francisco: Freeman, 1981.

Stanley, J.C., George, W.C., and Solano, C.H. *The gifted and the creative.* Baltimore: Johns Hopkins, 1977.

Stein, B.S. The effects of cue-target uniqueness on cued recall performance. *Memory and cognition,* 1977, *5,* 319–322.

Stein, M.I. *Stimulating creativity, Vol. 1: Individual procedures.* New York: Academic Press, 1974.

————. Creativity and culture. In Mooney, R.L., and Razik, T.A. (Eds.), *Explorations in creativity,* New York: Harper, 1967.

Stein, M.I., and Heinze, S. (Eds.). *Creativity and the individual.* Chicago: Free Press, 1960.

Stone, C.A., and Day, M.C. Competence and performance models and the characterization of formal operational skills. *Human development*, 1980, *23*, 323–353.

Storr, A. *The dynamics of creation.* New York: Atheneum, 1972.

Strom, R., and Strom, C. Creative curriculum for grandparents. *Journal of creative behavior*, 1984, *18* (2), 133–141.

Summerfield, J.D., and Thatcher, L. (Eds.). *The creative mind and method.* New York: Russell and Russell, 1964.

Szent-Gyoergyi, A. On scientific creativity. *Perspectives in biology and medicine*, 1962, *5*, 173–178.

Tagano, D.W., Fin, V.R., and Moran, J.D. Divergent thinking and hemispheric dominance for language functioning among preschool children. *Perceptual and motor skills*, 1983, *56*, 691–698.

Taylor, C.W. Some knowns, needs, and leads. In Taylor, C.W. (Ed.), *Creativity: Progress and potential*, New York: McGraw-Hill, 1964a.

————. *Creativity: Progress and potential.* New York: McGraw-Hill, 1964b.

————. The identification of creative scientific talent. *The American psychologist*, 1959, *14*, 100–102.

Taylor, C.W., and Barron, F. *Scientific creativity: Its recognition and development.* New York: Wiley, 1963.

Taylor, C.W., and Holland, J. Predictors of creative performance. In Taylor, C.W. (Ed.), *Creativity: Progress and potential.* New York: McGraw-Hill, 1964.

Taylor, I.A. A retrospective view of creativity investigation. In Taylor, I.A., and Getzels, J.W. (Eds.), *Perspectives in creativity.* Chicago: Aldine, 1975a.

Taylor, I.A., and Getzels, J.W. (Eds.). *Perspectives in creativity.* Chicago: Aldine, 1975b.

Taylor, I.A., and Sandler, B.E. Use of a creative product inventory for evaluating products of chemists. *Proceedings of the 80th Annual Convention of the American Psychological Association*, 1972, *7*, 311–312.

Terman, L.M. *Genetic studies of genius.* Stanford, Calif.: Stanford University Press, 1925.

Terrell, D.L. The TCB in clinical-forensic psychological evaluation: A case study of exceptionality. *Journal of non-white concerns*, *10*, 1982, 64–72.

Tisone, J.M., and Wismar, B.L. Microcomputers: How can they be used to enhance creative development? *Journal of creative behavior*, 1985, *19* (2), 97–103.

Tolstoy, L.N. *What is art?* Oxford: Oxford University Press, 1898 (reprint).

Torrance, E.P. Can we teach children to think creatively? *Journal of creative behavior*, 1982, *6*, 114–143.

————. *The search for satori.* Buffalo, N.Y.: Creative Education Foundation, 1979.

————. Creativity and the older adult. *Creative child and adult quarterly*, 1977, *2*, 136–144.

————. Creativity research in education: Still alive. In Taylor, I.A., and Getzels, J.W. (Eds.), *Perspectives in creativity.* Chicago: Aldine, 1975a.

———. Sociodramas: A creative problem-solving approach to studying the future. *Journal of creative behavior,* 1975, *9,* 182–185.

———. *Verbal test booklet A, Torrance tests of creative thinking.* Bensenville, Ill.: Scholastic Testing, 1974a.

———. *Verbal test booklet B, Torrance tests of creative thinking.* Bensenville, Ill.: Scholastic Testing, 1974b.

———. *Creativity.* Belmont, Calif.: Fearon, 1969a.

———. What is honored: Comparative studies of creative achievement and motivation. *Journal of creative behavior,* 1969b, *3,* 149–154.

———. *Rewarding creative behavior.* Englewood Cliffs, N.J.: Prentice-Hall, 1965.

———. Education and creativity. In Taylor, C.W. (Ed.), *Creativity: Progress and potential.* New York: McGraw-Hill, 1964.

———. *Creativity.* Washington, D.C.: National Education Association, 1963a.

———. *Education and the creative potential.* Minneapolis: University of Minnesota Press, 1963b.

———. *Guiding creative talent.* Englewood Cliffs, N.J.: Prentice-Hall, 1962.

Torrance, E.P., and Myers, R.E. *Creative learning and teaching.* New York: Dodd, Mead, 1972.

Torrance, E.P., Peterson, P., and Davis, D. *Revised originality scale for evaluating creative writing.* Minneapolis: University of Minnesota, 1963.

Torrance, E.P., and Templeton, D.E. *Manual for verbal form A, Minnesota tests of creative thinking.* Minneapolis: University of Minnesota, 1963.

Torrance, E.P., and Torrance, J.P. *Is creativity teachable?* Bloomington, Ill.: Phi Delta Kappa Educational Foundation, 1973.

Treffinger, D.J. Research on creativity. *Gifted child quarterly,* 1986, *30* (1), 15–18.

———. Review of the Torrance tests of creative thinking. In Mitchell, J.V. (Ed.), *The ninth mental measurements yearbook.* Lincoln: University of Nebraska, 1985.

———. George's group: A creative problem-solving facilitation case study. *Journal of creative behavior,* 1983, *17* (1), 39–48.

———. The progress and peril of identifying creative talent among gifted and talented students. *Journal of creative behavior,* 1980, *14,* 20–34.

Treffinger, D.J., Isaksen, S.G., and Firestein, R. Theoretical perspectives on creative learning and its facilitation: An overview. *Journal of creative behavior,* 1983,, *17* (1), 9–17.

Treffinger, D.J., and Poggio, J.P. Needed research on the measurement of creativity. *Journal of creative behavior,* 1972, *6,* 253–267.

Treffinger, D.J., and Renzulli, J.S. Giftedness as potential for creative productivity: Transcending IQ scores. *Roeper review,* 1986, *8* (3).

Treffinger, D.J., Renzulli, J.S., and Feldhusen, J.F. Problems in the assessment of creative thinking. *Journal of creative behavior,* 1971, *5,* 104–112.

Treffinger, D.J., Ripple, R.E., and Dacey, J.S. Teachers' attitudes toward creativity. *Journal of creative behavior,* 1968, *2* (4), 242–248.

Trostle, S.L., and Yawkey, T.D. Facilitating creative thought through object play in young children. *Journal of creative behavior*, 1983, *17* (3), 181–189.

————. Creative thinking and the education of young children: The fourth basic skill. *Journal of early childhood*, 1982, *14* (2), 67–71.

Vaillant, G. *Adaptation to life*. Boston: Little, Brown, 1977.

Vance, M. *Creative thinking*. Chicago: Nightingale-Conant, 1982.

VanGundy, A.B. *Managing group creativity*. New York: Amacom, American Management Association, 1984.

Von Frange, E.K. *Professional creativity*. Englewood Cliffs, N.J.: Prentice-Hall, 1959.

von Oech, R. *A kick in the seat of the pants*. New York: Harper and Row, 1986.

————. *A whack on the side of the head*. New York: Warner Books, 1983.

Wade, S. Differences between intelligence and creativity: Some speculation on the role of environment. *The journal of creative behavior*, 1968, *2*, 97–102.

Walkup, L.E. Creativity in science through visualization. *Journal of creative behavior*, 1967, *1*, 283–290.

Wallach, M.A., and Kogan, N. *Creativity and intelligence in children's thinking*. New Brunswich, N.J.: TRANS-action, 1967.

————. *Modes of thinking in young children*. New York: Holt, Rinehart and Winston, 1965.

Wallas, G. *The art of thought*. New York: Harcourt, Brace, 1926.

Ward, W.C., and Cox, P.W. A field study of nonverbal creativity. *Journal of personality*, 1974, *42*, 202–219.

Weissman, P. Psychological concomitants of ego functioning in creativity. *International journal of psycho-analysis*, 1968, *49*, 464–469.

Welsh, G.S. *Figure preference test: Preliminary manual*. Palo Alto, Calif.: Consulting Psychologists Press, 1959.

Werner, H. "The concept of development from a comparative and organismic point of view." In Harris, D.B. (Ed.), *The concept of development: An issue in the study of behavior*. Minneapolis: University of Minnesota Press, 1957.

Wertheimer, M. *Productive thinking*. New York: Harper, 1945.

White, L.A. Genius: Its causes and incidence. In White, L.A. (Ed.), *The science of culture. A study of man and civilization*. New York: Farrar, Straus, 1949, 190–232.

White, R. Motivation reconsidered: The concept of competence. *Psychological review*, 1959, *66*, 297–323.

Whiting, C.S. *Creative thinking*. New York: Reinhold, 1958.

Wicker, F.W. A rhetorical look at humor as creativity. *Journal of creative behavior*, 1985, *19* (3), 175–184.

Wilder, R.L. The role of intuition, *Science*, May 1967, *156* (3775).

Williams, A.J., and Poole, M.E. The school experience of talented adolescents. *The creative child and adult quarterly*, 1981, *4*, 103–108.

Wilson, R.C., Guilford, J.P., Christensen, P.R., and Lewis, D.J. A factoranalytical study of creative thinking abilities. *Psychometrika*, 1954, *19*, 297–311.

Witken, H.A., Dyk, R.B., Faterson, H.P., Goodenough, D.R., and Karp, S.A. *Psychological differentiation.* New York: Wiley, 1962.

Witken, H.A., Lewis, H.B., Hertzman, M., Machover, K., Meissner, P.B., and Wapner, S. *Personality through perception.* New York: Harper, 1954.

Wittmer, J., and Myrick, R. *Facilitative teaching.* Pacific Palisades, Calif.: Goodyear, 1974.

Yawkey, T.D. Creative dialogue through sociodramatic play and its uses. *Journal of creative behavior,* 1986, *20* (1), 52–60.

———. Effects of social relationships curricula and sex differences on reading and imaginativeness in young children. *Alberta journal of educational research,* 1980, *26* (3), 159–168.

———. Sociodramatic effects and sex differences on selected cognitive academic and play-related abilities in five-year-olds. *Contemporary educational psychology,* 1983, *2,* 24–35.

Yawkey, T.D., and Hrncir, E.S. Pretend play tools for oral language growth in the preschool. *Journal of creative behavior,* 1982, *16* (4), 265–271.

Zaidel, E., and Sperry, R.W. Memory impairment following commissurotomy in man. *Brain,* 1974, *97,* 263–272.

Zegans, L.S., Pollard, J.C., and Brown, D. The effects of LSD-25 on creativity and tolerance to regression. *Archives of general psychiatry,* 1967, *16,* 740–749.

Zwerling, I. The creative arts as real therapies. *Hospital and community psychiatry,* 1979, *30* (12), 841–844.

Index

Author Index

Subject Index

About the Author

John Dacey is director of the Graduate Human Development Program at Boston College. He received his Ph.D. from Cornell University in 1966, doing his dissertation on the relationship between divergent thinking and programmed instruction.

He is the author of a number of books, among them *New Ways to Learn* (1976), *Adult Development* (1982), and *Adolescents Today* (3rd ed., 1986). He is also the author of twenty-one articles, including three in the *Journal of Creative Behavior*. He resides with his family in Lexington, Massachusetts.

DE